T0283666

A
WHOLE
NEW
GAME

NEIL LONGLEY

A WHOLE NEW GAME

ECONOMICS, POLITICS, AND THE TRANSFORMATION
OF THE BUSINESS OF HOCKEY IN CANADA

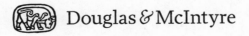 Douglas & McIntyre

Douglas & McIntyre (2013) Ltd.
P.O. Box 219, Madeira Park, BC, V0N 2H0
www.douglas-mcintyre.com

Edited by Derek Fairbridge
Indexed by Colleen Bidner
Dust jacket and text design by Dwayne Dobson
Printed and bound in Canada
Printed on 100% recycled paper

Canada Council   Conseil des arts
for the Arts   du Canada

BRITISH COLUMBIA
ARTS COUNCIL

BRITISH
COLUMBIA
Supported by the Province of British Columbia

Douglas & McIntyre acknowledges the support of the Canada Council for the Arts, the Government of Canada, and the Province of British Columbia through the BC Arts Council.

Library and Archives Canada Cataloguing in Publication

Title: A whole new game : economics, politics, and the transformation
    of the business of hockey in Canada / Neil Longley.
Names: Longley, Neil, author.
Description: Includes bibliographical references and index.
Identifiers: Canadiana (print) 20230506127 | Canadiana (ebook) 2023050616X |
    ISBN 9781771623803 (hardcover) | ISBN 9781771623810 (EPUB)
Subjects: LCSH: Hockey—Economic aspects—Canada. |
    LCSH: Sports administration—Canada.
Classification: LCC GV847.4 .L66 2023 | DDC 796.96206/9—dc23

CONTENTS

INTRODUCTION:
A HALF CENTURY
OF CHANGE

IT WAS MAY 2, 1967, a little less than two months away from Canada's 100th birthday. Canadians everywhere were preparing for a summer of centennial celebrations, schoolchildren were singing Bobby Gimby's catchy song "Ca-na-da," and the country was filled with optimism, hope and pride. Only four days earlier, the Expo 67 world's fair had opened in Montreal to rave reviews. With its futuristic theme of "Man and his World," over 300,000 people attended the exposition on its first day alone. Canada seemed to be on top of the world.

Hockey was also doing its part to contribute to the celebratory mood. On Carlton Street in downtown Toronto that night in early May, Maple Leaf Gardens was filled to capacity for the sixth game of that year's Stanley Cup final. The hometown Toronto Maple Leafs were ahead three games to two against their archrivals, the Montreal Canadiens, and a Leafs victory would clinch their 13th Stanley Cup championship.

The two clubs were the National Hockey League's (NHL's) only Canadian franchises at the time, and their battles were always sure to captivate the country. The matchup that year was particularly intriguing. It was only the third time in 17 years that the two clubs had met in the final, despite the NHL being only a six-team league. The Canadiens were two-time defending Cup champions, but the Leafs had assembled a roster of aging veterans in an attempt to pull off the upset. The Leafs had an unheard-of seven players on their roster over the age of 36, including Johnny Bower (42), Allan Stanley (40), Red Kelly (39) and Tim Horton (37), all of whom were well past their prime, but who were intent on taking one final shot at Stanley Cup glory.

Between the two of them, the clubs had won the past five Stanley Cups, and 18 of the past 23. They were the dominant teams of the NHL in that era, and their rivalry was fierce. The rivalry was a complicated one, and somewhat unique in North American sport, in that the Leafs-Canadiens matchups were never *just* about the game on the ice—it was always much more than that. The Canadiens, with a francophone-heavy roster, had long been the pride of French Canadians, while the Leafs had a strong following not just in Toronto and Southern Ontario, but throughout English Canada. While often not acknowledged explicitly, the on-ice battle between the Leafs and Canadiens was yet another chapter in the difficult, and sometimes tense, history of French-English relations in Canada.

Leafs fans ultimately went home happy that night. Their club would skate to a 3–1 victory, clinching the series and winning the Stanley Cup. Even at the time, though, fans must have known they were witnessing history, and that the NHL was on the cusp of a abrupt and dramatic change. The game marked the official end of what is now known as the "Original Six" era, a period of 25 years where the same six clubs—the Leafs and Canadiens, along with the Chicago Black Hawks,[1] Boston Bruins, Detroit Red Wings and New York Rangers—composed the NHL.[2] As Leafs fans savoured the Cup victory that night in early May, it would be a little more than five months before the NHL's membership would instantly double. Six new teams—but none in Canada—would make their debut in October 1967.

That doubling of franchises was just the beginning for the NHL. Over the next half century, the league would expand several more times, with many of these new franchises granted to non-traditional hockey markets in the US—cities such as Atlanta (twice), Nashville, Tampa and Las Vegas. It would also face direct competition from a rival league—the World Hockey Association (WHA) in the 1970s— with the NHL ultimately being forced to absorb four teams from that league in order to eliminate the WHA's competitive threat. The six NHL teams of 56 years ago have become 32 teams today.

For Canadians old enough to remember that time, the Leafs' 1967 Cup victory often evokes nostalgia. Part of this is no doubt due to the fact it was the last Stanley Cup final of the Original Six era, an era that spanned the formative childhood years of many of Canada's now-aging baby boomers. The 1967 Stanley Cup final has taken on even added significance over the years because the Leafs, the most financially valuable franchise in Canadian sport, and arguably the most popular, have not won the Stanley Cup in the over half a century that has passed since that time. In some ways, these two stories have become intertwined for many fans, with 1967 evoking images of a simpler, more genuine time—less driven by commercial interests and more connected to the grassroots foundations of hockey in Canada.

The sense that the game of hockey was very different 50 years ago is further reinforced by examining the rosters of the two teams competing for the 1967 Stanley Cup. Every single player on the two teams was born in Canada. The Leafs and Canadiens were in no way unusual—Canadians composed almost 100% of the players in the NHL at the time; today, that number has fallen to under 50%. For francophones in Quebec, the drop in numbers has been even more drastic. The 1966–67 Canadiens' roster was heavily dominated by homegrown talent—eight of the top 10 scorers on the Canadiens' roster that year were of French Canadian descent. In contrast, of the Canadiens' top 10 scorers in the 2021–22 season, not a single player was French Canadian. The notion of 50 years ago that the Canadiens hockey club was a sporting manifestation of francophone culture and society may have been true then, but is very far from today's reality.

THE DRAMATIC TRANSFORMATION OF CANADIAN HOCKEY

In 1967, the entire Canadian hockey landscape was on the cusp of an enormous structural change. This was driven largely by the NHL's strategic shift, as the league moved away from a parochial mindset that characterized its past to one that was driven by a more corporatist and modern business perspective.

While Canada did not receive any of the six new NHL franchises[3] in the 1967 expansion, by the early 1970s, the number of Canadian-based professional hockey franchises would grow significantly. First, Vancouver would finally get its NHL team—it was denied a franchise in the 1967 expansion, purportedly due to opposition from the Leafs and Canadiens, who were unwilling to split their CBC broadcast revenues a third way. Then, in 1972, a much more dramatic change occurred that shook the hockey world. The upstart WHA formed to directly challenge the NHL, with the new league placing charter franchises in previously unserved Canadian markets: Calgary, Edmonton, Winnipeg, Ottawa and Quebec City. Now, cities that would never have been granted an NHL franchise—at least not until decades into the future—suddenly had a major professional hockey team. Not only that, the WHA brought a flair and showmanship not found in the NHL, and gained immediate credibility when NHL superstar Bobby Hull left the Chicago Black Hawks to sign with the new league's Winnipeg Jets.

The WHA lasted seven tumultuous seasons, finally merging[4] four teams into the NHL in 1979, but not before forever changing the pro hockey landscape in the country. It left as its legacy Canadian NHL teams in Edmonton, Winnipeg and Quebec City (the latter two ultimately relocated to the US) and was one of the primary impetuses for the European migration of hockey talent into North America, ultimately filling roster spots that had previously belonged almost exclusively to Canadians.

Junior hockey—technically amateur hockey, but always with a strong spectator following in Canada—was also on the precipice of major change in 1967. For decades, junior clubs had been "sponsored" by NHL teams, who essentially used these junior clubs as part of their farm system. NHL teams would sign players, some as young as 14 (like Bobby Orr, in 1962), and then allocate them to one of their various clubs across the country. However, with the NHL's doubling in size in 1967, and with its plans for more expansion in the early 1970s, the league decided to replace this sponsorship system with a draft system, with the first draft occurring in 1969.[5]

With the sponsorship system on its way out, the newly independent junior hockey clubs began to reorganize and consolidate their operations. They moved away from the more fragmented and decentralized system of the sponsorship era, where many different, but often small and localized, leagues operated, and toward a system where elite-level talent was funnelled into one of three "major junior" leagues across the country. Two of today's three major junior leagues—the Western Hockey League (WHL) and the Quebec Major Junior Hockey League (QMJHL)—had their roots in the late 1960s. The WHL (known then as the Western Canada Hockey League) formed in

1966, and would ultimately siphon away most elite-level players (as well as several entire teams) from the provincial-based leagues in the four western provinces (such as the Alberta Junior Hockey League and the Saskatchewan Junior Hockey League). Three years later, the QMJHL began operations, also with a goal of consolidating high-end talent into a single league.

The end of the paternalistic sponsorship era made junior hockey clubs solely responsible for their own financial well-being. It ultimately moved them toward a more businesslike, profit-driven model, to the point today where they have adopted many of the business strategies of their NHL counterparts, complete with a player draft system that allocates players to teams within the league. No longer can junior hockey clubs be viewed as simply an outgrowth of the amateur hockey systems in the communities in which they operate; most are now simply commercial operations, focused on the bottom line, often with absentee ownership, and with rosters composed of largely non-local players. Major junior hockey leagues have essentially become small-scale versions of the NHL.

SPORT WITHIN AN EVOLVING CANADA

Hockey does not live in a vacuum. Changes in the hockey world both reflect and are driven by changes in the broader social, political and economic structures that it operates within. If these structures change, hockey will change.

It is not surprising, then, that the dramatic post-1967 changes in the Canadian hockey world have parallels in the non-sport world. In fact, the year 1967 has become somewhat of a metaphor in Canadian popular culture, symbolizing a turning point in the nation's development, away from the relatively stable, benign and harmonious two decades that followed the Second World War toward a period of greater economic, social and political challenges and conflicts. The iconic Canadian author Pierre Berton even wrote a book about the year, simply titled *1967: The Last Good Year*. As the book's name suggests, Berton argues that the year represented pride and optimism for Canadians—with the excitement surrounding the country's centennial celebrations, with Montreal hosting the Expo 67 world's fair and, of course, with the Leafs-Canadiens Stanley Cup—but that it turned out to be the high point for Canada, the end of an era and the simultaneous beginning of a series of disruptive and destabilizing changes that would fundamentally alter the country.

To fully appreciate the nature and impact these changes would have on Canadian society, some historical context is in order. Canada is a nation that has always defied geographic logic. The second-largest country in the world by land mass, Canada's relatively small population (now about 40 million residents) lives primarily along a narrow strip within 150 kilometres of the us border, but is spread over 5,500 kilometres from east to west. Added to this geographic complexity, Canada was settled by two predominant European cultures—French and English—each with its own language, values and beliefs.[6] The combination of a geographically dispersed population and two distinct settler cultures has always meant that the interests of Canadians—whether those interests be economic, political, social or cultural—vary widely from region to region across the country. In the face of these natural forces that may tend toward divisiveness, successive federal governments throughout Canada's history have been tasked with managing and adjudicating these interests and with explicitly promoting national unity.

Federal governments have also faced a parallel challenge. With Canada's proximity to the us, and with Canada having about one-tenth the population of its powerful southern neighbour, there have always been fears in Canada of being overwhelmed and consumed by the us, particularly economically and culturally. With the wide east-west span of Canada, Canadians often have stronger economic (and sometimes cultural) links with their us neighbours immediately to the south than they do with Canadians in other parts of the country.

In response to these various natural forces, federal governments throughout Canada's history have adopted interventionist policies. In the high-paying manufacturing sector, for example, jobs were protected through trade barriers like tariffs and quotas, mechanisms that increased the price of foreign-made goods. On the cultural front, organizations like the Canadian Radio-television and Telecommunications Commission (crtc) were created to preserve Canadian content in the arts and broadcasting, an effort to counteract less-expensive American content from flooding unfettered into Canada's radio and tv broadcasting.

As the 1970s arrived, the seemingly stable and harmonious economic and social system that existed in Canada during the postwar years was beginning to face threats. Disruptive forces were on the horizon on several fronts: The 1973 opec[7]–driven oil shocks seriously damaged the world economy. A long period of stagflation—simultaneously high unemployment and high inflation, something which, to that point, economists didn't believe could occur together[8]—plagued most Western industrial countries for the remainder of the 1970s.

Technology was also progressing rapidly, and advances in the telecommunications and transportation sectors were beginning to allow Canadians a greater exposure to the rest of the world—in some ways, it was the beginning of a more globalized and modern perspective. The nature of Canada's internal labour market was also transforming. Lesser-skilled jobs were being lost to developing countries with low-cost labour; meanwhile, the demand for skilled workers in Canada was increasing—a demand that was met, in part, through increased immigration. Potential immigrants with job-related skills or with funds to invest in businesses were given greater priority. This immigration was, in itself, a driver of further changes. It fundamentally shifted the social and cultural makeup of the country, with immigrants bringing in languages, customs, cultures and histories that were very different from those of most Canadians at the time.

Agriculture, always a critical industry in Canada, was also undergoing a major revolution. The emergence of automated labour-saving technologies allowed farms to produce more output with fewer workers, massively reducing the demand for agricultural workers and, in turn, creating a population shift away from rural areas and to the cities. This strong trend toward urbanization was further reinforced by increased immigration; cities (rather than rural areas), particularly Toronto and Vancouver, were the destination for many immigrants, with these cities becoming increasingly multicultural and heterogeneous.

Parallel with all of this, by the late 1970s, economic and political ideologies that espoused free markets were taking hold around the world. The rise of Margaret Thatcher in the UK, Ronald Reagan in the US and Brian Mulroney in Canada would become manifestations of this ideology. Economic efficiency became the new mantra— competition and free markets, it was argued, would allocate societal resources more effectively than would government policy-makers. The result would be lower production costs and lower prices to consumers, while resulting in higher-quality products, better service and more innovation.

To achieve this, as the argument goes, both business and government had to become sleeker and leaner, eliminating slack and inefficiencies. Governments in Canada espousing this view, both federal and provincial, took action on several fronts. First, they began to reduce their commitments to the social welfare structure, a structure that had been growing since the end of the Second World War. Proponents of such reductions argued that Canadians had become too reliant on the cradle-to-grave welfare state. By reducing the size of the social welfare state, the argument went, governments would not only motivate Canadians to work harder and become more self-sufficient, but also allow for a commensurate reduction in taxes.

Governments also began to reduce their direct role in industry. Crown corporations were sold at both the federal and provincial levels—most provinces, for example, sold their government telephone companies, partly so emerging companies could compete in what had traditionally been a monopoly market. Deregulation of business also emerged. Transportation industries such as airlines and trucking—long subject to oversight by regulatory boards that controlled critical factors like routes and prices—were now subject to market forces rather than regulatory control. Much of the stated goals of government intervention in these industries had been to ensure residents in less populated areas had adequate access to services, whether it be telephone systems and electricity in rural areas or airline service to smaller cities.

Parallel with these domestic initiatives to reduce the role of government, an analogous situation was occurring on the international front, where reducing trade barriers became a key focus. These barriers, primarily tariffs and quotas, increased the price of foreign goods, thereby favouring domestic production over imports. In economic-efficiency terms, trade barriers were viewed negatively since they did not allow resources to be allocated to their most productive use.

Many countries began to negotiate agreements with their neighbours. The Canada-us Free Trade Agreement—a product of Prime
Minister Mulroney and President Reagan's compatible ideologies and
close personal friendship—came into effect in 1988. Ultimately, it was
extended to include Mexico three years later, when the pact became
known as the North American Free Trade Agreement (NAFTA). Free-
trade agreements imposed external discipline on the political and
economic markets in Canada, so no longer could Canadian governments protect certain segments of the population as they once had.

The emergence of these forces that ultimately transformed
Canadian society—freer internal markets, globalization, immigration and urbanization—were not particularly unique to Canada.
Some version of these changes were occurring in most Western
industrial countries. Canada, however, faced an additional challenge. While the geographic dispersion and cultural diversity of
the country meant that regionalism and national unity issues have
always been present, tensions in these areas began to increase rapidly during the 1970s, at the same time that the external changes
discussed above were also starting to occur.

Most of the tensions were focused on Quebec sovereignty. While
there had always been a significant element in Quebec society
favouring sovereignty, Canadians outside of Quebec became much
more acutely aware of the issue in 1967, when French president
Charles de Gaulle controversially proclaimed "Vive le Québec libre"
("Long live free Quebec") in a speech in Montreal. This was just a
prelude to a cascade of events in Quebec during the 1970s—including
a rapid rise in political violence, and the election of an overtly
sovereigntist premier who would lead a provincial referendum on
the issue—that would shake national unity to its core. The Quebec
situation continued to consume much of the federal political capital
throughout the 1980s and into the 1990s, with two failed attempts

at constitutional amendments (the Meech Lake Accord and the Charlottetown Accord), both of which included language recognizing Quebec as a "distinct society."

While the prospects of Quebec sovereignty dominated the national news during that period, there was another unity issue brewing almost simultaneously in Western Canada. So-called Western alienation has its roots in the belief that federal policies long favoured the Central Canadian provinces of Ontario and Quebec. One example was the aforementioned trade policy, where a system of tariffs and quotas historically protected manufacturing in (voter-rich) Central Canada. Many Western Canadians viewed this as unfair, in that they received few of the job-creation benefits of these protectionist policies, but were forced to bear a significant portion of the costs in the form of higher prices.

The economic foundations of the Western provinces have historically been based on the primary industries of agriculture and natural resources—for example, lumber and fisheries in BC; oil and cattle in Alberta; wheat, oil and potash in Saskatchewan, et cetera. Unlike the manufacturing sector in Central Canada—which produced primarily for the domestic market, and which needed protection from foreign competition—the industries of Western Canada produced largely for the export market and relied on Canada having access to foreign markets. In many ways, then, the economic interests of Western Canada were diametrically opposed to those of Central Canada, at least with respect to trade issues.

Added to this long-standing sense of unfairness felt amongst many Western Canadians, a new, more volatile issue emerged in the 1970s. The OPEC oil embargo of 1973 caused world oil prices to sky-rocket, ultimately sending the world economy into a deep recession for several years. In an effort to decrease the country's dependency on foreign oil, the Liberal government of Pierre Trudeau adopted in

1980 an energy policy that introduced price controls for domestically produced oil. As a result, the price paid to domestic producers in Canada was below the world price of oil. This was met with intense opposition in Alberta, the country's leading oil-producing province, and was the backdrop to an almost decade-long battle between Peter Lougheed, Alberta's premier, and the Trudeau government.

This specific issue regarding oil, combined with the more general view amongst many Western Canadians that their concerns were not adequately heard in Ottawa, revealed itself in the electoral process. During Trudeau's time in office, the Liberals performed very poorly in Western Canada, rarely winning more than a handful of seats in the four Western provinces. Trudeau himself was a polarizing figure, and was generally very unpopular in the West. Electorally, Western Canada became a wasteland for the Liberals during most of his time in office, which set the foundation for a Western separatist movement that gained considerable momentum during the 1980s, particularly in Alberta.

While this is a book about the profound transformation of Canadian hockey over the past half century, it is not a book that is just about hockey—it can't be if it is to provide any meaningful insights into the transformations that have occurred. Changes in the hockey industry did not occur in isolation or in a vacuum, but rather were a manifestation of a complex set of economic, political and social changes that occurred in broader Canadian society. The freer movement of goods and services, globalization, immigration, urbanization, Quebec sovereignty, Western alienation—all were factors, in some form or another, that influenced the Canadian hockey industry. Sometimes the effects of these on hockey were quite direct, sometimes they were more indirect.

Looked at the opposite way, hockey not only is influenced by societal change, it *reflects* these broader changes in society; in a sense, hockey becomes a metaphor for the world around it. The nature of hockey—with its high public visibility, relative transparency as a business and widespread following amongst large segments of the population—makes it a particularly unique vehicle to witness societal shifts and transformations.

Each chapter of this book examines a particular hockey story that emerges from these broader societal changes. An early focus of the book is on the transformative impacts these changes had on the Montreal Canadiens franchise—and, relatedly, on the francophone player in professional hockey—viewed through the lens of the NHL's increasing corporatization, and at a time of a growing sovereignty movement in Quebec. Regional issues also come into play in the West, where both the WHA's emergence in the early 1970s and the "Battle of Alberta" of the 1980s are seen as intricately linked with increased Western alienation at the political level.

The book also examines changes in what could be termed the *development level* of hockey—i.e., the level before players reach the NHL. For example, it identifies the social and economic reasons behind the dramatic shifts in the geographic sources of NHL talent and why Canada—and, more particularly, certain regions within Canada—have plummeted in their production of future NHLers. And finally, no discussion of the economic and social aspects of Canadian hockey can be complete without examining the always controversial junior hockey system in the country—how, organizationally, it's changed with the times, but how it still operates in the same exploitative manner as it has for almost a century.

A recurring theme of the book is that there were moments in history when hockey in Canada could have adopted more of a European model—a model where clubs often formed organically as grassroots endeavours of the local population and where every country has its own independent domestic professional league, regardless of the sport (soccer, basketball, hockey, et cetera). Instead, hockey (and other professional sports) in Canada quickly got subsumed into a us-style model, where leagues and teams are privately owned and formed as explicit profit-seeking entities. This resulted in Canada being largely a "branch plant" for us sport leagues, with no real domestic influence or control over the industry.

CHAPTER 1:
AN EMPIRE FALLS

IN HOCKEY PARLANCE, it was a game where the home team came out completely "flat"—lethargic, unfocused and seemingly unprepared to compete. The visitors capitalized immediately, scoring just three minutes into the first period and then quickly adding a second goal at the eight-minute mark. While the home side briefly appeared to be back on track when it responded less than a minute later with a goal of its own, the visitors proceeded to pour in another three goals before the first period was over, taking a commanding 5–1 lead into the intermission.

The second period was no better for the hosts, as the visitors scored four more unanswered goals. They added two more in the third period and won the game 11–1, one of the most lopsided score lines in modern NHL history.

The fans at the Montreal Forum that night in early December of 1995 were certainly not accustomed to their team suffering such an ignominious defeat. After all, the Montreal Canadiens were a club rich in tradition, with a long and illustrious history of on-ice success. The club had won 24 Stanley Cups—more than any other

NHL franchise, by a wide margin—with 15 of these coming in an incredible 24-season run spanning from 1956 to 1979.

However, in the 15 years since the 1979 Cup win, the club seemed to be on a steady, albeit slow, decline. While they had actually won the Cup as recently as the 1992–93 season, that particular championship was very much unexpected. The team had only a mediocre regular season, at least by the Canadiens' standards—finishing seventh overall in the league standings—but then went on an improbable playoff run that was fuelled by an uncanny success in games that went into sudden-death overtime. Of the 16 playoff games the Canadiens won that year on their march to the Cup, 10 of those victories came in overtime, where the sudden-death aspect creates a situation where randomness and good fortune take on an increased importance in determining the outcome.

While the 11–1 loss to the Detroit Red Wings that night in 1995 was bad enough for Canadiens fans, it was far from the only story that unfolded that evening. The final score was almost secondary to the bizarre series of events that occurred between Canadiens star goalie Patrick Roy and head coach Mario Tremblay. Tremblay was a rookie coach, having been appointed less than two months earlier —and six games into the season—as a replacement for the fired Jacques Demers. There had been a simmering tension between Tremblay and Roy ever since the coach's appointment, and, arguably, even before that, back to when the two were Canadiens teammates —a tension that boiled over in a very public way on the night of the 11–1 defeat.

Most knowledgeable hockey observers felt Tremblay should have replaced Roy at the end of the first period, after the goalie had already allowed five goals. This would have been standard practice, where coaches "protect" a goalie who is having a bad game from further embarrassment. Tremblay did not do this, nor did he do it when Roy allowed three more goals in the first part of the second period. Roy was becoming increasingly agitated on the ice and was clearly seeking to be replaced. It wasn't until Detroit scored their ninth goal of the game, at 11:57 of the second period, that Tremblay finally replaced Roy. By that point Roy was furious at Tremblay and stormed off the ice. The Canadiens president, Ronald Corey, was seated just behind the team bench, and Roy was heard to tell Corey that he would never play another game for the club. Two days later, Roy—who had been a crucial component in the Canadiens' Stanley Cup victory only two years earlier—was traded to the Colorado Avalanche, where he would go on to lead his new club to two Stanley Cup titles and would be inducted into the Hockey Hall of Fame in 2006. Tremblay was fired as the Canadiens coach at the conclusion of the 1995–96 season and never coached again in the NHL.

The humiliating 11–1 defeat, combined with the Roy-Tremblay public dispute and the subsequent trade of Roy, was undoubtedly one of the lowest points in the Canadiens' illustrious history. In a way, it was a bottoming-out for the once-proud franchise, and if there was ever any doubt, it signified that the Canadiens' long dynasty had ended. The Canadiens' franchise was hockey royalty, but the royals had now aired their "dirty laundry" in a very public and embarrassing way.

In the three decades since that infamous night, the Canadiens have not won another Stanley Cup. In fact, before the Canadiens made their unexpected run to the Stanley Cup final in the COVID-shortened 2020–21 season, only three other NHL franchises had a longer drought in not even making an *appearance* in the final—the Toronto Maple Leafs, the New York Islanders and the Phoenix Coyotes/Winnipeg Jets. In stark contrast to their glory days, the Canadiens are now just like any other NHL club; there is nothing special about them—they have some better seasons, some worse seasons and some seasons of mediocrity. In sports parlance, they have "come back to the pack." The magic that surrounded the franchise for so long is now but a distant memory.

However, the on-ice rise and decline of the Canadiens is a story that goes beyond just hockey; there is a concurrent and parallel story about a minority society struggling to maintain its culture and language in the face of encroaching external economic and political forces. A defining feature of the Canadiens during their glory years was a roster that relied heavily on homegrown French Canadian players. The club was a point of immense pride amongst francophone Quebecers.

This strong francophone identification with the club and its successes was not unrelated to what was occurring in broader Quebec society at the time; in the mid-1950s, Quebec was still very much an insular society that was defined by its language and religion, and that, in many ways, was quite removed from everyday life in the rest of Canada. Quebec was in the midst of a struggle with how to shape its future and whether that future would be inside or outside Canada. Within this environment, the Canadiens became a symbol of francophone achievement and independence in what some francophones viewed as an outside world that threatened their cultural autonomy.

By the late 1960s—at a time when the issue of Quebec sovereignty was beginning to dominate political discourse, not only in Quebec, but in Canada as a whole—the NHL was contemplating its own future direction. Emerging economic forces were precipitating a strategic shift in the league, as the league moved from a parochial mindset to one that was driven by a more corporatist and modern business perspective.

As part of this shift, and in what would ultimately be a death blow to the dominance of the Canadiens, the league decided to radically transform its allocation system for incoming players, essentially removing the Canadiens' ability to secure the best francophone players entering the league. So, while the Patrick Roy–Mario Tremblay fiasco of 1995 was a headline-grabbing example of organizational dysfunction, the Canadiens' long-term on-ice decline probably had much less to do with any slide into poor management practices and much more to do with a single policy change implemented by the NHL.

THE CANADIENS IN MID-CENTURY QUEBEC

The Montreal Canadiens played their first game in 1910 as part of the National Hockey Association (NHA), forerunner to the NHL. From the beginning, the club was unabashedly French Canadian. Its founder, J. Ambrose O'Brien (ironically, an anglophone from Ontario), formed the club to explicitly appeal to the city's francophone population, serving as an alternative to the crosstown NHA team, the Montreal Wanderers, whose following was resoundingly anglophone.

When the NHL was formed in 1917, the Canadiens became a charter member of the new league. As with most fledging leagues, the early years of the NHL were somewhat tumultuous and chaotic, with franchises coming and going at a regular pace. It took over two decades—until 1942—for the league to settle into a group of franchises that would endure. By the 1942–43 season, NHL had taken shape as a six-team league.

While the Canadiens were winning Stanley Cups almost since their inception—their first came in 1916, when they were still in the NHA[9]—it wasn't until the 1950s that the club became a powerhouse. Starting in 1956, the Canadiens began a period of dominance that has been unmatched in any North American professional league to this day—over a 24-year span, they would win the Stanley Cup 15 times.

At the dawn of this Canadiens' dynasty, Quebec society was in
the midst of an era that would become known as the *Grande Noir-
ceur*—the Great Darkness. It was governed by the Union Nationale
party of Premier Maurice Duplessis, a populist and social conservative. It was a time when the Catholic Church was all-powerful, even
controlling critical social institutions like education and health care.

While francophones constituted about 80% of Quebec's population at the time, they comprised only about 20% of Canada's population as a whole—relatively few francophones lived outside the
province of Quebec. Francophones in Quebec were somewhat of an
island—a (large) cultural and language minority in the sea of anglophones that dominated the rest of North America.[10] For Quebec
francophones, the preservation of their language and culture, and
the resistance to subjugation by the majority, were always critical
social and political goals.

In mid-century Quebec society, then, the Montreal Canadiens
were so much more than just a hockey club—they were the sporting
embodiment of the francophone culture and community in which
they played. The Canadiens franchise was profoundly unique in
North American professional sport—no other club, in any sport,
came even close to being as embedded with the cultural and
social fabric of its surrounding community. The Canadiens didn't
just represent a physical or geographic space—a city, a province
or a state. What they represented went much deeper than that
—they represented an entire culture, a way of life, unified by a
common language.

What made the Canadiens hockey club particularly appealing to
francophone fans was that the roster was predominantly composed
of French Canadian players. NHL rules at the time gave the Canadiens a distinct advantage in securing the best francophone players,
not only immensely benefiting the club on the ice, but also enabling

the club to build a strong cultural and language compatibility with its fan base.[11]

Dynamic right winger Maurice "Rocket" Richard was the centre-piece of this synergy between culture and hockey. Richard was a kind of cult hero in francophone Quebec, bringing style and cha-risma, a prolific scoring talent and, perhaps most of all, a willingness to challenge the anglophone majority that ran the NHL at the time. Richard's suspension for the remainder of the 1955 season, including the playoffs, due to a March 13 on-ice physical altercation with a lines-man sparked the infamous "Richard Riot" in downtown Montreal. While attending a game at the Montreal Forum on the night of March 17, NHL president Clarence Campbell, the man who had imposed the suspension days earlier, was accosted by fans who felt the punishment was too severe. The mood inside the Forum turned hostile, and Montreal police chose to suspend the game partway through, with the violence ultimately spilling out into the sur-rounding streets. French Canadian fans had long believed there was an anti-francophone bias in the NHL, and saw the Richard suspen-sion as just another example of this.

A CHANGING QUEBEC

By the time the 1950s were coming to a close, the long postwar boom had begun to fundamentally alter many aspects of North American society. The decade of the 1950s was a time of optimism and hope, of renewal and change. The war years had created a huge pent-up demand that was finally released—gross domestic product grew rapidly, unemployment was low and consumer incomes grew to levels previously unseen.

There was also a focus, at least in Western industrial countries, on opening international markets and lessening trade and investment

barriers. These efforts were driven by the desire to avoid the disastrous impacts of protectionist and nationalistic policies of past
decades. International agreements were enacted to facilitate more
open economies: the Bretton Woods Agreement of 1944 provided
structure to the world's monetary system;[12] the General Agreements on Tariffs and Trade (GATT, the forerunner to today's World
Trade Organization), of which Canada was one of 23 founding
member-countries, was formed in 1948 to reduce trade barriers;
and so on.

In addition, advances in technology were starting to make the
world a "smaller" place. Commercial air travel was in its early
stages and would ultimately break down distance barriers, providing people with the ability to see ways of life beyond their own.
Communication technology was also improving—by the end of
the 1950s, there were televisions in about 90% of Canadian homes,
again resulting in more exposure to outside (i.e., non-local) forces
and influences.

These macro-level trends posed particular challenges for Quebec.
In an increasingly integrated world, with freer movement of goods
and services and greater cross-cultural exposures, it was becoming
ever more difficult to preserve the distinctiveness of the insular and
homogeneous francophone society of the 1950s.

Provincial politics in Quebec reflected these new external influences. Premier Duplessis died in office in September 1959, and
within a year his Union Nationale party was defeated at the polls.
The Liberal Party's Jean Lesage became premier, and his government
ushered in a new era through a process of adaptation that would
become known as the Quiet Revolution. It was an effort to modern-
ize Quebec society, and to move it beyond its parochial history—the
outside world was changing, and Quebec risked being left behind
if it did not adapt.

As inevitable as change was, resistance to change was also unavoidable. With the province moving toward greater modernization, certain segments of Quebec society began to more actively address the idea of sovereignty—a formal separation from the rest of Canada. The fear amongst sovereigntists was that a more open society would inevitably weaken, if not destroy, the unique francophone culture within the province.

The sovereignty movement would steadily gain momentum during the 1960s, ultimately setting the scene for a turbulent 1970s. The political violence carried out by the terrorist group Front de Libération du Québec (FLQ) during the early part of the decade, along with the 1976 election of the first openly sovereigntist government in the province's history, brought the issue of Quebec separation to national prominence, and put French-English tensions on the front burner of political discourse in Canada. While the Montreal Canadiens were never a politically active entity in any way, to many francophones the club represented independence from the outside anglophone world, and was a proud symbol of francophone accomplishments.

In his acclaimed book *The Game*, former Canadiens star goaltender Ken Dryden, an anglophone, recalls the night in November 1976 when the Parti Québécois won the provincial election. The Canadiens were playing at home that night, against the St. Louis Blues, and Dryden writes about how the atmosphere in the Montreal Forum was different from usual, as if the minds of fans were elsewhere. When, in the middle of the third period, the message board announced the PQ victory, Dryden recalls thousands of fans standing and cheering, with the Forum organist joining in and playing the PQ anthem.

The Canadiens' enormous on-ice dominance and its fervent support amongst the francophone community—at a time of deteriorating relations between English and French Canadians—often made the team a symbol of an increasingly divided Canada. In some ways, the Canadiens' immense popularity in Quebec was matched by a downright hostility toward the team in many parts of the rest of Canada, particularly in the West. While some of this hostility was no doubt related to blatant anti-French biases, there was also a view amongst some fans that the Canadiens' successes were based on an "unfair" advantage the club had in securing francophone players, an issue that would soon come front and centre as the NHL faced its own competitive threats and challenges.

THE NHL AND THE END OF COMPLACENCY

Just as Quebec society was on the cusp of enormous change during that era, so too was the NHL, particularly the Montreal Canadiens. In fact, the very forces driving transformation in Quebec also drove transformation in the NHL. Like Quebec society at the time, the NHL was itself a very parochial and conservative institution and increasingly vulnerable to outside threats that challenged its traditional approaches and mindset. The NHL ultimately responded with policy changes that—while not necessarily intended to do so —had disproportionately harmful impacts on the Montreal Canadiens franchise, essentially setting in motion the beginning of the end of the club's dynasty, all at a time when the club's core fan base in francophone Quebec was facing critical questions about its own future.

By the early 1960s, the NHL's Original Six teams had lived a comfortable existence for almost two decades. Storm clouds, however, were gathering. The postwar boom had created a burgeoning middle class, with increased leisure time and more discretionary income. The NHL, like the other three major North American professional leagues, had long been accustomed to operating as a monopoly— as such, it was always in the leagues' interests to create artificial scarcity, accomplished, in part, by very slow (if any) growth in the number of franchises. The Big Four—Major League Baseball (MLB), the National Football League (NFL), the National Basketball Association (NBA) and the NHL—were able to consistently reject expansion because the leagues were not governed by any type of external regulatory body; it was the existing owners of franchises in a league who made all decisions regarding possible expansion.

With a growing and more affluent population in North America, and with established leagues like the NHL failing to expand, many viable markets were left unserved. Because owners of established leagues unilaterally controlled expansion decisions, no entrepreneur could simply create a club and gain entry into a particular league. Instead, the only way owners in the established league could be threatened was if a *group* of entrepreneurs created an entirely new league, known as a rival league.

The NFL was the first of the Big Four to pay the price for this non-expansion strategy of the 1950s. The American Football League (AFL)—an eight-team league with franchises in such unserved markets as Boston, Denver, Houston and Buffalo—began play in 1960. The AFL would go on to inflict serious damage on the NFL, signing many star college players and driving up salaries in the process. The AFL gained a full merger with the NFL in 1966, with all eight of its charter members joining the NFL.[13]

Basketball was next. The American Basketball League (ABL) was formed in 1962 to challenge the NBA but played only one season. A more formidable competitor to the NBA would ultimately emerge in 1967, when the American Basketball Association (ABA) began play. The ABA employed a similar business model to the AFL by focusing on emerging but unserved markets such as Dallas, Indianapolis and Pittsburgh. Ten years later, the ABA, like the AFL before it, would also get a merger with the established league, but not before the ABA and

NBA had inflicted so much damage on each other (due to rapid salary escalation) that both leagues were near financial collapse.[14]

The NHL knew, then, what was coming. With only six teams, the NHL was practically inviting a rival league to form; it knew it must expand if it was to have any hope of pre-empting the development of a rival. However, the NHL faced a problem: the existing six teams already had an extensive network of affiliations with junior clubs in Canada (the only source of NHL talent at the time). Under this so-called sponsorship system, the six clubs had essentially tied up every amateur player in Canada.[15] The NHL decided to end this system in 1963 and instead joined the NFL and NBA and introduced a draft system to allocate incoming amateur players.[16] However, even though the sponsorship system technically ended that year, its effects were felt for another five years. For the 1963 through 1968 drafts, only those players not already under a sponsorship contract to an NHL club were eligible to be selected. It was not until the 1969 draft that the effects of the sponsorship era had fully dissipated, ensuring that all of the best draft-age players that year were available.

Ending the sponsorship system had a devastating impact on the Canadiens. They would no longer have any advantage in securing francophone players, the lifeblood of their franchise. The Canadiens were now like any other team, and if they wanted francophone players, they would have to draft them, just like everyone else. However, in a seeming acknowledgement by the NHL that the Canadiens bore the brunt of the costs of abolishing the sponsorship system, it gave the club a type of parting gift. In the NHL's first "true" draft of 1969, it decided to award the Canadiens the first two picks. The club then selected the two players considered the best prospects available that year, Réjean Houle and Marc Tardif. Not coincidently, both players were francophone.

THE MONOPOLY CONNECTION

Quebec sovereigntists of the 1960s argued that outside (anglophone) forces were a threat to their distinctive francophone culture and way of life—that francophones, as a minority group in Canada and North America, risked being assimilated into the broader anglophone world that surrounded them.

The extent to which this actually occurred in Quebec society as a whole is debatable, but it unquestionably did occur in hockey. The ability of the Montreal Canadiens to build a roster that reflected the francophone majority in Quebec was lost when the NHL implemented the draft system. The power brokers of the NHL at the time, in places like Toronto and New York, determined that the Canadiens' unique synergy with the francophone community was expendable.

The natural question, then, is why did the NHL feel the need to introduce the draft? After all, European soccer leagues to this day do not have a draft, and clubs recruit incoming young talent by means similar to the NHL's original sponsorship system. The European system allows clubs, if they choose, to field teams with a stronger local connection. Take for example Athletic Bilbao, a club in Spain's first division, La Liga. The city of Bilbao is located in Spain's fiercely proud Basque region, and the club only employs players from that region. Despite the ever-increasing commercialization and player movement that has occurred in elite-level soccer, Athletic Bilbao has still been able to enjoy on-field success with such a limiting recruiting policy.

The answer to this question is ultimately rooted in the fundamentally different economic structures found in professional sports in North America versus Europe. The North American Big Four leagues have long been characterized by monopolistic, anti-competitive structures and practices, and the draft system is just one component of these. The Big Four employ draft systems for a simple reason—

because their market power allows them to. In contrast, the European soccer market is much more open, competitive and free-market oriented—highly controlling and restrictive practices like player drafts would not be practical or useful in such a market structure.

The Big Four operate as "closed" leagues—in which the roster of clubs is constant from year to year. There is no promotion and relegation, as in European soccer. These closed leagues employ a "franchise" model, where new clubs can only be granted admission to the league with the approval of owners of the existing clubs. Generally, these existing owners would only grant such approval in cases where their own financial interests are served by admitting a new member. The number of franchises is tightly restricted, and new entrants are generally only approved for markets not already served by the league, no matter how large the market might be. Toronto, Canada's largest city, for example, has only one NHL team, despite the fact that its size and hockey-mad populace could easily support a second team, if not a third. These so-called territorial rights ensure that existing franchise owners have exclusive monopolies in their local markets, without fear of intrusion from other teams in the league.[17]

There is more. On the players' side, with no rival leagues to which they can sell their services, and with international leagues not a realistic option because of their relatively low salaries,[18] the Big Four also have absolute monopsonistic (i.e., single-buyer) power over their players. Historically, the Big Four have used this monopsonistic power to have mechanisms in place that ensure players are not able to freely move amongst teams in the league. The player draft is one such mechanism. It allows leagues to allocate talent across their franchises in a way that ensures these franchises do not compete against each other for incoming players, and, by extension, it suppresses these players' salaries.

In contrast to the Big Four, the economic structure of European soccer leagues is different in almost every way. First, domestic leagues are "open" rather than closed, meaning the roster of clubs changes from year to year, with some clubs being relegated to a lower tier, and other clubs being promoted from that lower tier. In addition, most European soccer clubs have much more organic foundations than their North American counterparts; their formation was not due to a monopoly league granting them a franchise, but rather was a natural outgrowth of the environment in which they were located.[19] This allows for the possibility of multiple clubs from the same city or regional area—London, for example, has had as many as eight clubs in the 20-team top tier in a single season (1989–90).[20] The Leafs' monopoly status in their market is protected in a way that none of the soccer clubs in London could ever hope to enjoy.

A second important difference is that the various domestic soccer leagues across Europe compete with each other for players. Unlike in North America, soccer players in Europe always have options to play in one of several top-level leagues. If a domestic league, like, say, the Premier League in England were to implement a draft system to allocate young incoming players, the players and their agents could circumvent the system by simply signing with a club in Germany's Bundesliga, or Spain's La Liga, or Italy's Serie A, et cetera.

So, while it *is* true that the NHL's expansion plans in the 1960s probably did render the sponsorship system obsolete, they didn't necessarily imply that the draft system was the only option—the draft system is merely one way to allocate players, and there was no inherent reason why the NHL needed to adopt it. The NHL could have, for example, simply mandated that the Original Six franchises divest themselves of their existing network of junior affiliates and that the expansion clubs adopt their own development systems. All teams would then scout and sign amateur players on a first-come, first-served basis, and then place these players with teams in their development system—essentially the model still used in European soccer today.

However, such a system would not have provided the NHL with the huge economic benefits that the draft system provided, in that it would not have suppressed its member clubs from competing against each other to sign players. The NFL and NBA had already shown the benefits of implementing draft systems in monopoly leagues, and the NHL was eager to follow suit.[21] It is no coincidence that the NHL's first draft in 1963 was only one year after a 14-year-old Bobby Orr fielded offers from multiple NHL teams to sign with them. The Bruins ultimately won the competition, but the NHL was eager to avoid such a free-market bidding war in the future.

FORCING THE ISSUE

Despite the ending of the Canadiens' advantage in securing the best francophone players, the club continued to dominate the NHL throughout the 1970s; they won six more Stanley Cups, including four straight from 1976 to 1979. This continued dominance was due to two reasons. First, many of the core players on the roster during those years, even during the latter part of the 1970s, were acquired by the Canadiens during the pre-draft era. For example, the 1979 Stanley Cup–winning roster still included star francophone players—such as Guy Lapointe, Serge Savard, Jacques Lemaire and Yvan Cournoyer—who were acquired by the Canadiens during the sponsorship era. It wasn't until almost three years later—March 9, 1982, to be exact—that the last vestiges of the sponsorship era finally ended for the Canadiens, with the trading of defenceman Guy Lapointe to the St. Louis Blues for a second-round 1983 draft pick.

The second reason for the club's continued success during the 1970s was that the Canadiens were ahead of the curve regarding strategies to manage the (relatively new) draft. Canadiens GM Sam Pollock understood the vital importance of acquiring elite-level young talent and adopted a policy of trading aging (often past-their-prime) veteran players to the new expansion teams—instantly giving those teams players with name recognition as they were attempting to build a fan base—in exchange for high picks in the draft. The most famous payoff of this strategy occurred in the 1971 draft. The Canadiens had just won the Stanley Cup less than a month earlier, but still had the first-overall pick in the draft thanks to Pollock's shrewd trade almost one year earlier with the California Golden Seals. Pollock gambled that the 1970–71 Seals would be the NHL's worst team, and they were, thus giving Pollock the Seals' first-overall pick. That first pick was francophone Guy Lafleur, who went on to become a Canadiens legend.[22]

However, the success of this type of draft strategy was inevitably short-lived. The Lafleur case in particular showed expansion clubs the folly in trading high draft picks for aging veterans. Teams like the New York Islanders—who entered the NHL as an expansion franchise in 1972—had what was then a novel strategy of building through the draft, and avoided trading their high picks for more immediate help. In their first five years of existence, they drafted such players as Denis Potvin, Clark Gillies, Bryan Trottier and Mike Bossy, who, as a group, formed the nucleus of the Islander clubs that would win four consecutive Stanley Cups in the early 1980s. Other clubs saw this success and copied the Islanders' strategy of retaining draft picks.

With the sponsorship system gone, and with newer clubs increasingly unwilling to make the type of one-sided trades that allowed Montreal to draft a player like Lafleur, the competitive advantage that the Canadiens had long enjoyed in securing incoming players had now evaporated. The Canadiens were just like any other team in the NHL, and unless the club had some inherent and sustained ability to make better draft selections than their league competitors—something which years of subsequent research by sports economists suggest is not likely for any team in any league—then it was almost assured that the club would suffer significant on-ice declines.

However, the draft era presented another problem for the Canadiens: it complicated the ability of the club to sustain its strong francophone flavour; with the draft system, all clubs now had the same access to incoming francophone talent. During the late 1970s and into the 1980s, the Canadiens sometimes tried to force the issue, often drafting French Canadians ahead of where many other club's would have drafted such players.[23] This overvaluing of the francophone factor ultimately resulted in the Canadiens drafting several players who would drastically underperform. Here are some of the club's more spectacular misses:

- Norm Dupont, drafted 18th overall in 1977: 35 career games and only one goal with the Canadiens
- Dan Geoffrion, drafted eighth overall in 1978: 32 career games and zero goals with the Canadiens
- Alain Heroux, drafted 19th overall in 1982: never played a single game in the NHL
- Jocelyn Gauvreau, drafted 31st overall in 1982: played in only two NHL games (both for the Canadiens)
- Jose Charbonneau, drafted 12th overall in 1985: 25 career games and only one goal with the Canadiens
- Éric Charron, drafted 20th overall in 1988: three career games for the Canadiens
- Martin St. Amour, drafted 34th overall in 1988: played one game in the NHL (for Ottawa)
- Steve Larouche, drafted 41st overall in 1989: played 26 games in the NHL for three different clubs (none with Montreal)

Ironically, the Canadiens' biggest draft mistake of that era (and perhaps of all time) occurred in the reverse situation, where the club passed on a prominent and widely touted French Canadian to select an English Canadian. The club had the first-overall pick in the 1980 draft (again, due to a clever Sam Pollock trade, this one four years earlier with the lowly Colorado Rockies). They selected Doug Wickenheiser of the Regina Pats rather than Denis Savard of the Montreal Juniors, despite the fan base's strong preference for the hometown Savard (who was ultimately selected third overall by the Chicago Black Hawks). In fairness to the Canadiens, Wickenheiser was larger than Savard and was coming off a spectacular 89-goal season in the physically tough WHL, compared with Savard's 63-goal season in the wide-open, high-scoring QMJHL. Wickenheiser's size, effortless playing style and elite offensive ability reminded the club of Canadiens' great Jean Béliveau, and Wickenheiser was expected to be the cornerstone of the franchise for years to come.

Unfortunately for the Canadiens, these expectations were never met. Wickenheiser faced enormous pressure in Montreal and played parts of just four seasons with the club, scoring only 49 goals in total over that period. He was traded to the St. Louis Blues in 1983 and played the rest of his career mainly as a defensive forward, scoring 111 career goals in 556 NHL games. Savard, on the other hand, quickly became an NHL superstar, scoring 473 career goals during a career spanning almost 1,200 NHL games.

This draft story has an interesting postscript: The Canadiens did end up acquiring Savard, in a 1990 trade with Chicago. However, the trade was consistent with the notion that the Canadiens often tried to force the issue in their attempts to acquire French Canadian players. The Canadiens overpaid for Savard, sending emerging star defenceman Chris Chelios to the Blackhawks. Savard's talents had already begun to decline significantly, and he was never the

high-impact player for the Canadiens that he was in his earlier days
in Chicago. Chelios, on the other hand, went on to become an NHL
icon, winning two more Norris Trophies as the league's top defenceman, and playing a staggering 26 seasons in the NHL (tying Gordie
Howe for the league record).

DECLINING NUMBERS

The Canadiens gradually realized that overreaching for francophone
players had its costs. Under a draft system, where all teams now had
equal access to all players, regardless of the player's origin, any biasing
of decisions toward less-talented francophones, simply because they
were francophones, would lower team quality. Competitive markets
penalized teams that made draft decisions based on factors other
than simply a player's talent; in this reality, there was a (potentially
high) cost to the Canadiens indulging a cultural preference. This
notion didn't just apply to the draft; it was also true for trades and
free-agent signings.

This realization led to a long and steady decline in the number
of francophones on the Canadiens' roster. In their glory years
from the mid-'50s to the late '70s, the Canadiens' rosters each year
were awash with francophone players; on average, francophones
accounted for a remarkable 55% of the club's roster spots in any given
season across their 24-year dynasty, reaching as high as 67% in the
Canadiens' 1970–71 Stanley Cup–winning season.[24] Even by the
late 1970s—ten full years after the NHL draft was introduced—the
Canadiens were still very francophone-heavy. The Canadiens' 1978
Stanley Cup–winning roster was 61% francophone; the 1979 roster
close behind at 55%.

The 1979 Cup victory marked the end of the dynasty. The Canadiens would go on to win two more Stanley Cups, but the makeup and

persona of these teams was different from that of the glory years. The 1986 Cup winners had only a 22% francophone component. As well, only three of the top 10 scorers on the club were francophone.

At 48%, the francophone makeup of the 1993 Cup-winning team was much larger than on the 1986 club, and was within striking distance of the proportions found on the Canadiens' teams of the glory years. The 1993 club even had a francophone as its leading scorer—Vincent Damphousse. While Damphousse was a solid player, he was no Guy Lafleur, or Jean Béliveau, or Rocket Richard. The Canadiens were already Damphousse's third NHL club in his relatively short career to that point. Many of the other francophones on the club that year tended to be role players or fringe players, hardly household names, and players whose careers quickly plummeted after that 1993 Cup win—players like Gilbert Dionne, Stéphan Lebeau and Mario Roberge.[25]

The 1992–93 season turned out to be the last hurrah, not only for the Canadiens' Stanley Cup success, but for the strong presence of francophones on the club's rosters. In the years following that season, francophones composed an ever-decreasing proportion of Canadiens players. By the 1999–2000 season, the proportion had dropped precipitously, down to only 14%. Data from the 2013–14 to 2020–21 seasons shows the proportion has reached somewhat of a steady state in those years, settling in at around 10%, still much higher than every other team in the NHL, but a far cry from the 55% of the glory years. Even more revealing, during the Canadiens' surprise run to the 2020–21 Stanley Cup final, of the 22 skaters who appeared for the club during the playoffs, only one—Phillip Danault—was French Canadian.

The obvious explanation for the steadily declining proportion of francophones on the Canadiens roster was that the club lost its priority access to these players when the NHL ended the sponsorship system. However, there also may be another, more subtle, influence: it's possible that Canadiens fans simply care less about a heavily francophone roster that they did a half century ago. Increased immigration in recent decades has decreased the percentage of the Quebec population that is francophone (or, to be more precise, whose mother tongue is French), and a more diverse and enlightened fan base—with a more global perspective—may place less importance on the ethnicity of players than in eras past.

However, the issue has never been just about the *total* number of francophones on the Canadiens roster; it's also about the star power of these players. Not one of the star francophone (non-goalie) players in the NHL over the past 40 years—spanning players like Mario Lemieux, Ray Bourque, Luc Robitaille, Pierre Turgeon and Vincent Lecavalier—was drafted by the Canadiens. Arguably, the Canadiens' best francophone player over that time was the aforementioned Vincent Damphousse, a player originally drafted by the Toronto Maple Leafs, and a player who, while certainly a solid NHLer, was far from a superstar.

No longer are francophones the perennial leaders in club scoring. A francophone has not led the Canadiens in scoring in two decades (since the 2001–02 season). During that time, neither has a francophone even finished *second* in club scoring. This absence of francophone scoring talent extends even deeper on the roster; in both the 2015–16 and 2016–17 seasons, only one francophone even cracked the club's top 10 in scoring.

These types of numbers would have been unheard of during the Canadiens' dynasty years. Consider this: in the 24 seasons spanning 1955–56 to 1978–79, a francophone was the club's leading scorer in 19 of those seasons—in the other five seasons, a francophone finished second in club scoring. Not only this, but there was francophone scoring depth throughout the entire roster. For example, in the Canadiens' Stanley Cup–winning 1965–66 season, all of the club's top five scorers that year were francophone, as were eight of the top 10. It was complete dominance.

THE OTHER FRANCOPHONE CLUB

While the Montreal Canadiens were busy adjusting to the NHL's post-sponsorship world during the 1970s and '80s, there was a parallel story unfolding 250 kilometres to the northeast, in Quebec City.

In 1972, the Quebec Nordiques would become charter members of the rival WHA, giving the province of Quebec its second major pro hockey team. The franchise was originally slated for San Francisco, but ownership and financing issues there resulted in the team being sold to Quebec City interests just months before the start of the WHA's inaugural season. The Nordiques owners also owned the local junior team, the highly successful Quebec Remparts, who just one year earlier had won the Memorial Cup, led by future NHL superstar Guy Lafleur.

The Nordiques would exist for 23 seasons, the first seven in the WHA, and then the last 16 in the NHL after the two leagues merged in 1979. In 1995, facing serious financial issues in Quebec, the club was sold and moved to Denver, Colorado, becoming the Colorado Avalanche.

From the beginning, the Nordiques were openly and unabashedly francophone in a way the Montreal Canadiens never were. In their inaugural WHA season of 1972–73, the club's roster was 90% francophone, a figure far higher than any season in the Canadiens' long history. While most of these players had been career minor-leaguers who had never played in the NHL—and never would—the club did manage to sign star defenceman J.C. Tremblay away from the Montreal Canadiens. Granted, Tremblay, at age 32, was past his prime, but he still had been selected as a first-team NHL all-star in 1971, and his signing quickly established the Nordiques as a legitimate team.

The Nordiques even signed Canadiens legend Rocket Richard as their head coach that first season. Hiring Richard was more of a public relations move than a sound hockey decision—Richard, then 51, had never coached prior to his hire by the Nordiques. Just two games into the season (with a record of one win and one loss), Richard decided that coaching wasn't for him and abruptly resigned his position. He would never coach again in hockey.

Despite the Richard miscue, the Nordiques began to build a solid following in Quebec City that first year. The city's population at the time was almost exclusively francophone—unlike Montreal, where there was a somewhat greater ethnic and cultural diversity— so filling the Nordiques roster with francophones seemed like a wise move to build immediate identification with the fan base.

While the Nordiques were largely a collection of no-name players that first season—save for Tremblay—they upped their talent level considerably in their second year by convincing a pair of franco- phone NHL regulars to jump leagues and sign with the team. One was Serge Bernier, who was just coming off an impressive 22-goal season with the Los Angeles Kings. The other was Réjean Houle, who four years earlier had been selected by the Montreal Canadiens as the first-overall pick in the 1969 NHL draft.

Partway through the Nordiques' third WHA season, they added even more francophone talent, acquiring Marc Tardif—originally selected, also by the Canadiens, second overall in the 1969 draft, after Houle—in a trade with another WHA club, the Michigan Stags. Like Houle, Tardif had left the Canadiens and the NHL at the end of the 1972–73 season; both players were frustrated by their lim- ited roles and overall lack of playing time with the Canadiens. The Canadiens of that era assembled some of the most dominant teams in NHL history—led by established stars like Lafleur, Cournoyer, Lemaire and Pete Mahovlich—so, for players like Houle and Tardif, despite their promising talent, staying with the Canadiens likely meant being relegated to supporting roles for years to come.

The Nordiques' pursuit of dynamic francophone talent also extended to the major junior ranks. In 1974, the club drafted and signed junior sensation Réal Cloutier. Cloutier was coming off a prolific 1973–74 season with the local Quebec Remparts, scoring a staggering 93 goals and adding 123 assists and leading his club to the 1974 Memorial Cup final (which the Remparts lost to the Regina Pats). The Nordiques took advantage of the fact that the NHL draft age at the time was 20, so Cloutier, at 18, would not be eligible to enter the NHL for two more years. Cloutier was such a hot commodity that the Chicago Black Hawks still drafted him ninth overall in the first round of the 1976 NHL draft, even though he was under contract to the Nordiques.[26]

The Nordiques' collection of high-end offensive talent, all of it francophone, not only quickly endeared the club to fans in Quebec City, it made the team a WHA powerhouse. The club made it to the WHA finals twice in three years, losing in 1975 and winning in 1977. And their stars dominated the stat sheets. Tardif won two scoring titles, as did Cloutier; Tardif led the league in goals twice, Cloutier once; Réjean Houle had a 51-goal/103-point season; Serge Bernier had two seasons of 100-plus points; and so on. In the end, Tardif would become the all-time leading goal scorer in WHA history; Cloutier was third on that list (with Bobby Hull in between, at second) and Serge Bernier was sixth. These were heady times for the Nordiques, and for francophone hockey in Quebec.

For the Montreal Canadiens, the Nordiques and their WHA success was somewhat of a curiosity, a sideshow, a minor irritant at most, but certainly not a threat to either the Canadiens' on-ice success or their business brand. While both clubs were located in the province of Quebec, and both relied heavily on francophone players, that was as far as the similarities went.

First, they were in different leagues and therefore hadn't faced each other on the ice, so there was no fan rivalry of any sort. One could be both a Canadiens fan *and* a Nordiques fan—they were not mutually exclusive. Furthermore, the WHA was viewed by the NHL and many observers as a much inferior league, not really worth the attention of the mighty Canadiens or the NHL. Under this view, whatever the Nordiques were accomplishing had to be viewed within the context of them being in a second-tier league. In addition, the WHA's very limited national TV contract in Canada meant that its clubs often got minimal exposure outside their home cities. Unlike the Montreal Canadiens, who were on *Hockey Night in Canada* as often as twice a week—many people in Canada had never seen the Nordiques play, even on TV. For many, the Nordiques were strictly local—great for Quebec City, but not really a force beyond that.

Perhaps most importantly, though, the Canadiens were not only the most iconic franchise in hockey history, they were also in the midst of a particularly dominating run of seasons. During the seven years that the WHA existed, the Canadiens won five Stanley Cups. Not only that, they had some of the most impressive regular-season performances in NHL history; in 80-game regular seasons, they lost only 11 times in 1975–76, eight times in 1976–77 and 10 times in 1977–78. With this immense success and complete domination of their opponents, the Canadiens and their fans were too busy basking in their own aura to give the Nordiques much thought.

This would all change, though, and quickly. Less than five months after the Canadiens' 1979 Stanley Cup victory—their fourth in a row—the Quebec Nordiques entered the NHL as part of the partial merger between the NHL and WHA. No longer would the Canadiens have the province of Quebec to themselves. There was now market competition—for fans, for the hearts of francophones, for television deals and for sponsorship dollars.

While the Canadiens had the benefit of their long, illustrious history, the Nordiques' arrival in the NHL couldn't have occurred at a worse time for Montreal. In the summer of 1979, the core of the Canadiens' dynasty years was shaken with the departure of four critical components—star goalie Ken Dryden, forward Jacques Lemaire, iconic coach Scotty Bowman and long-time GM Sam Pollock.[27] If it seemed at the time like the beginning of the end for the Canadiens' dominance, it quickly proved to be true.

THE BATTLE OF QUEBEC

The Canadiens' fall was swift and unceremonious. In the first season following the WHA merger, the Canadiens lost in the second round of the playoffs—one of their earliest playoff exits in years. That was followed by the club being eliminated in the first round of the 1980–81 playoffs—a 3–0 series sweep at the hands of the underdog Edmonton Oilers. It was only the Oilers' second NHL season (like the Nordiques, they were orphaned by the defunct WHA), and while they would soon go on to become a dynasty of their own, they were not there yet in 1980–81, finishing 29 points behind the Canadiens in the regular-season standings. For Canadiens fans, the playoff loss to the Oilers was a devastating reminder that the glory years were finished. But things would get even worse. The 1983–84 version of the Canadiens lost more regular-season games than they won, the first losing record for the franchise since 1950–51, 33 seasons earlier.[28]

The Canadiens' decline provided the Nordiques franchise with an opportunity to quickly establish itself within the Quebec market as a legitimate NHL club. While the Nordiques struggled on the ice during their first NHL season—finishing last in their division—their future looked promising. They were able to retain stars Marc Tardif and Réal Cloutier when the leagues merged, and then added in the 1979 entry draft top prospect Michel Goulet. Cloutier, Tardif and Goulet would finish 1–2–3 in the club's scoring that first NHL season. Save for Guy Lafleur, these three players offered the Nordiques' high-scoring francophone talent that was just as good as the Canadiens', if not better.[29]

The Quebec franchise's fortunes got a further boost in the summer of 1980 when brothers Peter and Anton Stastny defected from Czechoslovakia and joined the Nordiques—two years later, their older brother Marián would also come aboard. Together, the three Stastnys brought an offence-oriented, European style of play to the club that blended well with the style of the Nordiques' large francophone contingent.

Not surprisingly, the Nordiques improved rapidly. In 1981–82, only their third NHL season, they made the playoffs for the first time. Perhaps fittingly, their first-round opponent that year was the Montreal Canadiens. The matchup was classic: the fledging Nordiques, battling for recognition in both the NHL and in the province of Quebec, against the once-mighty icons.

The Canadiens were heavy favourites, not only because of their history, but also because they had finished 27 points ahead of the Nordiques in the regular-season standings. However, it was not meant to be for the Canadiens; in one of the biggest upsets in years in the NHL, the Nordiques pulled off an improbable series victory, winning the fifth and deciding game in the venerable Montreal Forum, scoring 22 seconds into sudden-death overtime. However, the Nordiques were not done. They went on to eliminate the Boston Bruins in the second round, advancing to the Prince of Wales Conference final against the New York Islanders. Incredibly, the

Nordiques were now only one playoff series win from reaching the Stanley Cup final. The dream ended abruptly when they were swept by the Islanders (who would go on to win their third consecutive Cup), but the Nordiques had served notice that they had become, almost overnight, a legitimate Stanley Cup contender.

The Nordiques' upset of the Canadiens in the 1981–82 playoffs turned out to be the first instalment of the "Battle of Quebec," an intense rivalry that would develop during the 1980s. The two teams would meet in the playoffs four times in a five-season span, and the familiarity seemed to breed contempt. The 1983–84 playoff series between the two clubs was particularly acrimonious; the sixth game of their second-round series was marred by two brawls, one at the end of the second period, and another at the start of the third period. The Easter-weekend game became known as the "Good Friday Massacre"; ten players were ejected from the game, and over 250 minutes in penalties were called. It was one of the most violent hockey games of its era and lives in infamy to this day.

However, the Battle of Quebec was much more than just an on-ice rivalry; it also had strong business and political elements to it. On the business side, the two clubs were owned by competing breweries: the Canadiens by Molson and the Nordiques by Carling O'Keefe. Through-out the 1980s, the two breweries used their respective hockey clubs as vehicles to market their product. While corporate ownership of major sport franchises was not necessarily unusual during the era— in baseball, for example, Labatt owned the Toronto Blue Jays and Anheuser-Busch owned the St. Louis Cardinals—what *was* unusual was the level of animosity between these two corporate entities. Much of this went back to the 1979 NHL–WHA merger agreement, when, as part of the harsh terms the NHL imposed on WHA teams, the Canadiens/Molson insisted that the Nordiques receive no national TV money in Canada for five years. Molson Brewery not only owned the

Canadiens at the time, but had been the primary sponsor of *Hockey Night in Canada* broadcasts, so the Carling O'Keefe–owned Nordiques were not about to get part of this lucrative TV money anytime soon.

The third front in the Canadiens-Nordiques rivalry was politics. With support for sovereignty much higher in the Quebec City region than in the more ethnically diverse Montreal, the Nordiques acted as a kind of the symbol for sovereigntists, the Canadiens for federalists. So, in a way not seen in North American sports, but often found in European soccer, the Canadiens-Nordiques battles became proxies for underlying political tensions.[30]

That this politicization of the rivalry occurred should not be surprising. Time and place matter greatly. The Nordiques inaugural 1979–80 NHL season was played during the run-up to the province's first sovereignty referendum—the club's final game that season occurred only six weeks before the referendum. The tense, politically charged climate of the day could never be divorced from hockey.

As intense and heated as the Battle of Quebec was, it was relatively short-lived. By the late 1980s, all three fronts of this rivalry were fading fast. The beer wars officially ended in 1989 when Carling O'Keefe was bought by (ironically) Molson. In anticipation of the merger, the Nordiques were spun off and sold to a group of local Quebec City businesspeople. On the ice, the quality of the Nordiques' performance was plummeting, particularly as Carling O'Keefe seemed to be losing interest. By 1987–88, the Nordiques had fallen to last place in their division; one year later, they had the worst record in the entire NHL. By the late 1980s, even the political climate had cooled somewhat. The Parti Québécois had lost power in Quebec in 1985 and lost again in the 1989 provincial election.

For the Montreal Canadiens, the Nordiques' rapid rise during the early and mid-'80s was somewhat of a double-edged sword. On the positive side, it allowed the Canadiens to quickly redirect fan attention away from their fallen dynasty and toward a potentially new and exciting chapter in their existence, one where the intra-provincial rivalry would be front and centre. No matter the sport, regional rivalries can also be good for business, driving a variety of local revenues, like merchandise sales, sponsorship sales and so on.

However, as with many rivalries, there was an asymmetry in how the two clubs viewed the rivalry. It always seemed that the Canadiens had more to lose from the rivalry than to gain. The Nordiques had no reputation to uphold, the Canadiens did. If the Canadiens won, they were *expected* to win. If they lost, they were disparaged by their fans and the media for being unprepared or uninspired, for letting an upstart get the best of them.

So much changed for the Canadiens, so quickly. Just a few short years earlier they were winning Stanley Cup after Stanley Cup, solidifying their place as the greatest franchise of all time in hockey, if not all of North American sport. Now, they were suddenly engaged in a battle for supremacy within their own *province*—a battle for on-ice superiority, a battle for market share and a battle for the hearts of hockey fans across the province. For many in the club, it was a distasteful battle, one where their opponent was seen as merely a refugee from a much inferior league, not worthy of challenging the hockey royalty that was the Canadiens.

For all its manifestations, the Battle of Quebec can ultimately be distilled down to its most core element: the presence of the Nordiques threatened the Canadiens' long-held status and identity as *the* club of francophones. During the early to mid-'80s, the Nordiques "out-francophoned" the Canadiens on almost every front, and did so with a flair and gusto the now-staid Canadiens couldn't seem to match. Over the seven seasons spanning 1981–82 to 1987–88, the Nordiques averaged about 40% more francophones on their roster in any given season than did the Canadiens.[31] Not only that, with players such as Réal Cloutier, Marc Tardif and Michel Goulet, the Nordiques' francophones possessed more dynamic offensive star-power than did the Canadiens. The best the Canadiens could do on this front was an aging Guy Lafleur, whose skills by this point were rapidly declining, and who would go on to (abruptly) retire partway through the 1984–85 season.

The Canadiens' tendency during that period to "force the issue" and draft several francophones higher than their talent warranted was no doubt driven, at least in part, by trying to keep pace with the Nordiques' francophone talent. The Canadiens seemed like they were always trying to serve two masters: they wanted to win, but they also wanted to ensure a sufficient complement of francophones. The two were not always compatible.

The issue of sufficient francophone representation went beyond just the players. In that first-ever salvo in the Battle of Quebec—the high-profile 1982 playoff series in which the third-year Nordiques pulled a shocking upset—the Canadiens came under criticism from some Quebec nationalists for having anglophones in both the head coach (Bob Berry) and general manager (Irving Grundman) roles, in stark contrast to the Nordiques, who had francophones in each.

Perhaps coincidentally, but probably not, the Canadiens soon moved away from having anglophones in these key positions. Grundman was fired one year later, immediately following the 1982–83 season, to be replaced by Canadiens legend Serge Savard; Berry was fired partway through the 1983–84 season, replaced by another former player from the team's pantheon, Jacques Lemaire. In the more than 40 years since Grundman was fired, francophones have held the Canadiens GM position for all but seven of those years.[32] On the coaching side, the Canadiens' have had 13 permanent[33] coaches since Bob Berry; only one of these coaches, Pat Burns during the late '80s and early '90s, was anglophone.

Perhaps as a counter to the decreasing presence and impact of francophone *players*, the club has seemingly gone out of its way to maintain a strong francophone presence on the coaching and management side of the organization.[34] However, given the Canadiens' mediocre record over that time—including a 28-year run of not even *appearing* in a Stanley Cup final, let alone winning one—the club's preference for francophone coaches and general managers may itself be an example of overreaching. A question naturally arises: Had the club been hiring the best possible coaches and managers available, or, instead, had they been hiring the best *francophone* coaches and managers available? The two are not necessarily the same. Clubs that utilize hiring criteria—including ethnicity—that are not solely based on coaches' and managers' abilities will inevitably lose ground to their league competitors, and will pay the price in the form of reduced on-ice team performance.

A NEW ECONOMIC ORDER

By the time of the infamous Roy-Tremblay incident in December 1995, the Canadiens were on the precipice of entering yet another era, one in which financial turmoil and the blunt uncertainty of the franchise's mere viability were the new reality.

The Canadiens had long been accustomed to being the economic powerhouse of the NHL. During antitrust hearings before the US Congress in the late 1950s, it was revealed that the Canadiens' revenues consistently far exceeded that of their four US-based counterparts.[35] Consider the 1954–55 season, the last season before the Canadiens started their run of five successive Stanley Cups. The club's revenues that year were an astounding 50% greater than the average of the four US-based clubs.[36] While this may initially seem like an incongruity, given that Montreal had a much smaller population than

any of these US cities, the Canadiens were in the enviable position
of being located in a grassroots, hockey-mad market, where hockey
was inextricably linked to the core of the community's social
and cultural fabric, and where hockey was *the* spectator sport. In
contrast, the US–based NHL teams had only niche followings in their
local markets; hockey at that time was seen as an "imported" game
with no grassroots foundation, and as a spectator sport was largely
overshadowed by more prominent American sports options in
these cities.

The Canadiens' revenue-generating advantages directly translated into on-ice success—in basic economic terms, clubs that generate higher revenues can afford to pay higher salaries and buy better
players (think of baseball's New York Yankees). In the 1950s, when
there was no draft and no salary cap, and when amateurs generally
could be freely signed by any NHL club, the Canadiens' economic
power and greater ability to pay player salaries no doubt helped
them to convince many top prospects (particularly francophones)
to sign with the club.

The payroll numbers bear this out. Take the Canadiens' 1955–56
Stanley Cup–winning season, the first year of the club's 24-year
dynasty. The Canadiens' payroll (salaries and bonuses) that year
was almost 100% greater than that of the Chicago Black Hawks and
Boston Bruins, and 55% higher than the big-city New York Rangers!
Even more revealing, it was 45% higher than the club's biggest
on-ice rival of that era, the Gordie Howe–led Detroit Red Wings. So,
while the Canadiens dominated on the ice during the late 1950s, it
certainly wasn't a level playing field. They massively outspent their
competitors and, in present-day parlance, could have been accused
of "buying" Stanley Cup success.

Fast-forward three decades and not much had changed. In
1991—the year the business magazine *Financial World*[37] began esti-

mating the franchise values[38] of North American pro-sports teams—the Canadiens topped the NHL rankings, being listed by the magazine as the most valuable franchise in the league. So, despite the fact that their quarter-century dynasty had ended more than a decade earlier, and that their on-ice performance during the 1980s had largely slipped into mediocrity, the Canadiens were still a thriving *economic* entity. The iconic status of their franchise kept the Canadiens' brand strong.

By the *late* 1990s, however, financial uncertainties were beginning to surround the club, much of them driven by external factors. The economics of the NHL were undergoing a fundamental and dramatic change that altered the variables that drove economic success in the league and that would ultimately displace the Canadiens as the league's flagship franchise.

Under the old economic order, the local revenues of NHL clubs were first and foremost driven by gate receipts and, only secondarily, by (analog) TV contracts with regional providers. In this environment, as was seen during the 1950s, the mere population of a city was less important to a club's revenues than was the city's level and intensity of interest in the sport of hockey. It meant that clubs in smaller markets, particularly those in Canada with their deep-rooted passion for the game, were not necessarily at any significant financial disadvantage compared with those in very populous markets—clubs like the Edmonton Oilers and Calgary Flames could financially compete with clubs like the New York Rangers and the Chicago Blackhawks.

The emergence of digital technology began to change all of that, and quickly. The local TV contracts of the US–based franchises in markets with larger populations exploded, dwarfing those of most of the Canadian-based franchises and abruptly shifting the economic power base of the league.

Parallel with these technological changes were two other forces that reduced the power and influence of the Canadian franchises. The low value of the Canadian dollar caused enormous financial stress, since player salaries were paid in US dollars—as required by the NHL collective bargaining agreement (CBA)—but most revenues were earned in Canadian dollars. By the mid-'90s—when the Canadian dollar was trading at only about $0.70 USD—two of Canada's NHL franchises left for the US. The Quebec Nordiques relocated to Denver, Colorado, in 1995, and one year later the (original) Winnipeg Jets moved to Phoenix, Arizona.

The mid-'90s also saw the beginning of the Gary Bettman era in the NHL. A transplant from the legal departments of the NBA, Bettman became the first commissioner of the NHL in 1993.[39] His prime focus was to extend the NHL's geographic footprint in the US; the league had long struggled to gain a national following in that country, limiting its ability to gain lucrative national TV contracts. Bettman's strategy was to ensure that the NHL was in all the major US media markets, seemingly regardless of whether those markets had a traditional hockey following or not. By the end of the '90s, "Sunbelt" cities like Miami (Florida Panthers), Tampa, Atlanta, Nashville, Anaheim and San Jose had received expansion franchises. In addition, relocations of existing NHL franchises (the Winnipeg Jets, Minnesota North Stars and Hartford Whalers, respectively) saw the league enter markets in Phoenix, Dallas and Raleigh, North Carolina.[40]

Many Canadians, rightly or wrongly, vilified Bettman and saw him as undermining the game's fundamental connection to Canada and the north. Popular opinion amongst Canadian hockey fans suggested that Bettman's New York City birth, his roots in the NBA and his lack of any significant hockey background indicated he had very little interest in preserving the league's Canadian-based history.

For the Montreal Canadiens, so difficult were the times that the franchise was sold in 2001 to American George Gillett, whom many Canadiens fans feared had designs on moving the franchise to the us. Gillett was viewed with great suspicion in Montreal, and, as with Bettman, his nationality and his lack of any hockey-related history—not to mention his previous high-profile bankruptcy—did nothing to endear him to the club's fans.[41]

Gillett arrived on the scene at a time when the Canadiens, as a business entity, were in a free fall. The preceding decade had not been kind to the club: it went from being the most valuable franchise in the NHL in 1991 to seventh on the list by 2001—a very large decline in such a short time. Even more discouraging, this decline occurred in spite of the club moving into a new, state-of-the-art arena in 1996 (the Molson Centre, now Bell Centre), and commensurately benefiting from the increased revenue potential that went along with the new facility. By 2004, the financial situation had deteriorated even further, with the Canadiens falling to 10th place in franchise-value rankings. To put this in perspective, the storied Canadiens franchise was now only one spot above the much-less-than-iconic Minnesota Wild, who had entered the NHL only four years earlier as an expansion franchise.

The Canadiens' declining financial value (at least relative to their league counterparts) trickled down and ultimately inhibited their ability to compete in the players' market. In the 15 seasons between 1989–90 and 2003–04, the Canadiens' league ranking in team payroll dropped precipitously from fifth place[42] to 17th. The 16 teams that had higher payrolls than the Canadiens' in 2003–04 included three Canadian franchises—Toronto, Ottawa and Vancouver—so the Canadiens' fall could not be solely attributed to the struggles that all Canadian clubs were experiencing. Even more stark, the Canadiens' payroll in 2003–04 was just 50% of what clubs like the Red Wings and Rangers were paying, making it extremely difficult for the Canadiens to stay competitive on the ice, let alone seriously contend for the Stanley Cup.

It turned out that the 2003–04 season would mark the end of an era in the NHL, at least in a business and financial sense. As mentioned earlier, the development of digital technology created an explosion in local TV revenues for the large-market US clubs, allowing them to more fully capitalize on their mega-populations than what was previously possible in a primarily gate-driven league (where arena capacity was a limiting factor for gate revenues). The NHL knew it had an ever-increasing competitive balance problem in the league, where large-market/large-revenue teams were at a consistent on-ice advantage because of their larger payrolls.

With the CBA between the league and its players expiring at the end of the 2003–04 season, the NHL proposed the introduction of a hard salary cap, where every club's payroll would be required to fall within a narrow band, and where overall player salaries in the league would be a fixed proportion of league revenues. The players were strongly opposed to any type of salary cap, and a bitter year-long dispute between the two sides resulted in the cancellation of the entire 2004–05 season, the first instance in the history of North American sports where an entire season was lost due to a labour dispute.

When the two sides finally came to an agreement in the summer of 2005, the NHL got almost all of what it wanted, including a hard salary cap. For the Canadiens and most other Canadian clubs, it seemed like they had finally been thrown a lifeline; there was now some control on labour costs and the large-market US teams would have their unfettered payroll spending finally reined in.

The 2005 CBA also introduced a revenue-sharing scheme that transferred money from the largest-revenue clubs to the smallest-revenue clubs. While the league had always shared revenues from national TV contracts equally across all franchises, this was the league's first serious effort to share *local* revenues. Doing so brought it closer to what was happening in sports like baseball. Now, clubs like the New York Rangers and Detroit Red Wings, with their lucrative local TV deals, would not be able to keep all these proceeds for themselves.

For the Canadiens, as a business entity, the combination of the new CBA, a rising Canadian dollar[43] and a change of ownership from American George Gillett to the local Molson family not only stopped the franchise's downward spiral, but actually put the club on a strong upward trajectory. The club began to steadily move up the rankings of team values, going from 10th place in 2004 all the way to third in 2009.

With the salary cap levelling the playing field, and with the increase in the Canadian dollar lowering salary costs for the Canadiens, the club could compete again in the players' market. To illustrate the dramatic effects of the cap, consider this: in the final season before the introduction of the salary cap—2003–04—the Canadiens' team payroll was $40 *million* less than big spenders like the Detroit Red Wings and New York Rangers. With the highest-paid players in the league that season making about $10 million each, this $40 million payroll deficit of the Canadiens was equivalent to clubs like the Red Wings and Rangers having four more elite superstars than the Canadiens—an incredible advantage on a 20-player roster. By 2010–11, however, that gap had almost completely vanished; the Canadiens' payroll that year was approximately only $1 million less than either the Red Wings or Rangers.

Throughout the post-cap era, the Canadiens have remained one of the NHL's most valuable franchises: they placed third on the *Forbes* list in 2020–21, trailing only the New York Rangers and Toronto Maple Leafs. Their financial success, however, has translated into only very modest gains in on-ice performance. In the final 10 uncapped NHL seasons (1994–95 to 2003–04), the Canadiens had an overall points-percent of 0.495, dismal by their high standards, and the worst 10-year run for the club since the 1933–34 to 1942–43 stretch. Over that time, their average overall finish in regular-season standings was 17th in the league, and they failed to qualify for the playoffs in five of those 10 seasons.

By contrast, in the 18 capped seasons (through 2022–23), the club's average finish in the NHL standings has been 16th—better than the 17th they produced in the last 10 uncapped seasons, but only slightly. Their points-percent actually decreased, albeit marginally, from .495 pre-cap to .491 in the cap era.[44] So, whatever the reason—be it overreaching for francophone players and/or coaches, organizational culture issues or just plain ineffective decision-making at various levels in the organization—the club has not been able to escape its now decades-long on-ice mediocrity.

AMERICAN DOMINANCE

In the salary-cap era, the Canadiens as a business entity have unquestionably thrived—dramatically rising from the dark depths of 2004 to once again become one of the most valuable franchises in the NHL. Just like the 1950s—when US antitrust hearings first revealed the Canadiens' large financial advantage over their league competitors—the Canadiens of today are an economic powerhouse within the league.

But something is different this time around. Yes, the Canadiens are once again a strong business entity—a decorated history, combined with a highly knowledgeable and hockey-mad fan base almost guarantees a high degree of financial success. But all of this is against a backdrop of a world around them that has changed forever. And while older generations of hockey fans may still appreciate the Canadiens' iconic uniforms and insignia, for many fans under the age of 40, and particularly for those outside Quebec, the Canadiens are no longer special. They are just like any other franchise, with a revolving set of players drawn from various places around the hockey world, with an on-ice performance that is not particularly noteworthy, and with challenges on the business side that every other club in the league faces.

In their glory days, the Canadiens were a cultural institution, not only in Quebec, but in all of Canada. Today, they are a mere corporate brand, one franchise, just like any other, within a large American-dominated league. The flair, the mystique, the distinctiveness—all are gone.

Of the 124 franchises in the Big Four North American leagues—115 of which are in the US—the Montreal Canadiens have a history that is so utterly unique. The Canadiens were the pride and embodiment of a minority people struggling to maintain their identity. In this way, the Canadiens aligned more with many soccer clubs in Europe than with their North American counterparts, in that their fan base wasn't unified by mere geographic location, but by much deeper identifiers like social class, religion, language, culture and so on.

In Europe, these unique characteristics of clubs were largely preserved, even as the game became more commercialized. There are at least two reasons for this. First, leagues in Europe were domestic (not transnational), increasing the likelihood that club-specific peculiarities would be celebrated as part of the national mosaic and not lost in a sea of conformity-inducing transnational commercialism. Second, European leagues remained open leagues (i.e., with promotion and relegation), meaning the membership of any one club was not necessarily permanent and reducing the power of existing clubs to introduce monopoly practices, like player drafts and salary caps.

A European-style model would have meant no salary cap. The introduction of the cap in 2005 had conflicting impacts for a team like the Canadiens—while the hard salary cap brought much-needed short term cost control, it also ensured that the Canadiens, as an iconic franchise of the NHL, were constrained to spend essentially the same on salaries as more obscure clubs in lower-revenue markets like Atlanta (home of the Thrashers, now the second iteration of the Winnipeg Jets), Columbus and Miami (Florida Panthers). In other words, they had no way to reinvigorate their on-ice performance by significantly outspending their league counterparts, something that happens regularly in Major League Baseball with teams like the New York Yankees or the Los Angeles Dodgers, or in European soccer with clubs like Real Madrid or Manchester City.

The story of the Canadiens raises the question as to whether that club's fans, and Canadians in general, would have benefited had a "made in Canada" league developed in the early years. Canadian hockey, both at the junior level—as will be examined in Chapter 5 —and at the professional level, became heavily reliant and tied into a league (the NHL) that was driven first and foremost by American interests. While it is true that the NHL began operations in 1917 as an all-Canadian league, this was short-lived, with the league quickly adding six US–based franchises over the next decade.[45] From 1938 to 1970—a period that covered much of the NHL's crucial formative years—the league had only two Canadian franchises: the Leafs and the Canadiens.

In the NHL's first half century (i.e., to 1967) and even beyond, the American owners of the US franchises were entirely dependent on Canada as the source of players to stock their rosters. The US produced essentially no NHL–calibre players itself, and the European "invasion" of players was still years away—Canada was the exclusive source of top-level hockey talent. There was a significant geographic disjoint, then, between where the players were produced (Canada) and where the majority of the players were employed (the us).

In this environment, one might have thought the conditions were right for a major Canadian professional league to form. It did not. As a result, Canada's national game became forever caught up in a us-controlled league. Many Canadians associate the "Americanization" of the NHL with the 1967 expansion (when no Canadian teams were added), or with the reign of commissioner Gary Bettman, who oversaw the NHL's expansion into several Sunbelt cities across the us, while Winnipeg and Quebec lost their NHL teams to us cities. However, the Americanization happened much longer ago than these events.

In 1947, the NHL essentially took over the amateur hockey system in Canada, and explicitly turned it into a device of its own. The Canadian Amateur Hockey Association (CAHA), the governing body of amateur hockey in Canada, signed an agreement that gave NHL teams complete and unilateral control over all amateur teams and players in Canada. In return, the NHL provided cash injections to help amateur teams that were struggling financially in the immediate postwar environment.[46] As a result, hockey in Canada quickly became about *only* serving the NHL, and an independent Canadian league had virtually no chance of succeeding in this type of environment.

Canada may be the only country in the developed world to not have a domestic professional league for the country's most popular spectator sport. In Europe, for example, each country has its own independent domestic soccer league, regardless of the size of the country. Even tiny Andorra—with a population of only 75,000— has an eight-team domestic professional league.

There were probably moments in history when professional hockey in Canada could have adopted more of a European model—

one where clubs formed organically as grassroots endeavours of the
local population, and where a national governing body protects
the interests of the domestic game. These governing bodies—like
England's Football Association or the German Football Association
—are broadly similar in design to what the CAHA was intended to be.

The governing bodies in European countries have always jeal-
ously guarded the domestic game and have long resisted any talk of
transnational "super-leagues." While a country's top clubs will participate in the pan-European and high-profile Champions League, they
also participate in their own domestic leagues, and success in these
domestic leagues is always an important objective. Even for smaller
countries, while they often see their best national players eventually
migrate to high-revenue clubs outside the country, they still value
their domestic leagues as a matter of national pride and unity.

One would think this would have direct relevance to Canada,
where a strong domestic professional hockey league (or leagues)
could be a unifying force, while simultaneously celebrating the
regional differences and rivalries across the country. Instead, professional hockey in Canada quickly got subsumed into a US-style
sport model, where leagues and teams are privately owned and
formed as explicit profit-seeking entities, and have little to no oversight by outside forces. With such a US-style model, preserving the
unique history and culture of the Montreal Canadiens eventually
came at too great a cost for the NHL.

It was the fall of an empire.

CHAPTER 2:
FRANCOPHONES IN AN ANGLOPHONE WORLD

GILBERT PERREAULT WOULD HAVE been a perfect Montreal Canadien. A francophone from Victoriaville, Quebec, he was a smooth-skating, high-scoring superstar with the fabled Montreal Junior Canadiens of the Ontario Hockey Association (OHA), leading his club to successive Memorial Cup titles in 1969 and 1970. He was the exact type of player the Canadiens had a near-monopsony on during the NHL's sponsorship era, and he would have fit perfectly into the tradition of francophone greats who played for the team: Rocket Richard, Bernie Geoffrion, Jean Béliveau.

Had Perreault been one year older, and hence eligible for the 1969 draft, he almost assuredly would have joined the Montreal Canadiens. The 1969 draft was considered the NHL's first "true" draft—it was the first one in which the impacts of the sponsorship system had fully dissipated, and all draft-age players were available to all teams—but even that draft needs an asterisk because the Canadiens were given preferential treatment. As a final gesture to the club's francophone heritage, the NHL awarded the club the first two picks in the draft so as to allow the Canadiens to secure the two top draft-eligible French Canadian players that year, Réjean Houle and Marc Tardif—both also from the Montreal Junior Canadiens. Perreault, however, was certainly a better prospect than either Houle or Tardif, but was one year too young for the Canadiens to have taken him in 1969.

Perreault had to wait until the 1970 draft, where, for the first time ever, the Montreal Canadiens had become like any other NHL club. The expansion Buffalo Sabres had the first pick in the draft that year and selected Perreault. It turned out to be a wise choice, as Perreault went on to have a Hall-of-Fame career in the NHL— all 18 seasons with the Sabres—scoring 512 goals. To think what Perreault might have done for the Canadiens had they had access to him, consider this: the only players in Canadiens history to score more career goals for the club were Rocket Richard (544) and Guy Lafleur (518).

The following year, 1971, the draft class was particularly rich with high-end French Canadian talent. The first three players selected that year—and four of the top five—were French Canadian. While the Canadiens did acquire Guy Lafleur with the first-overall pick (due to a shrewd trade, rather than any preferential treatment), they saw Detroit draft Marcel Dionne second, Vancouver draft Jocelyn Guevremont third and Buffalo draft Rick Martin fifth. These players would have undoubtedly become Canadiens under the old sponsorship system.

Dionne turned out to be one of the best NHL players of all time. When he retired in 1989, he was second on the league's career goals-scored list, behind only Gordie Howe. Had the Canadiens' priority access to francophones lasted only two years longer, the club's dynasty could easily have continued well into the mid-to-late 1980s. Imagine a situation with Lafleur, Perreault and Dionne all playing for the same club at the same time.

While the demise of the sponsorship system dramatically altered the future of the Montreal Canadiens, it also had profound effects on the francophone hockey player. Perreault's entry into the NHL in 1970 signalled a new era for French Canadian players— one where these players, including potential superstars, would no longer automatically play for Montreal, but instead would be dispersed throughout the league. Somewhat ironically, Perreault's Sabres would reach the 1975 Stanley Cup final—in only their fifth year of existence—by defeating none other than the Canadiens in the semi-finals. Even more ironic, the Sabres' success that year was largely attributable to their "French Connection" line of Perreault, Martin and René Robert, who were the club's top three scorers, combining for 291 points.

The success of the French Connection line in Buffalo notwith- standing, the end of the sponsorship era created potential problems for francophone hockey players. Many of these players would have undoubtedly preferred to stay at "home" and play for the Canadiens; not only was the club a cultural icon that every boy in the province dreamed of playing for one day, but the insular society of Quebec during that era meant that a French Canadian playing for any of the other NHL teams would inevitably face significant cultural and language barriers. With the end of the sponsorship system and the corresponding rapid expansion of the NHL, the majority of French Canadian players would end up on teams outside their home prov- ince. As a minority group in the NHL, in a league long dominated and controlled by English Canadians, and with French-English tensions continuing to exist in Canada, the environment was certainly ripe for discrimination against French Canadians.

DISCRIMINATION IN SPORT

The idea that socio-political forces within a country can spill over and impact the sports world is not only a possibility, it is practically unavoidable. The romanticized notion of sport as a pure, idyllic escape from the realities and unpleasantries of everyday life, where an athlete's performance is all that matters, and not their ethnicity or the colour of their skin, is absolute fantasy.

In North America, the narrative of discrimination in professional sport has largely been an American narrative, focusing on how the country's history of racial tension and strife had an impact on the treatment of Blacks in sports like baseball, football and basketball. When the Second World War ended in 1945, the US South was still segregated and Blacks in all parts of the country faced limited economic, political and social opportunities. Over the next 30 years, radical changes would occur: the end of segregation, the dawn of the civil rights movement, race riots in major cities such as Los Angeles, Detroit and Chicago, and the emergence of controversial integration policies like "busing." Race issues had suddenly come to the forefront in mainstream American society.

Sport was no different. In 1945, there wasn't a single Black player on the roster of any team in the NFL or MLB. Professional sport was completely segregated. In baseball, Blacks had long been relegated to playing in the so-called Negro Leagues. In football, while some Blacks had played in the NFL during the league's early years, none had done so since 1934.

Football and baseball both broke the colour barrier in the years following the Second World War. In a well-documented story, Jackie Robinson, in 1947, became the first Black baseball player in the majors when he was called up to the National League's Brooklyn Dodgers from their Montreal minor league affiliate. Less well-documented was that the NFL broke the colour barrier the previous year, when

Woody Strode (who later played with the Calgary Stampeders of the Canadian Football League) and Kenny Washington joined the Los Angeles Rams. The Rams were playing their first season in Los Angeles, having relocated from Cleveland. As a condition of being allowed to play in the publicly owned Los Angeles Coliseum, the City of Los Angeles required the Rams to desegregate.

Despite these initial gains, the process of integration was long and slow. It took another 12 years for all MLB teams to integrate: the Boston Red Sox were the last, signing Elijah "Pumpsie" Green in 1959. Seven years earlier, Green had played a season for the Indian Head Rockets, an all-Black, semi-pro club based in Saskatchewan that travelled across the Prairies each summer in the early 1950s playing tournaments and sports days. Many talented Black players, unable to gain jobs in MLB—in 1952, 10 of the 16 MLB teams had yet to integrate—played for the Rockets.

The NFL was similar in that it also took 13 years, until 1959, for all teams to fully integrate. In this case, it was the Washington Redskins that were the holdout club. Many saw similarities between the Red Sox and Redskins, in that both had owners—Tom Yawkey of the Red Sox and George P. Marshall of the Redskins—who were often accused of holding prejudicial views toward Blacks.

Basketball was not much different. NBA teams played with predominantly white rosters throughout the late '40s and '50s. The league had formed in 1946, but didn't have its first Black player of particular notoriety until a decade later, when the Boston Celtics drafted Bill Russell out of the University of San Francisco. Even as late as 1958, a team with an all-white roster (the St. Louis Hawks) captured the NBA championship.

Even for those who did make it to the pros, life as an Black athlete in the post-segregation period was not easy, whether in baseball, football or basketball. At a minimum, players were often met with

exclusionary treatment—sometimes subtle, sometimes not—
whether from fans, from opponents or from teammates. At its worst,
they were sometimes victims of a much more overt racist behaviour.

Some players talked openly about what they encountered. Russell
was very vocal about his time in Boston, and had long been critical of
the city and its fans. Others, like basketball's Kareem Abdul Jabbar
and baseball's Hank Aaron, while perhaps not as confrontational as
Russell in their approach, were no less forthright about the racially
charged atmospheres in the sports in which they played. Many Black
players, however, were silent, fearing job loss if they spoke out. While
star Black players who spoke out had a level of protection against
retribution, the Black players who were less celebrated did not.

These struggles and controversies that the other three major
professional leagues had with race and integration issues in the
postwar period were not as pronounced in the NHL. For the most
part, far fewer American Blacks played hockey compared with the
other three sports.[47] At the time, few Americans, let alone *African*
Americans, played the game at any level. Even though the NHL had
four US–based franchises through these years—in Boston, New
York, Detroit and Chicago—the interest in hockey in these cities
was purely from a spectator perspective; in addition, the game itself
had little to no broader national presence in the US. While a handful
of Americans had played in the NHL from the time of its inception in
1917, the first American skater (non-goalie) to play *regularly* in the
league was Tommy Williams of the Boston Bruins in the early 1960s.

While the NHL through the 1970s was, for the most part, homogeneous in both nationality and race—the vast majority of players were white Canadians—it was certainly not homogeneous in
culture and language. People from the two European settler cultures that established the nation of Canada—English and French—
embraced the game in large numbers. However, with francophones

composing only about 20% of the country's population, they were
destined to be a minority group in the NHL, inevitably raising the
possibility, as with any minority group, of domination and/or exclusion at the hands of the majority.

That francophones would face barriers in the NHL seemed inherently possible, particularly given the broader historical context of
French-English relations in Canada. Throughout the country's history, French Canadians and English Canadians tended to live in
very separate worlds, both literally and figuratively, with often only
minimal crossovers and interactions between the two cultures and
societies. Part of this divide is geographic. Francophones compose
about 80% of the population of Quebec, but under 5% of the population in the rest of Canada. Their numbers are lowest in the three
western-most provinces (BC, Alberta and Saskatchewan), where only
about 2% of the population is francophone. This physical segregation of francophones and anglophones mirrors a great cultural and
social divide between the two groups. Nova Scotian novelist Hugh
MacLennan once described Canada as "two solitudes" —francophones and anglophones living within the same national boundaries, but in societies that are largely autonomous and removed from
each other. In many practical ways, then, Quebec has been a "country
within a country."

Throughout Canada's history, francophone Quebecers have
sought to preserve their distinct language and culture from subjugation by the country's anglophone majority. This was arguably somewhat easier up until the middle of the 20th century. The insular and
conservative nature of traditional Quebec society, with the Catholic
Church playing a central role in almost all aspects of daily life, provided a sort of natural barrier to outside forces.

However, as a more open and liberal Canadian society began to
emerge after the Second World War, threats to this parochial way

of life began to increase. Politically, changes began to take hold as
Quebecers moved away from Premier Duplessis's "Dark Ages" Union
Nationale government of the 1950s toward the more centrist and
modernist government of Jean Lesage's Liberals. While Lesage's
"Quiet Revolution" government of the early 1960s signalled the
beginning of a new era, not all Quebecers were on board, and a
growing and visible sovereigntist movement began to develop,
parallel with Lesage's increased openness. An element of this
movement resorted to violent tactics; the FLQ, formed in the early
1960s, conducted more than 200 bombings throughout the province
during the decade, culminating in 1969 with the bombing of the
Montreal Stock Exchange, and, in a separate incident, the bombing
of Montreal mayor Jean Drapeau's home.

By the time the 1970s arrived, the issue of Quebec sovereignty
had started to move to the forefront of the political stage in Canada.
Pierre Trudeau had been elected Canadian prime minister in 1968
on a federalist agenda, vowing to fight the threat of Quebec independence. The issue took a dramatic turn in October 1970, when
the FLQ kidnapped in Montreal the British trade commissioner to
Canada, James Cross. Then, a few days later, they kidnapped a second
public figure, this time Quebec's deputy premier, Pierre Laporte. He
was found a week later, in the trunk of a car, murdered; and while
Cross was eventually released by his captors, he was held for over
two months by the FLQ.

The kidnappings and the Laporte assassination set off a political
crisis in Canada. The Trudeau government implemented the War Measures Act, which was essentially a declaration of martial law. As army
tanks rolled through the streets of Montreal, Canadians debated
whether the Trudeau response was an overreaction—an action that
was a dangerous and unnecessary suspension of civil rights—or a
legitimate and appropriate counter to a critical national security threat.

While the hysteria and alarm surrounding the October Crisis—as it became known—eventually dissipated, the broader question of Quebec sovereignty continued to gain political traction in that province. By 1976, Quebec had its first openly sovereigntist provincial government, led by René Lévesque, a former Liberal who had left the party over the sovereignty issue. Within its first year in office, the Lévesque government passed the highly controversial Bill 101, which mandated French as the language of government, courts and the workplace in Quebec. In addition, all signage was required to be in French, and it became compulsory for children to attend French schools. Celebrated by Quebec nationalists, the bill was met with outrage by many anglophones in Quebec.

Before the end of Lévesque's first term as premier, he would take the sovereignty question directly to the Quebec public through a province-wide referendum in May 1980. The sovereignty side came up short, with 40% in favour of separatism. While the result was a setback for the sovereigntists, the outcome was closer than many outside observers had predicted. Particularly concerning for federalists was that 50% of francophones had voted in favour of sovereignty.

Over the subsequent 15 years, the Quebec question would almost completely dominate the political discourse across the country. Two attempts to amend the constitution—first, the Meech Lake Accord of 1987, and then the Charlottetown Accord of 1992—failed, the latter going down to a defeat in a federal referendum. The accords were attempts to clarify Quebec's place in confederation, and to further strengthen Quebec's status as a distinct society; both served to grant increased powers to provinces, reducing the role and reach of the federal government.

Out of the failed Meech Lake Accord, a new sovereigntist party emerged, this time at the federal level. The Bloc Québécois—led by Lucien Bouchard, a cabinet minister in the Mulroney government

who left the Progressive Conservative Party after Meech Lake—
formed in 1991 and would make an immediate impact, capturing
54 out of the 75 Quebec seats in the 1993 federal election and in the
process became the official opposition in the House of Commons.
The party would go on to dominate federal politics in the province
for almost two decades. The Bloc's successes in 1993 would also spur
a new sovereigntist push at the provincial level. In 1995, the Parti
Québécois, now under Premier Jacques Parizeau, conducted the
province's second referendum on sovereignty. As with Lévesque's
1980 referendum, the sovereigntists went down to defeat, but this
time the margin was razor-thin—50.58% to 49.42%—with 60% of
francophones voting for sovereignty. Despite the referendum result,
the Parti Québécois continued to be a major force in Quebec politics,
holding power until 2003, and then returning to power as a minority
government from 2012 to 2014.

Overall, then, this history of postwar French-English relations in
Canada reveals a rather tumultuous—at times outright adversarial
—relationship between the two cultures. In some ways, the differences between the two sides have been intractable. For many francophone Quebecers, federalism is inherently incompatible with the
preservation of their distinct culture and language within Quebec;
without provincial control, the argument goes, in areas such as
language, immigration and education, the non-francophone majority that resides outside Quebec will eventually overwhelm francophone interests.

On the opposite side, many people in English Canada correspondingly grew weary over time with the Quebec issue and its seemingly
constant place at the forefront of the national political agenda, often
at the expense, according to the critics, of other equally pressing
(or more pressing) national issues. As the country rolled from one
Quebec-related issue/crisis to another, attitudes toward Quebec

became more hardened, particularly in Western Canada, where few francophones reside. Federal policies protecting francophone rights outside Quebec—policies, for example, that required holders of certain federal government jobs to be bilingual, even where the francophone population in the area was relatively small—often met with particular contempt. More broadly, many anglophones were offended by what they saw as francophone Quebecers' disrespect and/or outright disdain for the rest of Canada and by the apparent desire of sovereigntists to break Canada apart.

The Quebec question, and broader French-English relations in Canada, cannot be divorced from hockey. As discussed in the previous chapter, the so-called Richard Riot of 1955 was a perfect early example of this. Another widely reported incident occurred in 1971, this time in junior hockey. The QMJHL's Quebec Remparts, led by future NHL Hall of Famer Guy Lafleur, were playing the OHL's St. Catharines Black Hawks in a best-of-seven series for the right to represent the East in the Memorial Cup final. St. Catharines' star player was francophone Marcel Dionne. Unlike Lafleur, Dionne had elected to forgo the Quebec league to play in the supposedly higher-quality Ontario league. Many in Quebec, however, viewed Dionne as a traitor, one who had abandoned his "homeland." Tensions ran high during the series. The first two games, in Quebec City, were marred by violence —not only amongst opposing players on the ice, but also between players and fans. In the end, with the series tied 2–2, and scheduled to head back to Quebec City for a pivotal Game 5, the Black Hawks refused to go, fearing for their safety. The Black Hawks were forced by the CAHA to forfeit the series, and the Remparts went on to the Memorial Cup final (which they won, against the Edmonton Oil Kings).

In *The Game*, Ken Dryden offers unique insights into French-English relations on the great Canadiens' teams of the 1970s, describing an overall professional compatibility, but with informal subgroups that tended to divide by language. Issues of language and ethnicity seemed to be never far from the surface in the politically charged world of 1970s Montreal. Dryden argues that when "incidents" occurred between Canadiens teammates—like the fight in a Cleveland hotel room between Pete Mahovlich and Mario Tremblay that landed Mahovlich in the hospital—the fans and media in Montreal inevitably wanted to portray it through their own lens and experiences of French-English animosity, rather than as simply a fight between two road roommates who let a drunken argument get out of hand.

In his book about hockey scouts, Canadian sportswriter Gare Joyce relates a more recent story that reveals the depth of French-English animosities sometimes found at hockey's grassroots level. Attending a game in Rimouski—a city in northeast Quebec that is almost exclusively francophone—Joyce observes that many fans stay seated during the playing of "O Canada," apparently a common occurrence in the QMJHL, and a gesture that many would interpret as a sign of disrespect to Canada. Joyce then overhears a nearby (presumably English Canadian) NHL scout admonishing an elderly fan that failed to stand, with the scout angrily saying, "I guess that means you won't be cashing your *Canada* pension cheque" (emphasis mine).

Other stories abound—many of which involve francophones being the target of disparaging comments. In 2005, English Canadian Sean Avery of the Los Angeles Kings, commenting on a hit on Avery's teammate Jeremy Roenick by French Canadian Denis Gauthier of the Phoenix Coyotes, said, "I think it was typical of most French guys in our league with a visor on, running around and playing tough and not backing anything up." After apparently receiving a call from the NHL office, Avery publicly apologized for the comment.

Five years earlier, Czech forward Vaclav Prospal of the Ottawa Senators called Canadiens defenceman Patrice Brisebois a "fucking frog" during a game. Prospal later issued a half-hearted apology, saying, "I do admit I said those things, that I said them in the heat of the battle...I do apologize to French Canadian people who may be offended by that comment but I never will apologize to the one Frenchman who caused this controversy." Prospal said he had heard other players use the offensive term and then laugh about it. The NHL responded to the incident by requiring Prospal to undergo sensitivity training.

The media itself has occasionally been at the centre of controversies. Don Cherry, the long-time, influential *Hockey Night in Canada* commentator, has often been accused by his critics of an anti-French bias. Cherry has cast aspersions on francophone players (as well as European players) for what he sees as their apparent "softness" on the ice. In 2004, his comments on francophones players' propensity to use visors created particular controversy. It prompted Canada's Office of the Commissioner of Official Languages to launch a formal investigation into whether Cherry's comments contravened the Official Languages Act. The incident also caused CBC Television to enact a seven-second delay on Cherry's live "Coach's Corner" intermission segment. This was not Cherry's first cultural imbroglio. Prior to the 1998 Winter Olympics in Nagano, Japan, Cherry dismissed Canada's flag bearer, gold-medallist Jean-Luc Brassard, as "a French guy, some skier that nobody knows about." About Quebec sovereigntists, he once said, "They don't like the Canadian flag but they want our money, we bail them out. I've never seen such a bunch of whiners in my life."

While stories such as these can provide a certain context to the issue of French-English relations in the hockey world and put a recognizable face to the issue, they are still merely anecdotal in nature and, as such, can never provide any deeper understanding of the problem, or allow for any broader analysis. Complicating matters

further, discriminatory acts or behaviours in hockey are likely to
be severely underreported. Those in power positions inside the
game—team owners, executives at both the league and team level,
coaches, et cetera—have an obvious interest in downplaying any
talk of bias. Furthermore, francophone players who feel they have
been targets of discriminatory behaviour are generally unlikely to
report such incidents for fear of jeopardizing their careers by being
branded a complainer or whistle-blower.

So, a general absence of discussion about discrimination by those
inside the game should never be taken as evidence that the issue
isn't a problem. Only through a more structured and systematic
approach can any meaningful insights about the issue be gained. In
this sense, the economics discipline offers some hope.

DETECTING DISCRIMINATION

University of Chicago professor Gary Becker won the 1992 Nobel Prize
in Economics, in part for his work studying discrimination in labour
markets. His work on discrimination actually began 35 years earlier,
in the late 1950s—a time when civil rights issues were beginning to
come to the forefront in the US. Becker was not so much focused on
identifying the underlying psychological reasons *why* people may
hold prejudicial views against others—that was largely beyond the
scope of what economists studied—but was instead interested in *how*
these prejudicial beliefs played out in employment markets.

His ideas and approaches ultimately laid the groundwork for
many economists that would follow, and the "economics of discrimination" has become a major sub-field within the economics
discipline. Economists consider employment discrimination to have
occurred when an identifiable group suffers inferior labour market
outcomes—whether that be lower salaries, underrepresentation

or even outright exclusion—that are unexplained by productivity differences, but are instead related to their personal identifiers, such as race, gender, nationality or ethnicity.

As economists see it, the extent of any discrimination will be directly related to the characteristics of the underlying labour market. If markets are relatively competitive, then employers with prejudicial biases pay a price for indulging these discriminatory preferences, in that, by essentially "undervaluing" those in the non-preferred group, they are allowing (non-biased) competitor firms to hire away these individuals at a beneficial productivity-to-wage ratio. The theory is that, eventually, the prejudiced employer will incur sufficient costs so as to change its behaviour. Alternatively, if labour markets aren't very competitive, then the non-preferred employees can't escape the discriminating employers; they have nowhere else to take their services, so discrimination in this case can persist indefinitely.

There may even be some cases where labour markets are competitive, yet discrimination still occurs. Sometimes employers discriminate against a group, not because of the biases of the firm's owners or managers, but rather as a rational response to the biases of the firm's stakeholder. For example, if the firm's other employees don't want those in the non-preferred group as their co-workers, then the firm may choose to indulge these preferences for fear of losing its other employees. The same holds for the firm's customers; if enough customers don't want to associate with the non-preferred group, they may take their business elsewhere unless the firm responds.

While economists can construct eloquent theories about how and why employment discrimination occurs, actually testing for discrimination in real-world settings is notoriously difficult. This testing is inhibited by a severe lack of data. Researchers would need access to detailed company records that identified, for each employee, a host of personal factors; however, these types of data are proprietary to the firm, highly confidential and almost never available to outside researchers.

This is where sport comes in. Cornell University economist Lawrence Kahn once called the professional sport industry a labour market laboratory, in that it provides a wealth of publicly available data about every employee that is simply unseen in any other industry. In sport, individual player salaries are known and widely reported, their current and past performance can be objectively and transparently measured, and their workplace environment—such as who their managers (coaches) and co-workers (teammates) are—can be readily determined. As well, researchers have available a variety of demographic information about each player, such as their age and experience, their previous training, and their race, nationality and ethnicity. All of this allows researchers to home in on the relationship between minority group membership and employment market outcomes (like salary), all the while allowing one to control for a host of variables that may otherwise confound the analysis (such as age or experience differences).

Studying the sport industry can serve two purposes. In the narrowest and most obvious sense, it can inform our understanding of the industry itself. Perhaps more importantly, though, sport can serve as a microcosm of the broader society in which it operates and can shed light on critical social and economic issues like discrimination, in ways not otherwise possible.

Applying this to a Canadian context, the NHL provides a particularly good opportunity to observe the employment outcomes of francophones who work outside Quebec and in industries dominated by anglophones. This type of situation is relatively uncommon in the non-hockey world: given the insular nature of Quebec society, there has seldom been a lot of outward migration by francophones into the broader Canadian labour market, making it difficult to conduct tests for discrimination.

Even in hockey, the outmigration of francophones from Quebec only began in earnest in the early 1970s. During the preceding sponsorship era, most French Canadians in the NHL stayed at "home" and played for the Montreal Canadiens. Those francophones that did play outside Montreal were, for the most part, role players rather than stars—in many cases, they were players the Canadiens didn't really want or need. While the Canadiens did still manage to let a few star francophones "get away" on them—Jean Ratelle and Rod Gilbert, both of whom starred for the New York Rangers during the late 1960s and early 1970s, are good examples—this was much more the exception than the rule.[48]

Everything began to change in the late 1960s. With the NHL doubling in size in 1967, and then expanding again in 1970, 1972 and 1974, the number of franchises in the league went from six to eighteen in a span of only seven years. With the commensurate increase in the demand for players, more and more francophone players began to enter the league, with most playing for franchises in the US. Many of these players were older, and had been so-called "career minor-leaguers," trapped in the farm systems of Original Six teams (most often, the Canadiens). Veteran minor-league pros like Noel Picard and André Boudrias were typical of this type of player. Picard was a 29-year-old rookie with the St. Louis Blues in the club's inaugural 1967–68 season. His only prior NHL experience was a brief 16-game stint with the Montreal Canadiens during the 1964–65 season. Picard went on to play over 300 games in the NHL, all with US–based franchises.[49]

Boudrias was another francophone trapped in the Canadiens system. After an illustrious junior career, he played four games as a 20-year-old for the Canadiens during the 1963–64 season, but then only three more games for the club over the next three seasons combined. With the NHL doubling in size in 1967, Boudrias was acquired by the expansion Minnesota North Stars and ultimately went on to play over 600 NHL games, none further with Montreal, scoring 150 career goals.

This expansion-induced influx of older francophone players into the NHL was not the only sea change that was occurring—*young* francophone players were also affected. With the NHL's introduction of the amateur draft in 1969, Montreal's priority access to securing the best francophone talent coming out of the junior system was now lost. Players like Gilbert Perreault and Marcel Dionne—who in the pre-draft era would have automatically been Montreal Canadiens, and who between the two of them would go on to play 35 NHL seasons and score 1,243 goals—ended up spending their entire careers playing for US-based clubs.

Combined, the effects of expansion and the introduction of the draft—which in themselves were related events—fundamentally and forever altered the landscape for francophones in the NHL. By the early 1970s, and for the first time ever in the NHL's history, the majority of francophones in the league were *not* playing for the Montreal Canadiens.

The numbers reveal the starkness of this transformation. Over the quarter century of the Original Six era (1942–43 to 1966–67), the Canadiens accounted for a whopping 62% of all French Canadians who played in the NHL during that time period,[50] despite composing only one-sixth (16.7%) of the teams in the league. Compare this with the subsequent 12 seasons—from 1967–68 to 1978–79[51]—when the corresponding percentage dropped to only 24%. So, while the Canadiens continued to employ a disproportionate percentage of francophones, even after the league's structural changes, the imbalance was greatly reduced relative to the sponsorship era.

In this new era that unfolded during the late 1960s and 1970s—
where three of every four francophones in the NHL now played in
the anglophone world, either in English Canada or in the US—most
francophones in the league were minorities in the cities in which
they played, facing the attendant language and cultural barriers
that came with playing outside Quebec. Scenarios like these—no
matter what the specific setting—are always ripe with potential for
the minority group to suffer biased or prejudicial treatment at the
hands of the majority.

However, the story was more complicated than just this. There
was a timing issue as well. The sudden and rapid flow of francophones to teams based outside Quebec occurred at a time when
French-English tensions in Canada were escalating quickly, driven
by the growing sovereigntist movement in Quebec and coming to
an apex with the October Crisis in 1970. With English Canadians
having a near monopoly on coaching and general manager positions across the league during that era, it is not difficult to see how
these political tensions could potentially spill over into hockey, to
the detriment of francophone players.

For many sovereigntists, the Gilbert Perreault story perfectly
exemplified their discontent. Here was a young francophone icon,
who, in their minds, should have been able to stay home and play
for the beloved Montreal Canadiens, but instead was "exported" to
the US under a set of rules developed by an anglophone-controlled
institution (the NHL), for the benefit of anglophones.

If there was ever any doubt that hockey in that era could somehow have been divorced from the time and place of the broader
world in which it operated, consider this piece of irony: On the
evening of October 10, 1970, Perreault made his long-anticipated
NHL debut, scoring a goal for his Buffalo Sabres in a 2–1 win over
the Pittsburgh Penguins. Perreault's debut, however, received little

fanfare in the Canadian media the next day. It had been overshad-owed by a much more important and serious news item. Less than two hours before Perreault stepped on the ice for his first-ever NHL game, the FLQ kidnapped Deputy Premier Laporte from his Montreal home. Laporte's kidnapping, and murder one week later, brought the smouldering October Crisis to a sudden flashpoint.

With all of this, then, it is not surprising that the 1970s also marked the beginning of academics taking an interest in the issue of discrimination in hockey. The question was straightforward: To what extent, if any, did French Canadians in the NHL experience inferior outcomes relative to their anglophone counterparts?

EVIDENCE FROM THE RESEARCH

Somewhat ironically, it was not a Canadian but an American, sociol-ogist David Marple, in 1975, who first wrote about the possibility of discrimination against francophones in the NHL. Marple saw the situation of francophones in hockey as comparable to that of Blacks in the other three major professional leagues.[52]

By the time the 1980s arrived, a robust debate was beginning to unfold, with two competing camps emerging. On one side, there was University of Ottawa economist Marc Lavoie and his colleagues, whose various research studies tended to show evidence of discrim-ination. Heading up the opposing view—what could be termed the "no-discrimination" side—was William Walsh and his University of Victoria colleagues. The debate took place largely in the pages of the academic journal *Canadian Public Policy*, with various back-and-forths, points and counterpoints, spanning more than a decade.

Lavoie and company fired the first salvo, arguing in a 1987 study that French Canadians in the NHL were, on average, better performers than their anglophone (both Canadian and American) counterparts.

They found francophones to be superior offensive performers (as measured by points-per-game), and no worse in terms of defensive performance (measured by plus/minus rating and short-handed goals).[53] In economic terms, the implication of this apparent performance disparity was that the overall talent level in the league could be improved if NHL teams hired more francophones and fewer anglophones; in other words, there were francophones unable to gain NHL jobs who were presumably better performers than some anglophones who *were* in the NHL. Francophones apparently faced a higher standard of entry into the league than did anglophones. The effect of this barrier would be most felt, not by star francophones —they would always have a place in the league—but by marginal players, who were much more replaceable by (presumably less talented) anglophones.

Walsh quickly (in academic terms) responded. He agreed that evidence supported that francophones were better offensively than anglophones, but argued that they were both poorer defensively and of smaller physical size, two attributes that lessened their value to NHL teams. In Walsh's mind, it was these factors, and not any type of discrimination, that explained why francophones might have (mistakenly) appeared underrepresented in the league. Walsh's results were based on a measure of defensive performance (voting on the Selke Trophy)[54] quite different from those of Lavoie and his colleagues. In a rebuttal to Walsh, they then developed still other measures of defensive performance,[55] which, they argued, supported their original claim that francophones were no worse defensively, and allowing them to reassert their view that francophones were underrepresented in the NHL.[56]

This controversy surrounding the measurement of defensive performance obviously becomes critical to the debate. If French Canadians were, in fact, worse (on average) defensively than English

Canadians, to the point where this inferior defensive performance more than offset their superior offensive skills, then their underrepresentation was simply a legitimate market response, rather than evidence of any type of discrimination. However, it is also possible that French Canadians have been *perceived* to be inferior defensively, when in fact they have not been. In other words, there may be widely held, but untrue, systemic biases amongst hockey decision-makers who underestimate, sometimes unintentionally, the defensive skills of francophones. These biases and perceptions can have a life of their own, and become almost a mantra, an article of faith. They can be found in many other labour markets, not just in hockey. The unfounded notions, for example, that women are less proficient in math and sciences than men, or that Blacks lack the attributes to play quarterback in the NFL, are similar manifestations of this type of stereotyping.

One problem is that defensive ability is notoriously difficult to measure in hockey. Defensive attributes tend to be more subtle (like, for example, correct positioning) and multi-dimensional than offensive attributes (like scoring goals), making defence less amenable to objective quantification. Another problem is that hockey is a continuous-flow game, meaning that players (forwards and defencemen) on the ice at any given time simultaneously play offence and defence. As a result, players who play more offensively aggressive in an attempt to score goals also run the risk of putting themselves out of position to prevent the opposition from scoring. In hockey, offence and defence cannot be separated into neat, discrete tasks as they are in sports like baseball and football, so disentangling the two is exceedingly difficult and always open to conjecture and debate.

Another argument sometimes heard to justify the underrepresentation of francophones is that language and cultural barriers can often make them less valuable to employers, relative to native English-speakers. Under this view, the underrepresentation of francophones is not so much evidence of discrimination, but rather a legitimate and natural market response by employers to the additional integration costs they face when employing francophones. In other words, if these integration costs were significant enough, teams may have had an economic incentive to substitute anglophone players for francophones, all else equal; in essence, given the choice between an anglophone and francophone of equal playing talent, the team would always choose the (lower-cost) anglophone.

There is no question that players coming out of the insular Quebec society of past eras would be abruptly thrown into environs that were often completely foreign to them, being forced to adapt to a world where both the language and culture were alien, making it very difficult to achieve any sense of belonging. This made interacting with their club's fan base, or dealing with the local media, particularly challenging for some of these players. Perhaps more importantly, it made communicating with their largely anglophone coaches and teammates more difficult, possibly to the detriment of the team's on-ice success.

To make matters even worse, very few support systems existed for the player, either within the team or outside the team. With the former, since so few francophones played outside Montreal, those players who did inevitably had few, if any, francophone teammates. This was somewhat similar to the early days of integration in the NFL and MLB, when most teams had only one or two Black players, making it an isolating experience for those players. Outside the team, francophone NHL players lived in cities that were hundreds of kilometres from home, where little or no French was spoken and where developing any sense of connection to the local community was next to impossible.

As Quebec eventually became a more open and outwardly integrated society, these situations gradually became less pronounced, but were far from eliminated entirely. Even the great Mario Lemieux—who was drafted first overall by the Pittsburgh Penguins in 1984, and who went on to become one of the most celebrated NHL players of all time—spoke no English when he arrived in Pittsburgh. While Lemieux's prodigious talents were more than enough to offset the increased communication costs he would inevitably impose on his club (at least until he learned English), unilingual francophones of lesser talent than Lemieux's may not have always been given such a grace period.

While this debate on underrepresentation was occurring, a parallel research stream emerged that examined a different type of possible discrimination: whether francophones who *did* make it to the NHL were paid the same as their anglophone counterparts of comparable performance levels. Again, both Lavoie and Walsh, along with their respective colleagues, drove much of the early work in the area. This time, they were in agreement, at least initially, both concluding that salary discrimination against francophones did not appear to be a serious issue. Walsh and his colleague Colin Jones examined the 1977–78 season and found no evidence of discrimination against francophone forwards or goaltenders, although they did find some (relatively weak) evidence that francophone defencemen were underpaid. Lavoie and his colleagues examined the 1989–90 season and, like Walsh and Jones a decade earlier, also did not detect any discrimination.[57]

However, as I have pointed out in a series of academic studies spanning the mid-1990s through to the early 2000s, the problem with all of these early approaches to test for discrimination—whether related to entry or salary—is that they lumped all French Canadians in the NHL into a single group, and in the process failed to consider how team location may influence the findings. There was no distinguishing, for example, between a francophone playing for the Montreal Canadiens versus, say, the Calgary Flames or the New York Rangers. Since one would not inherently expect the Montreal Canadiens (or the Quebec Nordiques, when they were in the NHL from 1979 to 1996) to have biases against francophone players, and since these teams traditionally employed a disproportionate number of the league's francophones, any discrimination against francophones playing for teams outside the province of Quebec may be statistically obscured—the result being that one could reject the notion of discrimination, when, in fact, it is present (at least for some players).

In my 1995 study—a study that, like Marc Lavoie's, examined the 1989–90 season—I separated the data to isolate every specific combination of cultural grouping (francophone, anglophone, American and European) and team location (Quebec, English Canada and the US). Of these 12 possible combinations, only one salary anomaly appeared—that was for francophones playing for teams based in English Canada, who, on average, were paid a whopping 37% less than their English Canadian counterparts on those teams, *after* accounting for any performance differences between the two groups that may impact salary. It is particularly important to note that francophones playing on US–based teams did not suffer any salary penalty, nor did, for example, Europeans playing for English Canada–based clubs. The potential discrimination seemed to be isolated solely to the case of francophones in English Canada.

This finding generated a series of follow-up studies by other researchers. Ottawa's Lavoie studied the 1993–94 season and found francophones on English Canadian teams suffered a 36% penalty, an almost identical number to the 37% I had found for the 1989–90 season. (Unlike my study, however, Lavoie found that English Canadian teams also underpaid European and American forwards, not just francophones, leading him to hypothesize that such teams simply preferred "hometown" players—i.e., English Canadians—rather than having a specific bias against francophones). American researchers Michael Curme and Greg Daugherty also found similar numbers in their examination of the 1999–2000 season, putting the salary penalty for French Canadians on English Canadian teams at over 30%. This collection of studies, by different researchers, studying different seasons, were remarkably consistent in the magnitude of their numerical findings;[58] something very real certainly seemed to be driving these results.

However, there was more. Not only did English Canadian clubs apparently underpay their francophones players, they also employed disproportionately *fewer* of these players than did us–based clubs. The data here is quite stark and persists through time.

For example, starting with the Original Six era from 1943 to 1967 —a time when the Toronto Maple Leafs were the only English Canadian team in the NHL—almost all francophones not playing for the Montreal Canadiens played for one of the four us–based clubs. In fact, the Leafs were almost *four times* less likely to employ French Canadian players than an average us–based team! This is a profoundly large difference and would seem to indicate an intentional and sustained effort by the Leafs to stay away from francophones, for whatever reason.

Even as the league added more English Canadian teams in the post-1967 era—Vancouver in 1970, Winnipeg and Edmonton with the WHA merger in 1979 and Calgary in 1980—the situation didn't remedy itself. English Canadian teams still seemed very reluctant to hire francophone players. My work in the early 2000s showed that over the 30-year period from 1968 to 1998, there were about 50% more francophones on the typical American team roster in any given season compared with the typical English Canadian team roster.[59]

This underrepresentation also extended to the draft. Teams based in English Canada tended to draft proportionately fewer French Canadians that did us clubs, particularly in the later rounds of the draft, where indulging any discriminatory preferences would be less costly for teams than in earlier rounds. Also, the apparent unwillingness of English Canadian teams to employ French Canadians did not extend to European players, who were actually overrepresented on these clubs relative to their representation on us–based teams. This dichotomy would seem to invalidate any argument that English Canadian clubs were not actually discriminating against francophones, but were simply displaying a preference for hometown (i.e., English Canadian) players at the expense of all other player groups.

Some of the traditional arguments as to why francophones might be underrepresented in the NHL as a whole—they face language and cultural barriers on teams outside Quebec, they have deficient defensive skills relative to anglophones, et cetera—even if true, should apply equally to both English Canadian and us–based teams. However, since English Canadian teams have been less likely to employ francophones than us–based clubs, something else is apparently at work. The key is to find fundamental differences between clubs based in English Canada and those based in the us.

Clubs based in us and clubs based in English Canada differ in one important and fundamental way: their fans. If local fans of English Canadian clubs hold biases against francophones and correspondingly prefer not to see them on their teams, the management of those clubs would have a financial incentive to respond to such biases. Given the long-standing anglophone-francophone tensions in Canada, it would be entirely plausible that such tensions carry over to the NHL.[60]

The idea that these tensions are at the root of the issue is given further credence by the fact that the degree of underrepresentation of francophones on English Canadian teams increased markedly during the late 1970s, the years immediately following the election of René Lévesque as Quebec's premier, and leading up to the first sovereignty referendum in 1980—a period when French-English tumult was particularly high and visible. A similar spike in under-representation occurred during the mid-1990s, corresponding to the Bloc Québécois becoming the official opposition in Parliament in 1993, and to the Parti Québécois regaining power in Quebec in 1994 on the promise of another sovereignty referendum.

CHANGING TIMES

Almost 30 years have now passed since the last Quebec referendum. The defeat (albeit very narrow) of the sovereignty question in that 1995 referendum, combined with the gradual decline of the Bloc Québécois on the federal side, served to put the "Quebec question" on the political back burner, at least as far as those in English Canada saw it.

In hockey, a parallel change has also occurred, with francophone-related issues seemingly becoming less prominent. There are several reasons for this. The Montreal Canadiens, the long-standing manifestation of francophone pride, became a shell of their former selves. Employing progressively fewer and fewer francophone players with each passing year, their unique identity began to fade. On the ice, the team was certainly no longer special. Their last Stanley Cup win was in 1993, the same year the Bloc Québécois became the official opposition in Parliament, and two years before Jacques Parizeau's referendum defeat. It took 28 years (until 2020–21) for the Canadiens to even advance to another Stanley Cup final, where they lost to Tampa Bay after a highly improbable playoff run, after the Canadiens finished 18th overall during the regular season.

As well, the Quebec Nordiques, a club that throughout the 1980s had an even higher percentage of francophones on its roster than did the Canadiens, moved to Colorado in 1996. While the franchise never won a Stanley Cup while still in Quebec, the Nordiques had some strong teams during those years. To the extent, then, that there is/was an anti-francophone bias in English Canada, no longer are there any clubs in the NHL that are identifiably francophone. Without the "bad-guy(s)," perhaps the intensity, the passion, has simply faded.

In addition to the disappearance of the distinctly francophone *club*, there has also been a commensurate decline in prominence of *individual* francophone stars. For decades, many of the greatest players in the game were francophone—the '50s had Rocket Richard and Bernie Geoffrion, the '60s had Jean Beliveau, the '70s had Guy Lafleur and Marcel Dionne, and the '80s and '90s had Mario Lemieux. Francophone stars were often offensive dynamos and had a flair and mystique that gave them high profiles amongst fans and the media. While never composing more than about 10% of NHL players, francophones were an ever-present and dominant force in the league. Take the 1974–75 season, for example, when francophones held down a mind-boggling eight of the top 12 positions in the NHL scoring race (by comparison, the eighth-leading francophone scorer in 2018–19 placed 118th on the league's scoring list). Even in the rival WHA, there was francophone dominance. Of the WHA's top five all-time leading scorers, four were francophone.

However, since Mario Lemieux was drafted first overall in 1983, only three French Canadian skaters[61] have been drafted in the number one slot: Alexandre Daigle in 1993, by Ottawa, Vincent Lecavalier in 1998, by Tampa Bay, and Alexis Lafrenière in 2020, by the New York Rangers. Daigle was a complete bust—playing only five uneventful seasons in Ottawa, and then becoming a hockey

nomad for the next decade, eventually ending his career in the
Swiss league. Lecavalier, on the other hand, turned out to be a star,
leading the Tampa Bay Lightning to a 2004 Stanley Cup victory.
However, he never really became a truly iconic francophone figure,
perhaps in part because he left Quebec at a young age to play at
Notre Dame College (in Wilcox, Saskatchewan), but probably more
so because he spent the great majority of his NHL career in Tampa,
far from the epicentre of hockey culture and media.

One of Lecavalier's teammates in Tampa was Martin St. Louis,
who seemingly came out of nowhere to become the greatest francophone player of the past quarter century. When he retired after the
2014–15 season, he was the club's all-time assists and points leader.
St. Louis's Hall-of-Fame career[62] was hardly predicted—actually,
he was one of the most unlikely superstars in NHL history. St. Louis
played four years of college hockey at the University of Vermont—a
path not typically viewed (at the time, at least) as the route that serious NHL prospects would take.[63] St. Louis went undrafted and, after
his college career, signed as a free agent with the Calgary Flames.
His career with the Flames did not last long, and he scored only four
goals in 59 games before being released. He ultimately landed in
Tampa, seemingly the last chance to prolong his NHL career. Playing
on a team with Lecavalier and Brad Richards, a budding superstar
in his own right, St. Louis's career took off. He won the NHL scoring
title in 2003–04, capturing the NHL's MVP award in the process.

St. Louis's case stands out because it became the exception. Francophones are far from being the dominating force they once were.
This is not to say that there haven't been some highly talented
francophones in the league in recent decades. For example, Patrice
Bergeron of Boston has had a stellar NHL career, and is one of the
best players of his generation. However, Bergeron is what could be
termed an "all-around" player, known as much for his defensive

prowess as for his offensive capabilities. He is certainly not of the mould of the francophone scoring greats of eras past. Bergeron stands only 17th on the all-time point-scoring list of Quebec-born players, and is the only current NHLer (as of the start of the 2023–24 season) even in the top 50 on that list.[64] The steady long-term decline in talent coming out of Quebec has been so great, it even caught the attention of the venerable *New York Times*—an outlet not normally known for its attention to hockey, let alone *Canadian* hockey—which, in 2016, ran the article "Once a Hockey Lode, Quebec Now Yields Few Top Prospects." Politicians have also gotten involved, with Quebec premier François Legault announcing in November 2021 that he would be establishing a committee to investigate the reasons for the declining numbers.

Taken together, then, the loss of the Montreal Canadiens (and Quebec Nordiques) as a symbol of francophone identity, combined with the sharp drop in the quantity and overall quality of francophones in the NHL over the past 20 years, has served to take the edge off the French-English discrimination issue in hockey. In addition, as European and American players began to enter the NHL during the 1970s—a trend that fully took hold during the 1980s and '90s, and eventually reduced the percentage of Canadian players in the NHL from almost 100% to just over 40%—the issue of intercultural relations became more multi-faceted and complex, diluting the focus on just the French-English dichotomy. With this increased player diversity, the NHL became less of a symbol and manifestation of French-English tensions in Canada.

Not only did the player pool become much more diverse, but the hockey-consuming public did as well. In Canada, still very much the heart and soul of the NHL, immigration increased markedly over the past half century. Whereas the NHL's Canadian fan base during the league's first 50 years was almost exclusively from European

stock—predominantly English and French, of course—the massive
non-European immigration into Canada over the past half century
has fundamentally altered the nature of the consumer market, to
the point where the media has responded by offering broadcasts
in different languages.[65] With the majority of immigrants coming
from Asia, the Middle East or Africa—regions with no significant
hockey culture or history—it is certainly possible, if not likely,
that newer Canadians, unbound by the unending and unresolved
French-English tensions of Canada's history, simply don't care about
nationality or ethnicity when it comes to hockey.

However, in spite of all of these structural changes in hockey
and in Canadian society, recent data shows, perhaps surprisingly,
that not much has actually changed—francophones are still highly
underrepresented on the rosters of English Canadian teams, just
as they have been throughout the entire modern era of the NHL.
Over the six seasons spanning 2013–14 to 2018–19, the average
US-based franchise employs almost twice as many francophones
as the average English Canada–based franchise, a disparity that is
even higher than it was two decades earlier.[66]

These numbers would seem to indicate that French Canadian
players and English Canadian teams continue to be a poor match
for each other. One explanation of this new data is that, even with
the reduced French-English rhetoric of more recent times, underlying fan biases against francophone players still exist, forcing
teams to respond to such biases. However, a reverse explanation
is also plausible—that many francophones, preferring not to play
in English Canada, self-select away from those teams. This latter
scenario is more likely now than in past eras—in 2005, NHL players
gained increased free-agency rights, allowing some players (generally, those over the age of 27) the ability to freely change clubs upon
the expiration of their contracts. At least for these players, no longer

do clubs have the exclusive purview over where players will play, as they did in the "reserve clause" era that existed through much of the history of the NHL.[67] Whatever the specific causes, however, the geographic segregation of many francophone players away from English Canadian teams seems as prevalent today as it was a half century ago.

MOVING FORWARD

With French-English relations in both Canadian society and in hockey seemingly less prominent and intense than in the past, it is not surprising that the number of academic studies examining discrimination in the NHL has also markedly declined since it peaked in the 1990s.

However, the issue has not vanished altogether, and a new line of inquiry has emerged in recent years. This new research focuses on the behaviour of on-ice officials, and examines whether referees exhibit any biases in their penalty-calling. With the advent of big-data analytics in sport, these types of studies are now much more feasible than they were in past eras. Digitized play-by-play game reports allow researchers to track and code information on every single penalty called during a game—including which of the two referees called the penalty, which players were on the ice for both teams when the penalty was called, the game score at the time, et cetera. Research I published with Kevin Mongeon examined almost 2.7 million on-ice "shifts" over three seasons (2008–09 to 2010–11) and found that French Canadian referees are more likely to call penalties on English Canadian players than are English Canadian referees, after controlling for a host of other variables that could impact the results. While this finding of "reverse discrimination" should not necessarily be surprising, given the long history of French-English tensions, prior academic studies have found little to no evidence of discrimination *by* francophones *against* anglophones—it has almost always been the opposite.

Of course, despite decades of research, including this most recent line of inquiry that examines refereeing, it is still not possible to definitively claim that French-English tensions spilled over to the NHL. Academic studies can be notoriously nebulous, and the results of any one study are always a function of the particular data set used and the type of statistical model employed by the researchers. Nevertheless, the overall body of work is strongly suggestive that professional hockey has not been immune to French-English tensions.

In some ways, it doesn't take academic studies to shed light on the issue—simple common sense can often be revealing. Montreal native Rod Gilbert was a sports icon in 1960s and '70s New York City when he was a star player for the Rangers.[68] Part of Gilbert's immense popularity in New York, aside from the fact he was a very good hockey player, seemed to be *because* he was French Canadian. He had an exotic "foreignness" to him—his accent, his on-ice flashiness, his cosmopolitan lifestyle. All of these played very well in Manhattan.

This, however, begs a critical question: Would Gilbert have had the same appeal to local fans had he played with the Toronto Maple Leafs? Or, continuing along this line, what if francophone great Mario Lemieux had been drafted by, say, the Calgary Flames in 1983, rather than the Pittsburgh Penguins? Would he have been as adored in early-1980s Alberta—with its growing Western alienation, fuelled in part by its frustration with the Quebec question—as he was in Pittsburgh?

It would seem a large stretch to answer either of these questions in the affirmative.

CHAPTER 3:
THE WEST WANTS IN

THE EVENTS THAT NIGHT epitomized the drama that seemed to occur every time these two clubs met. It was April 30, 1986, and the Calgary Flames and Edmonton Oilers were playing Game 7 of the NHL's Smythe Division final. The Oilers were two-time defending Stanley Cup champions, having won in both the 1983–84 and 1984–85 seasons, and were looking to make it three in a row, a feat that would put them in the rarefied company of just a very small handful of teams throughout the NHL's long history. While the Flames were certainly a solid team, the Oilers were still heavy favourites. The Oilers had finished 30 points ahead of the Flames during the regular season, and featured their usual star-studded lineup that included the likes of future Hall of Famers Wayne Gretzky, Mark Messier, Paul Coffey, Jari Kurri, Glenn Anderson and Grant Fuhr.

Game 7 was, perhaps surprisingly, close. The Flames did not let their overwhelming underdog status deter them and were tied 2–2 with the Oilers at the end of the second period. The tension at Edmonton's Northlands Coliseum heading into the third period was palpable. For Oilers fans, the game and the series were much too close for comfort. It wasn't supposed to be this way—Oilers fans were expecting their club to dispense with the Flames quickly and easily.

Then, with just under 15 minutes to play in the third period, Oilers rookie defenceman Steve Smith scored to break the tie. But instead of elation for Oilers fans, it was horror. The problem? Smith had inadvertently scored in his own goal. Smith was behind the Oilers' net, and his clearing pass hit goalie Grant Fuhr on the skates, with the puck deflecting into the net behind Fuhr.[69]

With the goal, Calgary took a 3–2 lead. It was to be the last goal scored by either team in the game, and Edmonton was eliminated —the Oilers mini-dynasty, and their hopes for a three-peat, had abruptly and shockingly come to an end.

THE BATTLE OF ALBERTA

It was the NHL's fiercest rivalry of the 1980s—the Calgary Flames and the Edmonton Oilers. Their head-to-head battles in the playoffs, the first coming in the spring of 1983, were legendary. They were two clubs at the top of their game, only 300 kilometres apart along Alberta's Highway 2, but representing cities that, while both fuelled by the oil industry, were vastly different. Calgary was the swashbuckling, fun-loving Cowtown, while Edmonton was the buttoned-down centre of business and government.

What made this natural geographic rivalry even more special was that the two teams were extremely talented—in fact, they dominated the NHL during the 1980s. In the eight years spanning the 1982–83 to 1989–90 seasons, either the Oilers or the Flames were in the Stanley Cup final every single year—six appearances for the Oilers (with five wins), and two appearances for the Flames (with one win). It was undoubtedly the halcyon days of hockey in Alberta.

During the decade, the Flames and Oilers met in the playoffs a total of four times over a six-year span. The two teams' playoffs matchups were epic, and the rivalry quickly became known across Canada and the NHL as the "Battle of Alberta." The Flames' 1986 series with Edmonton would be the only one that Calgary won, but the relatively one-sided nature of the rivalry certainly did not diminish its intensity. Looking back, Steve Smith's infamous own goal that year is probably even more traumatic retrospectively for Oilers fans than it was at the time, given that the club rebounded to win the Stanley Cup again the following two seasons, meaning that this bizarre 1986 loss to Calgary possibly prevented the Oilers from winning five straight Stanley Cups, a feat achieved only once (by Montreal in the late 1950s) in NHL history.

While the game was undoubtedly the low point for the Oilers in that era, it represented a type of coming-out party for the Calgary franchise. The Flames had finally won a playoff series against the seemingly invincible Oilers, after having been eliminated by the Oilers in the Smythe Division final in two of the prior three seasons, one of which was a Game 7 loss. After upsetting Edmonton, Calgary went on to defeat the St. Louis Blues in the 1986 Campbell Conference final, sending the club to its first-ever Stanley Cup final. While they lost the final that year, to Montreal, the Flames would return to the final three years later, again playing Montreal, but this time emerging victorious. The 1989 Cup win was the first—and to this day, only—Stanley Cup championship for the Flames franchise.

While the Flames–Oilers rivalry was compelling hockey drama for nearly a decade—evoking notions of great sport rivalries of the past, like the Celtics–Lakers in basketball, the Dodgers–Yankees in baseball and the Canadiens–Maple Leafs in hockey—it had a unique twist: both clubs were very new to the NHL. In 1983, when the two teams met in the playoffs for the first time, neither club had even been in the NHL just four years earlier. The Oilers entered the NHL in only the fall of 1979, a transfer from the rival WHA when the two leagues agreed to merge. Calgary's NHL franchise was even younger, beginning play one year later than Edmonton, in the fall of 1980, when the NHL's Atlanta Flames relocated to Calgary.

The fact that neither Edmonton nor Calgary gained their franchises through any proactive expansion decision of the NHL was curious in itself. The NHL had repeatedly sent the signal over the years that neither city was NHL material—both were simply considered too small and, while unspoken, perhaps too parochial in the eyes of the Eastern-centric NHL power brokers. It would take forces outside the NHL, fighting long odds, to ultimately change this perception.

ECONOMICS, POLITICS AND THE TRANSFORMATION OF THE WEST

The Oilers-Flames battles of the 1980s—and how that intense rivalry put Alberta at the centre of the hockey world, for at least a brief while—is really a story that began 40 years earlier.

It was February 13, 1947, a day that would become a landmark in Canada's economic history. Canadians were less than two years removed from the end of the Second World War. The postwar boom that would ultimately take full hold during the 1950s was still in its early stages. But on that winter day in 1947, Canada's economy—and particularly that of Alberta—would be suddenly and dramatically changed forever. A major oil reserve was discovered at Leduc, Alberta. The so-called Leduc No. 1 well was, in the parlance of the petroleum industry, a gusher.

Normally, countries or regions experience economic growth very gradually, through time, often over many decades. This is because the forces that drive growth—such as the education and abilities of the workforce, and the physical capital and technology the economy possesses—are relatively fixed and unchangeable in the short run. But Leduc was different—literally overnight, everything changed.

The Leduc discovery would quickly and radically transform Alberta—its wealth, its social systems, its politics and its stature within the rest of Canada. Before the Leduc find, Alberta was economically and demographically not much different than Saskatchewan, its neighbour to the east. In the 1941 census, Saskatchewan actually had about 100,000 more residents than Alberta—Saskatchewan's population was just under 900,000, while Alberta's was just under 800,000.[70] Thirty years later, by the 1971 census, the different trajectories of the two provinces were clearly evident: Alberta's population had grown dramatically, to about 1.7 million, while Saskatchewan's population was relatively stagnant, increasing only marginally, to just over 900,000.

Alberta's oil was not the only driver of postwar economic growth in Western Canada, but it was the largest. Saskatchewan—long dependent on agriculture, particularly grain crops—ultimately had several significant oil discoveries of its own, albeit of a much smaller scale than Alberta's. As well, Saskatchewan was found to be situated on large potash reserves, first discovered in 1943 when geologists were drilling for oil. In northern Saskatchewan, uranium—an input in the burgeoning postwar nuclear industry—began to be mined in the 1950s.

Changes were also occurring on the West Coast. British Columbia had long been a province known for its natural resources—particularly fishing and lumber—but its relatively remote location put the province, and its primary city of Vancouver, thousands of kilometres from the business and financial hubs of Central Canada. However, the 1950s brought rapid advances in transportation. Not only did commercial air travel experience sizable growth, but the

automobile culture took hold nationwide, facilitated by large
government investments in infrastructure projects like the Trans-
Canada Highway. BC's geographic isolation was becoming a thing of
the past.

The West's emergence from hinterland status was reflected in
its postwar population growth—not only an absolute growth, but,
more importantly, a growth relative to the rest of Canada. Most of
this growth occurred in BC and Alberta—the two provinces composed
only 14% of the Canadian population in 1941, but by 1971 this had
jumped to 18%.[71]

By the early 1970s, Alberta was a quarter century into its oil
boom, and over those years, the province's economy had been fundamentally and forever transformed. The economy looked nothing
like it had in 1947, when the Leduc discovery occurred. In contrast,
Alberta's political scene had changed very little over that time. The
Social Credit Party had ruled Alberta since 1935, beginning its reign
in the midst of the Great Depression and the Dust Bowl years. The
party was a rural-based, socially conservative, populist party, led
by premiers William Aberhart from 1935 to 1943, and by Ernest
Manning from 1943 to 1968. Both Aberhart and Manning were
deeply religious—Aberhart, nicknamed "Bible Bill," was a Baptist
minister, and Manning, an Aberhart follower, became a well-known
radio evangelist.

With Manning retiring from politics following his party's 1968
election victory, Harry Strom became leader of the Social Credit
Party and Alberta premier. It soon became apparent that Strom
lacked the personal popularity and charisma of his predecessors,
and the party's fortunes began to decline. The reasons for the
decline, however, went well beyond Strom's leadership. There was
a growing sense amongst many Albertans that a new direction was
needed in Alberta politics—one that moved the province away from

its agrarian and populist roots and toward a more modern and urban focus. There was also a concern amongst many Albertans that the province's political influence within Canada had not kept pace with its strong economic and population growth in the oil-boom era. This concern was further heightened with the election of Pierre Trudeau as Canada's prime minister in 1968. Trudeau had strong voter support in Quebec and Ontario, but Westerners were leerier, concerned that Trudeau's Central Canadian base would make him less responsive to the interests of Western Canada.

For the Social Credit in Alberta, it all ended with the 1971 provincial election. The party went down to a crushing defeat to Peter Lougheed's Progressive Conservative Party, ending the 36-year reign of the Socreds. Lougheed, a lawyer and Harvard MBA, represented a profound departure from the Socred premiers that had preceded him. The election of Lougheed was the beginning of a dramatic change in Alberta's—and, to a lesser extent, the West's—more assertive approach to the Central Canadian establishment.

For many in the West, their initial concerns regarding Pierre Trudeau proved to be well-founded. At best, many of his favourite policy initiatives—bilingualism, federalism and Quebec sovereignty, constitutional issues, et cetera—seemed distant (both literally and figuratively) and far removed from the everyday issues facing Western Canadians. At worst, several of his policies seemed to actively work against the interests of the West, and Trudeau himself was often accused of being dismissive and confrontational when it came to issues facing Western Canada. In the end, the Trudeau government managed to alienate a broad range of voters, from farmers to oil workers. There seemed to be little understanding, or interest in understanding, the concerns and psyche of Western Canadians.[72]

HUNTER, MUNRO AND HATSKIN

While the quarter century following the Second World War saw Western Canada's *economy* emerge from its hinterland status, professional hockey in the region certainly did not follow suit—in fact, it remained as irrelevant as ever amongst the NHL's power brokers. The 1967 NHL expansion was a huge disappointment for Western Canada; Vancouver in particular had been hoping to receive one of the new franchises, but all six went to US cities, including non-traditional hockey markets St. Louis, Los Angeles and Oakland. The Toronto Maple Leafs and Montreal Canadiens had reportedly opposed the Vancouver bid, not wanting to share the lucrative Canadian TV contract a third way.

While Vancouver did eventually get its NHL franchise—in 1970 —other cities in the West, like Edmonton, Calgary and Winnipeg, still sought major professional hockey franchises, but it was understood that this was unlikely to occur in an NHL dominated by interests in the US and Central Canada. Westerners had long been forced to make do with the old Western Hockey League. Not to be confused with the current junior league of the same name, the WHL was what could be termed a minor pro league, employing players not able to make NHL rosters. Over its 22-year history (1952–53 to 1973–74), it had, at one time or another, franchises in several Western Canadian cities, including Edmonton, Calgary, Vancouver, Victoria, Saskatoon, Regina and Brandon, Manitoba. Despite its relative longevity and reasonably high quality of play, the league was never able to fully escape the perception amongst fans of being a second-tier operation, and a league nowhere near on par with the NHL.

Three men set out to change this reality, to lift Western Canada out of the proverbial dark ages of professional hockey. Bill Hunter, Scotty Munro and Ben Hatskin were long-time acquaintances. Each was an icon in the amateur hockey world of their respective cities— Hunter in Edmonton, Munro in Calgary and Hatskin in Winnipeg. All three were franchise owners in the West's premier junior league, the Western Canada Hockey League (WCHL)—forerunner to today's Western Hockey League. They knew their markets well, and each believed his city could support a major professional hockey team. Hatskin, in fact, had attempted to gain an NHL franchise for Winnipeg as part of the league's 1967 expansion, an attempt that ultimately failed.

All were staunch Westerners. Hunter and Munro were both originally from Saskatchewan—Hunter from Saskatoon and Munro from Swift Current. Hatskin was born and raised in Winnipeg, a child of Russian Jewish parents, and had played professional football with the CFL's Winnipeg Blue Bombers. As importantly, the three were not afraid to challenge the status quo and hockey establishment. Hunter was probably the most controversial of the group. In 1966, he personally founded the WCHL, a breakaway renegade league that upended the long-standing junior-hockey order.

Hunter owned the Edmonton Oil Kings[73] junior team and moved his club to the WCHL for the league's 1966–67 charter season. One season later, Scotty Munro's Calgary Centennials and Ben Hatskin's Winnipeg Jets (not to be confused with Hatskin's WHA team of the same name) joined Hunter's league.

In the early 1970s, Gary Davidson, a young Southern California lawyer and sports entrepreneur, along with his business partner Dennis Murphy, had an idea to establish a new professional hockey league—a league that would seek to challenge the monopoly dominance of the NHL. The upstart World Hockey Association (WHA) was about to radically change the face of professional hockey in North America. Hunter, Hatskin and Munro, with their deep knowledge of the Western Canadian hockey scene and their track record of challenging the establishment, fit perfectly with Davidson's plan.

RIVAL LEAGUES

The WHA was born in 1972, right in the very middle of what could be termed the "rival league era" of North American professional sport. The era spanned the period between 1960 and 1985 and saw the formation of no less than seven rival leagues across the four major North American professional team sports. In addition to the WHA, two other leagues—the American Football League (AFL) and the American Basketball Association (ABA)—would ultimately go on to gain mergers with the established leagues against which they were competing.

The 1950s had ended with each of the four sports controlled by a single (i.e., monopoly) league—the NFL,[74] the NBA, MLB and the NHL. All were what economists call "closed" leagues, in that the league membership was fixed, and the only means by which new franchises could enter the league was to get the existing owners in that league to agree to expand. The problem was that these owners had little incentive to expand. The leagues, like any monopolist, benefited from artificially restricting their own output, thereby creating scarcity, and thus driving up the value of their product. A good analogy is OPEC, the international oil cartel, by which member countries restrict their oil output so as to keep prices high.

For the monopoly sports leagues, the output restrictions manifested themselves in the effort to keep the number of franchises at an artificially low level. For example, both the NHL and MLB ended the 1950s with the same number of franchises, in the same cities, as what they had started the decade with (six franchises in the NHL and sixteen in baseball). The situation was even more pronounced in the NFL and NBA—both leagues actually had fewer franchises at the end of the 1950s than at the beginning (one fewer in the NFL and three fewer in the NBA).[75]

This unwillingness of owners to increase the size of their leagues during the 1950s was juxtaposed against a rapidly evolving postwar economic and social climate in North America. Average incomes were rising, leisure activities were becoming increasingly afford-able, the baby boom was well under way, and the population in North America was shifting westward. All of this meant there were more cities that could viably support a professional sport franchise, but instead these markets remained unserved by the established leagues. Not only that, but some of the very largest markets, while served, in that they did have a franchise in the league, were often "underserved"—i.e., their population could have supported an additional franchise or franchises. Think, for example, New York with football or baseball, or Toronto with hockey.[76]

The established leagues, seemingly overconfident about the dominance of their position and comfortable in their belief that no credible rival could present a challenge, severely miscalculated. It was the AFL that first exposed the fallacy. Dallas oilman Lamar Hunt had long sought an NFL franchise for his rapidly growing city, but was always rebuffed by the league, being told throughout the late 1950s that it had no interest in expansion. Hunt decided to take matters into his own hands and formed the eight-team American Football League. As with the rival leagues that would follow, Hunt's strategy was to place a few of the franchises of the new league in major media markets already served by the NFL—so as to gain increased media attention—but to place the remaining franchises in growing but unserved markets.

In the AFL's case, they competed head-to-head with the NFL in New York, with the AFL's Titans (later Jets) going up against the NFL's Giants, and in Los Angeles, where the AFL's Chargers were opposite the NFL's Rams. The other six franchises were awarded to Boston, Buffalo, Minneapolis, Denver, Dallas (owned by Hunt himself) and Houston. In a tactic by established leagues that would become commonplace in the future, the NFL suddenly dispensed with its moratorium on expansion, and announced, even before the AFL had played its first game, that it had granted expansion franchises to Dallas (the Cowboys) and Minnesota (the Vikings). Lamar Hunt elected to keep his AFL franchise in Dallas (the Texans) to compete directly with the NFL's Cowboys, but the AFL franchise initially destined for Minnesota was shifted to Oakland (where they became the Raiders) before the start of the league's first season. Hunt ultimately found that competing with the NFL's Cowboys was too much, and after three years in Dallas he moved his Texans franchise to Kansas City (where they became the Chiefs). Other than this move by the Texans, and a move by the Chargers to San Diego after the AFL's first season, the new league had a remarkable franchise stability for a fledging rival league, with no other franchises shifting cities throughout the league's 10 years of existence.

It wasn't just the NFL's unwillingness to expand into emerging markets that provided an opportunity for the AFL. It was also that the NFL drastically underpaid its players—in the sense that players generated far more revenues for their clubs relative to what they were paid—thereby making the AFL a potentially attractive alternative for current or prospective NFL players. NFL policies at the time prohibited voluntary player movement across its teams, perpetually binding players to the club that drafted or signed them. This greatly reduced players' bargaining power and served to suppress their salaries well below a competitive level.

The AFL, and the rival leagues that were soon to follow it, capitalized on this and enjoyed a situation where many star players were quite willing, for the right price, to entertain a move to the upstart league. Before the AFL's very first season, the Houston Oilers signed reigning Heisman Trophy winner Billy Cannon out of Louisiana State University, signing him out from under the Los Angeles Rams, the NFL team that had drafted him, and in the process giving the AFL instant credibility, signalling that the new league would be a force to be reckoned with. An even bigger signing occurred three years later, when the AFL's New York Jets signed University of Alabama star quarterback Joe Namath. The loss of Namath, with his larger-than-life personality and national celebrity status, was a blow that was simply too much for the NFL and convinced the league to begin serious merger talks with the upstart league. Three years after the Namath signing, in 1966, the two leagues did finally agree to merge, with 10 AFL clubs joining the NFL—all eight of the AFL's original franchises, as well as two other clubs that had been granted AFL expansion franchises but had not yet begun play.[77]

One year after the AFL first launched in 1960, a new rival baseball league was also to enter the market. The Continental League, as it was known, adopted a model similar to the AFL, with a franchise in New York, but otherwise largely focused on placing franchises in unserved markets, cities like Minneapolis, Atlanta and Buffalo. Major League Baseball had only 16 franchises in 1960—eight in the National League, and eight in the American League—the same number as it had in 1901. MLB had not expanded in almost 60 years, despite the US population more than doubling during that period. It was an extreme case of artificial supply limitations, and had persisted even in the face of several US congressional hearings during the 1950s that sought answers for the reasons why baseball wasn't expanding.

The Continental League's first president was Branch Rickey, a baseball icon who, as GM of the Dodgers, had overseen the breaking of MLB's colour barrier in 1947 when he brought Jackie Robinson to Brooklyn. One of the other architects of the new league was William Shea, a New York City lawyer who had been tasked by that city's mayor to find a replacement for the New York Giants and Brooklyn Dodgers, both of whom had vacated the New York market in 1958 to relocate to California—the Giants to San Francisco, and the Dodgers

to Los Angeles. The owners of these two franchises—Horace Stoneham of the Giants and Walter O'Malley of the Dodgers—had been
unable to negotiate deals to get new stadiums in New York to replace
the old, outdated facilities their clubs had been playing in, and
abruptly decided to move westward. Major League Baseball's
unwillingness to expand, particularly to California and the rapidly
growing West, created an opportunity for Stoneham and O'Malley
to move their franchises.

Ultimately, the Continental League never played a single game.
They faced a critical, and ultimately insurmountable, problem: they
had no access to quality players. MLB had essentially tied up thousands of players in its minor league systems—players who had no
reasonable prospect of ever making it to the majors, but who were
nonetheless restricted by the "reserve clause" in their contracts
that perpetually bound them to their clubs. While such a practice
would have been considered highly anti-competitive, and illegal,
in almost any other industry, baseball had an explicit exemption
from US antitrust law based on a 1922 US Supreme Court case. The
Continental League lobbied Congress to (at least partially) overturn
the exemption, and to force MLB teams to control no more than 100
players in their minor league systems. The matter made it all the
way to a Senate vote in 1960, but the vote to repeal the antitrust
exemption ultimately went down to a narrow 45–41 defeat, largely
due to senators from states that had MLB teams voting to retain
the exemption. The Continental League's fate was sealed, and the
league disbanded shortly thereafter.

As a postscript to the story, even if the league had been victorious
in that vote, it would have faced other, perhaps insurmountable
problems. The threat of a legitimate rival entering the market
prompted MLB to abandon its nearly six-decade moratorium on
expansion, and the National League announced that it would grant

franchises to New York (the Mets) and Houston (the Colt .45s, later the Astros) to begin play in 1961. With the New York market being such a central part of the Continental League's strategy to fill the gap there left by the departure of the Giants and Dodgers, the arrival of the Mets essentially nullified the new league's viability.

Despite the setbacks encountered by the Continental League, the early success of the AFL buoyed the spirits of those sports entrepreneurs seeking to form other rival leagues. In basketball, the short-lived American Basketball League began play in 1961. Despite being headed by Harlem Globetrotters founder Abe Saperstein and having future New York Yankees owner George Steinbrenner as one of its franchise owners, the league only survived one season. However, a more formidable challenger to the NBA arrived in 1967, when the ABA started play. The league was founded by Gary Davidson and his business partner Dennis Murphy, who would, of course, go on to create the WHA in the early 1970s. Like the AFL before it, the ABA made an immediate impact in the players' market. The Oakland Oaks signed reigning NBA scoring champion Rick Barry, who was only the first in a long line of high-profile players that would ultimately join the upstart league. Future NBA stars like Julius Erving and Moses Malone started their pro careers in the ABA, with Malone being signed directly out of high school at a time when the NBA was requiring incoming players to have played four years of college basketball.

The ABA was a much more unstable and tumultuous business entity than was the AFL, with the ABA experiencing multiple franchise shifts and foldings, and a seemingly constant stream of ownership changes. The league did, however, survive nine seasons, and during that time inflicted large-scale damage on the NBA, primarily through bidding up players' salaries to the point where both leagues were on the verge of financial collapse. A tentative merger agreement in 1970 between the two leagues was overturned because it did not receive antitrust approval,[78] but a merger did eventually occur in 1976, one that saw four ABA teams join the NBA, the New York (now Brooklyn) Nets, the Denver Nuggets, the Indiana Pacers and the San Antonio Spurs.

Before the rival league era came to a close in 1985, three other challenger leagues would form—the WHA, along with two football leagues, the World Football League (WFL) and United States Football League (USFL). The WFL, another Gary Davidson/Dennis Murphy creation, their third, would not have the same success as their two earlier leagues, and folded in July 1975, midway through only its second season. Most of its owners were woefully underfinanced, but the league did make headlines before its inaugural season when the Toronto Northmen[79] signed the trio of Larry Csonka, Jim Kiick and Paul Warfield, star players from the defending Super Bowl–champion Miami Dolphins. The USFL entered the football market almost a decade later, in 1983, playing in the spring rather than the fall, the more traditional football season. Despite a better-financed group of owners (including future US president Donald Trump) and the signing of many college stars, like Heisman Trophy winners Doug Flutie, Herschel Walker and Mike Rozier, the league made several strategic missteps, and lasted only three years. It filed an antitrust suit against the NFL and actually won the case, but the courts awarded the USFL only $1 in damages (trebled to $3 under US antitrust law), thereby extinguishing any hopes for its revival.

The USFL's collapse in 1985 would ultimately mark the end of the rival league era—there has not been another legitimate rival league in any of the four major sports since then. The two key conditions that led to rival leagues forming—the existence of viable markets left unserved by the established league, and players so underpaid in the established league that they are willing to risk defecting to the rival league—gradually eroded. The established leagues got smarter, recognizing that they needed to voluntarily expand in order to pre-empt the entry of a rival. As well, players' associations got stronger, ultimately winning the free-agency rights that gave players voluntary mobility within the established leagues and allowing them to use this internal competition to dramatically increase their salaries without the need to jump to a rival league.

THE WORLD HOCKEY ASSOCIATION

The WHA, then, was far from a unique enterprise; it was simply one in a long line of rival leagues that formed in that era. Like those of the other leagues, the WHA's basic business model was to place franchises in unserved markets and then lure star players to the league by offering salaries above what the established league was offering. The WHA, however, was different from other rival leagues in one important way: the distinct Canadian market was a central (if not critical) element to its business strategy. While other rival leagues had focused almost exclusively on the US market,[80] the game of hockey had only a niche following in the US at the time, and certainly had a much narrower appeal than traditional "American" sports like football, baseball and basketball. While the league would also have several US-based franchises, the ability of the WHA to get a strong foothold in Canada would go a long way to determining its ultimate success or failure.

This is where Hunter, Hatskin and Munro came in. They were Western Canadian "hockey men" who not only knew the game extremely well, but were legends in their own communities for their backgrounds as operators of their local major junior clubs. Gary Davidson knew when he founded the WHA that getting this trio of esteemed junior hockey men on board would be critical to the new league's success.

Davidson, of course, already had a track record. His founding
of the ABA in 1967—a league that was still operating as a going
concern five years later in 1972, when the WHA was forming—
gave him credibility as a visionary sports entrepreneur, and one
whose ideas worked. There was a problem, though. Davidson, by his
own admission, knew nothing about hockey.[81] His law offices were
in Newport Beach, California—about as far away as one could get,
literally and figuratively, from the unglamorous hockey circuit
of the Canadian Prairies. Davidson admitted that, prior to his
founding the WHA, he had never been to a hockey game—for Davidson, this was purely about a business opportunity, not about a love
of hockey.

Howard Baldwin, the charter co-owner of the WHA's New England
Whalers, described the charismatic Davidson as a "surfer type,"
with Robert Redford good looks—a sharp contrast to the gruff and
serious Hunter, Haskin and Munro. These differences in background
and perspective, not to mention age—Davidson was in his 30s when
the WHA was formed, while Hunter, Hatskin and Munro were all in
their mid '50s—made for a difficult and often tense relationship
between Davidson and the Canadian trio. In Davidson's 1974 book
Breaking the Game Wide Open, he complains about Hunter, Hatskin
and Munro—the "Canadian block," as he called them—saying they
resented his lack of knowledge about hockey and wanted to "take
over," demanding, amongst other things, the league office be in
Canada, with a Canadian commissioner.

Of the three, Davidson found Hunter particularly difficult. While he
admired Hunter's maverick streak and his willingness to challenge
the NHL establishment, Davidson saw him as "hard to handle"—an
explosive personality who was always threating to walk out and
take Munro and Hatskin with him. Eventually, at least according
to Davidson, Hunter and Davidson came to somewhat of a truce,

with Hunter begrudgingly acknowledging that Davidson ultimately had the final say.

When the WHA announced its formation in the fall of 1971, its initial franchise roster consisted of 10 cities—the aforementioned three in Western Canada, along with seven US franchises: in Miami, Los Angeles, Chicago, Long Island, Dayton, San Francisco and Minnesota. Unlike the three Canadian franchises, most of these US franchises were owned by individuals who could be termed hockey "outsiders," men who had no prior connection to the game, but simply saw the new league as a fun and potentially lucrative investment. This lack of hockey knowledge, however, hampered the league because it often led owners to hire the wrong people for their organizations.

Because of the risk and uncertainty inherent in launching a new league, finding suitable owners was often difficult. As with many rival leagues, some WHA owners were woefully underfinanced and did not have the capacity to withstand the inevitable early financial losses that would occur. Davidson knew going in that he couldn't afford to be too selective—he needed individuals who were willing to pay him the $25,000 franchise fee to gain admission to the league, and there was often very little other vetting that would occur.

Not surprisingly, there were ownership changes and franchise shifts even before the first puck dropped in the league's inaugural season. The Calgary franchise, nicknamed the Broncos, encountered immediate problems when owner Bob Brownridge[82] passed away unexpectedly, putting the franchise in limbo, and ultimately resulting in it being sold and then moved to Cleveland.[83] This was all very disappointing news for those in southern Alberta. Calgary's WHA experience ended almost as quickly as it began, and what was to be the trifecta of Prairie franchises was now suddenly down to two.

Other franchise shifts also occurred: the Miami Screaming Eagles became the Philadelphia Blazers, the Dayton Aeros became the Houston Aeros, the San Francisco Sharks (owned by Gary Davidson himself) became the Quebec Nordiques, and the franchise originally slated for Long Island was relocated to Manhattan in response to the NHL deciding to place an expansion franchise on Long Island (the New York Islanders) beginning in the 1972–73 season. All these changes occurred without the WHA ever having played a single game. In addition, two more franchises—in Ottawa (the Nationals) and in Boston (the New England Whalers)—were added to the initially announced group of 10 franchises, bringing the WHA to a 12-team league for its first season, four of which were in Canada.

For any rival league, the ability to quickly capture fan and media interest was critical, and the most effective way to accomplish this was in the players' market. Rival leagues needed to sign at least *some* players, preferably high-profile players, who would have otherwise played in the established league. Otherwise, the rival league could be simply dismissed as being of minor-league status, a second-tier operation that shouldn't be taken particularly seriously, and one that posed no threat to the one true major league. For the AFL, it was the signing of Billy Cannon; for the ABA, it was Rick Barry. The WHA needed something similar.

They got it, and in the most spectacular way possible.

Bobby Hull was an NHL superstar, a hockey icon of his generation. In the spring of 1972, he had just come off a 50-goal season for the NHL's Chicago Black Hawks, his fifth season of 50 or more goals, and the second-best goal output in the entire NHL during the 1971–72 season.

Hull shocked the hockey world by signing a million-dollar contract with Ben Hatskin's Winnipeg Jets. Hull received a $1 million signing bonus and a yearly salary of $250,000 per season.[84] This was in an era when the average NHL annual salary was only about $25,000, and when even star players often made less than $50,000 per year. Because Hull's presence in the WHA would benefit all franchises, not just the Jets, the other owners agreed to equally split the $1 million cost of the signing bonus.[85]

Davidson talked about how the WHA targeted Hull over other stars of the day, like Boston Bruins defenceman Bobby Orr. Davidson saw Hull as being more charismatic and fan-friendly, a player who could not only give the WHA credibility on the ice, but would also be invaluable to its off-ice marketing efforts.

Many other big-name NHLers joined Hull in the WHA for its first season. The defending Stanley Cup champion Boston Bruins were particularly hard hit, losing Gerry Cheevers to the Cleveland Crusaders, Derek Sanderson and Johnny McKenzie to the Philadelphia Blazers, and Ted Green to the New England Whalers. Sanderson and Cheevers were particularly prominent signings for the WHA, with each player commanding $200,000-plus a season, an unheard-of amount by NHL standards of the day. The Toronto Maple Leafs were another team to suffer large defections. They lost not only veteran goalie Bernie Parent to the Philadelphia Blazers, but a trio of young upcoming defencemen to the New England Whalers in Rick Ley, Brad Selwood and Jim Dorey. The year after they lost Hull, the Black Hawks got hit hard again in the WHA's second season, losing star defenceman Pat Stapleton to the crosstown Chicago Cougars— Stapleton signed with the WHA for $90,000 per year, almost double his NHL annual salary of $55,000.

It was not coincidental that the Chicago Black Hawks, Boston Bruins and Toronto Maple Leafs were the NHL teams that suffered the heaviest losses. All had owners that were considered the old guard—hard-liners who were outraged by the salary offers the WHA was making to NHL stars and who were steadfastly refusing to get into a bidding war. Toronto had Harold Ballard, Boston had Charles Adams, and Chicago, Bill Wirtz. Wirtz was instrumental in scuttling a proposed merger between the two leagues at the end of the WHA's first season, a merger that would have seen all 12 of the WHA franchises join the NHL.

Many NHL teams, so accustomed for decades to being in a monopsony position with their players—that is, being the only buyer for a given player's services—often seemed unprepared for the new reality. In the absence of a rival league, players had little to no negotiating power with owners, resulting in the players being relatively underpaid, in that their salaries were far below the revenue they generated for their respective clubs.

The WHA used this to their advantage, knowing that many NHLers would certainly consider a move to the new league if it meant a significant salary increase. NHL players often faced a difficult decision: while the WHA was offering a major salary increase, it also presented more risk. The league was new, unknown and unproven. For a player like Hull, the move to the WHA was a huge leap of faith.

Of course, WHA clubs could not afford to fill their entire roster with NHL-calibre players. Being a new league, WHA teams had nowhere near the revenue-generating potential of their NHL counterparts. So, the WHA adopted a strategy of signing only select NHL players—enough to gain the new league immediate attention—but still ultimately filling the majority of their roster spots with players who would otherwise be considered career minor-leaguers.

Another avenue the new league took was to target young players coming out of junior hockey. These players were often somewhat less expensive than veteran NHLers, but they still provided the WHA with a significant level of publicity, at least in Canada. A key element of the WHA's strategy was to target so-called "underage" juniors, i.e., those players who were not yet 20 years old, the age at which the

NHL drafted juniors. The first big signing came in May 1973, when the Houston Aeros signed Mark Howe, an 18-year-old who had just led the Toronto Marlboros to a Memorial Cup victory. Howe had been brilliant, capping the tournament with a two-goal and three-assist performance in the championship game, and being named tournament MVP. Howe was still two years away from being eligible for the NHL draft, but the WHA offered Howe an opportunity to start his pro career immediately. Mark Howe was part of a package deal that saw the Aeros sign Mark's older brother Marty— a much lesser prospect than Mark—and their father, Gordie, the NHL's all-time leading goal scorer at the time, who came out of retirement at 44 years of age to join his two sons with the Aeros. Both Mark and Gordie had illustrious WHA careers, first with the Aeros and then later with the New England Whalers.

The following year, the NHL lost another Memorial Cup star when the Regina Pats' Dennis Sobchuk, widely considered to be the best prospect in junior hockey, signed with the WHA's expansion Cincinnati Stingers. The 18-year-old Sobchuk had led the Pats to the 1974 Memorial Cup, scoring three goals in the final game. He would likely have been the first-overall pick in the NHL draft that year had he been eligible.[86]

In 1978, the WHA's Birmingham Bulls took the signing of under-age juniors to a whole new level, essentially building their entire roster around such players, and in the process acquired the moniker of the "Baby Bulls." The Bulls were owned by Toronto's John F. Bassett, who had moved the franchise from Toronto (where they were known as the Toros) to Birmingham, Alabama, one year earlier. Bassett signed a plethora of OHL stars, most of whom would ultimately go on to notable NHL careers: Ken Linseman, Mark Napier, Rick Vaive, Pat Riggin, Craig Hartsburg, Rob Ramage, Gaston Gingras and Michel Goulet.

The signings of these underage players were actually part of a larger WHA strategy. The summer of 1978 had seen new negotiations about a possible merger between the two leagues. But the negotiations ultimately broke down, with the NHL again rejecting a merger agreement. In the aftermath of this breakdown, the WHA decided that it had to increase the pressure on the NHL if it was to get the latter league to ever agree to a merger. With these signings, the WHA was now beginning to accumulate a critical mass of young players, not to mention the bad publicity that went along with it.

The WHA's ultimate underage signing came later that same year, when the Indianapolis Racers' owner, Vancouver native Nelson Skalbania, signed 17-year-old Wayne Gretzky to a personal services contract. Gretzky had already been a hockey sensation throughout Canada during most of his childhood, so signing him was a major coup for the WHA. Gretzky played only seven games for the Racers before Skalbania sold his contract to Peter Pocklington, owner of the Edmonton Oilers.

THE AFTERMATH

The WHA survived seven tumultuous seasons. The league's instability had many sources—underfinanced owners, substandard and often outdated playing venues, and franchises in questionable hockey markets. Only three franchises played the entire seven years of the WHA's existence in the same cities in which they started, and all three were Canadian—Edmonton, Winnipeg and Quebec City.

In May 1979, these three franchises, along with the New England Whalers (who were renamed the Hartford Whalers upon their entry into the NHL) were merged[87] into the NHL, with the remaining three WHA franchises, along with the league itself, folding. As part of the merger agreement, the WHA franchises were stripped of most of their players upon entering the NHL, but the Edmonton Oilers were allowed to keep the young Gretzky—this fortuitous decision, along with some shrewd selections in the NHL draft, would set the foundation for the Oilers' dynasty of the 1980s.

In many ways, the WHA achieved what any rival league's ultimate goal is: to inflict enough damage on the established league so as to force a merger, preferably at a reduced entry price. The four surviving WHA clubs were admitted into the NHL for an expansion fee of $6 million each. This was the same amount that the Buffalo Sabres and Vancouver Canucks paid as expansion fees almost a decade earlier, in 1970. With inflation being high during that decade, the $6 million paid by the WHA teams amounted to only $3.2 million in 1970 dollars; thus, the WHA teams received a highly discounted entry price, indicative of the NHL's strong desire to see the end of the WHA. Of the four WHA teams to merge, only the New England Whalers had the same owner (Howard Baldwin) as when the WHA was founded. Two of the three Canadian-based franchises had relatively new owners, buying in just before the merger. Peter Pocklington bought control of the Oilers in 1977,[88] and a group headed by Michael Gobuty and Barry Shenkarow bought the Jets in 1978, when the club was experiencing severe financial difficulties. The Nordiques owner at the time of the merger was Maurice Filion, who had bought the club in 1974.

The merger was not easy. The initial vote saw all three of the Canadian NHL clubs—the Canadiens, Leafs and Canucks—vote against the agreement, apparently not wanting to share the lucrative Canadian TV market with the three Canadian WHA teams. However, the decision met with outrage in much of Canada, with Molson Brewery, the owner of the Canadiens, feeling particular pressure and facing potential boycotts of its product. The pressure worked— a few days later, NHL owners re-voted, and Montreal and Vancouver switched their vote to yes, thus providing enough votes for the merger to be approved. In the space of a matter of minutes, the WHA was dead, and the number of NHL teams in Canada doubled.

For hockey fans in Canada, the postscript on the WHA offered a mixed bag. On one hand, the WHA was the vehicle by which the cities of Edmonton, Winnipeg and Quebec City got their NHL teams—an outcome that almost assuredly would never have occurred had the WHA not forced the hand of the NHL. Other Canadian cities, however, didn't fare as well: franchises in Vancouver, Calgary, Toronto and Ottawa all folded or relocated at some point during the WHA's existence. Ottawa actually had two franchises fail: the charter Ottawa Nationals—who played only two seasons in Ottawa before relocating to Toronto, where they became the Toros—along with the Ottawa Civics. The Civics franchise illustrated the bizarreness that often plagued the league. The Denver Spurs were granted an expansion franchise for the 1975–76 season, but struggled so badly at the gate early on that the franchise relocated to Ottawa halfway through the team's first season, on January 2, 1976. The relocated Spurs, now the Civics, somewhat astonishingly folded on January 17, 1976, only two weeks after they had moved to the nation's capital. Such was life in the WHA.

Toronto's WHA franchise, the Toros, played in the city for three years, from 1973 (upon their arrival from Ottawa) until 1976. The team had reasonable success at the gate; in 1974–75, for example, they averaged a very respectable (for the WHA) 10,400 fans per game at Maple League Gardens, trailing only the Edmonton Oilers in attendance. Despite this, Toros owner John F. Bassett eventually grew tired of dealing with Leafs owner Harold Ballard. Ballard owned Maple Leaf Gardens, and generally made life miserable for his WHA counterpart and long-time foe.[89] Ballard eventually decided to no longer let the Toros play at all in Maple Leaf Gardens; without another viable arena in the city, Bassett promptly moved the franchise to Birmingham. The Toros' respectable attendance numbers did, however, show that the Toronto market could support two major professional hockey franchises. To this day, however, Toronto still has only a single major professional hockey team, the Leafs. With the demise of the WHA and the corresponding return to monopoly conditions in the professional hockey market, along with the continued existence of the NHL's territorial rights, the Leafs have maintained a seemingly absolute power to block any new competitors entering their market.

In the West, both Vancouver and Calgary were just brief stops on the WHA franchise merry-go-round. The Vancouver Blazers began play in 1973–74—the WHA's second season—a transfer from Philadelphia, where the Philadelphia Blazers had been a charter franchise in the WHA.[90] After two years in Vancouver, competing with the NHL's still relatively new Canucks, Blazers owner Jimmy Pattison decided to move the team to Calgary in 1975, where the club became the Calgary Cowboys. Calgary finally had its WHA team, three years after the charter Broncos franchise abruptly folded before the WHA's inaugural season. By 1977, however, the WHA was beginning to enter its death throes, and it was becoming apparent to many that the league would not survive much longer. Pattison knew that it was unlikely the Cowboys would be part of any merger with the NHL—the Stampede Corral, Calgary's multi-purpose venue, was simply too small to meet NHL standards[91]—so he ceased the club's operations at the end of the 1976–77 season, after just two seasons in Calgary.

Edmonton, Winnipeg and Quebec City were obviously the Canadian success stories of the WHA. None faced competition from other NHL teams in their markets, all were moderately to highly successful on the ice, and all were playing in arenas that, at least by WHA standards, were more than adequate. The Winnipeg Jets were by far the most successful team on the ice, in the WHA's short history. Led by

Bobby Hull, along with their large group of Swedish imports, they won three WHA championships and lost in the league final two other times. The Winnipeg Arena was still relatively new (at least by the standards of that era—it opened in 1955), and the combination of the team's on-ice prowess and an above-average playing facility resulted in the Jets leading the league in attendance most years.

While the fortunes of the Edmonton Oilers and Winnipeg Jets took very different turns upon their arrival in the NHL—the Oilers went on to win four Stanley Cups in five years during the mid-1980s, while the Jets struggled on and off the ice, with the franchise eventually leaving Winnipeg in 1996—the Oilers had nowhere near the success of the Jets during the WHA years. The Oilers generally had relatively mediocre teams, with few star players, not counting, of course, Gretzky, who only arrived partway through the WHA's final season. The Oilers never won a WHA title and only ever made it to the final once, losing to the Jets in 1977. On the business side, the club was hampered during its early years by being forced to play in the old Edmonton Gardens, a facility built in 1913 that had a capacity of only about 5,000. Upon the completion of the 15,000-plus-seat Northlands Coliseum in 1974, the Oilers moved into the new building and saw their attendance improve dramatically. Northlands would give the Oilers the largest arena capacity of any of the four WHA clubs that eventually joined the NHL.

In Quebec City, the Nordiques had built a large and extremely loyal following during their WHA days. The club very explicitly targeted their almost exclusively francophone fan base; in the early years, the club's roster was made up almost entirely of French Canadian players. With the implementation of the NHL draft in 1969 gradually forcing the Montreal Canadiens to become less francophone by default, the Nordiques were busy making up the difference. Like the Winnipeg Jets, the Nordiques were playing in a still-serviceable arena, Le Colisée de Québec (built in 1949), and drew well at the gate, always at or near the top of WHA attendance figures.

The WHA's impact in Canada, however, went beyond just these three cities that received NHL franchises. Calgary was a particularly interesting case. In terms of population and wealth, Calgary was at least on par with Winnipeg and Edmonton, but came out of the merger with no NHL team. Calgary had had tough luck in the WHA —with the relocation of the Broncos and then the folding of the Cowboys franchise—but these problems seemed to be situational, and were not necessarily a reflection of the overall quality of the market potential.

Like Edmonton and Winnipeg, Calgary would get its NHL franchise through the "back door"—in other words, not through a proactive decision by the NHL to locate an expansion franchise in the city, but rather through a reactive process, and with seeming reluctance. Calgary's NHL franchise came by way of Atlanta, Georgia. The Atlanta Flames had joined the NHL in 1972 as an expansion franchise, along with the New York Islanders. In their eight years in Atlanta, the Flames were never able to generate a significant following, despite offering a credible on-ice product for many of those seasons. In May 1980, Nelson Skalbania bought the Flames franchise and moved the club to Calgary.[92] In the space of two years, the Prairies—the birth-place of so many NHL players over the years—had gone from zero to three NHL franchises.

Only three years after the Flames' relocation, the Prairies came very close to adding a fourth franchise. In 1983, Edmonton Oilers founder Bill Hunter agreed to buy the NHL's St. Louis Blues, with the intention of moving them to Saskatoon, his hometown. The finan-cially struggling Blues were owned by Ralston Purina, the St. Louis–based pet-food company that had been trying to off-load the team for several years. At the time, Saskatoon's population was only

150,000, which would have made it the smallest market in the NHL, by a very wide margin. The spring of 1983 was a surreal time for the people of Saskatoon and Saskatchewan, when the far-fetched dream of securing an NHL franchise suddenly seemed close to reality. The dream, however, ended abruptly on May 18 of that year. The NHL's board of governors voted 15–3 against approving the franchise transfer, with only the Blues, Calgary Flames and Montreal Canadiens voting in favour. The NHL power elites never wanted a franchise in Saskatoon, and were shocked and angered that long-time owners Ralston Purina had created the scenario where such an outcome could occur.[93]

THE PARALLELS OF SPORT AND POLITICS

It took the emergence of a brash, often swashbuckling rival league to put the Canadian Prairies on the professional hockey map. The legacy of the WHA was that it showed the hockey world that the Prairies were not just a *source* of hockey talent—talent that in the past would ultimately be exported elsewhere—but was a region where major professional hockey clubs themselves could locate. And not only could these clubs survive, they could thrive; this was no better evidenced than by the Flames and Oilers' domination of the NHL during the 1980s. The geographic alignment had abruptly and radically shifted. Within a little over a decade, the Prairies had gone from the hinterlands of professional hockey to its centre of power.

The emergence of the WHA did not happen in a vacuum. It was a product of a time and place, not just in the hockey world, but in the broader social and political environment that surrounded it. The parallels between the formation of the WHA and the election of the Peter Lougheed government in Alberta were particularly strong. While the WHA railed against the hockey establishment—as embodied by the Eastern-centric NHL—the Lougheed government railed against the Canadian political establishment, embodied by Pierre Trudeau and the federal Liberal Party. Both reflected the emergence of a "new" Alberta—more confident, more assertive and much more willing to push back against the Eastern establishment. Sometimes the parallels bordered on the uncanny. Consider this: Peter Lougheed became Alberta's premier on September 10, 1971; just three days later, on September 13, 1971, the WHA was officially founded.[94]

Pierre Trudeau got off to a bad start with the West. In late 1968, mere months after being elected prime minister, Trudeau famously quipped to Saskatchewan farmers, "Why should I sell your wheat?" The rhetorical question pertained to the Canadian Wheat Board, the agency that was the monopoly seller of all wheat and barley produced in Western Canada. As the Economist put it almost 40 years later, "By daring to question the existence of the Canadian Wheat Board, [Trudeau] helped relegate his party to perennial fringe status in the prairie provinces."

Six months after the Wheat Board comment, in July 1969, at a speech in Regina, Saskatchewan, Trudeau said to a young protester who had thrown wheat at him, "If you don't stop that, I'll kick you right in the ass." The animosity between Trudeau and the West never really subsided during his entire tenure as prime minister. In August 1982, only two years before Trudeau would retire from politics, another infamous incident occurred, this one in Salmon Arm, BC. Trudeau was taking a train trip through the Rockies with his young sons, and as the Trudeaus' train stopped in Salmon Arm, protesters pelted it with eggs and tomatoes, prompting Trudeau to give the proverbial "one-finger salute" to the assembled crowd.

Davey Steuart—a Liberal senator from Saskatchewan appointed by Trudeau, and the one-time leader of the Saskatchewan Liberal Party—said of Trudeau, "He tended to say things offhand or give people the finger or something. I think that was some of the reasons that people didn't like him." Allan Blakeney, the respected New Democratic Party (NDP) premier of Saskatchewan (1971–82)—whose left-of-centre ideology was not dissimilar to that of Trudeau—was somewhat more eloquent and diplomatic than Steuart regarding Trudeau, but nonetheless still critical, saying the prime minister "had no particular feel for Western Canada as an agriculture and resource-based area."

Initially, Westerners seemed willing to give Trudeau a chance. In the 1968 federal election in which he swept to power, Trudeau's Liberals won 27 of 68 seats in Western Canada—not spectacular, but certainly respectable for a party that had long run second to the Progressive Conservative Party in that region. It was the Liberals' best showing in the West since the 1949 federal election, when Prime Minister Louis St. Laurent swept the region, winning 41 of 71 seats.

Any fascination or curiosity the West may have had about Trudeau was short-lived. In Trudeau's first re-election test, in October 1972, Westerners resoundingly changed their minds. The Liberals' 27 seats in the West in 1968 shrank to just seven in 1972. This collapse of the Liberal vote in the West was a major reason why the party wasn't able to retain a majority in Parliament, winning only two more seats than the opposition Progressive Conservatives, and being forced to operate as a minority government.

By the time of the 1972 election, a new assertiveness had begun to emerge in Western Canada—particularly Alberta—when it came to perceived Eastern domination. The dawn of this new era, and mindset, was signalled by the election of Peter Lougheed as Alberta premier one year earlier, who was already on his way to becoming a more aggressive and formidable foe than what Ottawa was ever accustomed to.

The tensions of the early 1970s between the West and Trudeau's

Liberals were just the beginning. It would be Trudeau's energy policies—driven by the 1973 OPEC oil embargo that dramatically raised the world price of oil—that provided the flashpoint for full-scale confrontation with Alberta. To protect consumers in Eastern Canada from the full effects of the higher world prices, the Trudeau government created what was essentially a "made in Canada" price for oil, where the price paid to domestic producers in Western Canada (primarily Alberta) was well below the world price.

If the WHA's official formation just three days after Peter Lougheed became premier in 1971 symbolized the beginning of the pushback to Eastern domination in both hockey and politics, the league's eventual ending also had uncanny political parallels. The WHA played its final game on May 20, 1979, when the Winnipeg Jets defeated the Edmonton Oilers for the league championship. While the WHA was disbanding, the Oilers and Jets were not. For fans in Winnipeg and Edmonton, and the Prairies in general, it was a milestone—the NHL had finally arrived!

Just two days after that final WHA game, on May 22, 1979, many Western Canadians celebrated another type of victory, this one in politics. Alberta's Joe Clark was elected prime minister, defeating Pierre Trudeau and his Liberals in the general election. Clark became not only the first Alberta-born prime minister, but the first ever to have been born in Western Canada. East of the Manitoba border, the Liberals did fine in the election, taking a majority of the seats—111 of the 205 seats. In the West, though, the party was decimated, winning only three of the 77 seats across the four Western provinces.

Clark's victory had raised hope that the West would now begin to have a stronger voice in national politics. That hope was quickly dashed. Clark's minority government was brought down when it lost a non-confidence motion in Parliament just six months after he had taken power, with his Progressive Conservatives then getting trounced in the subsequent February 1980 general election. During the campaign leading up to that election, Liberal senator and key campaign organizer Keith Davey[95] quipped, "Screw the West, we'll take the rest." Davey's words were prophetic. The Liberals did indeed "take the rest," winning 71% of the seats east of the Manitoba-Ontario border, ensuring a strong majority in Parliament regardless of what happened in the West. Not unexpectedly, the West was a disaster for the Liberals—not, in Davey's view, that it mattered for them—winning only two of 14 seats in Manitoba and failing to capture any of the 63 combined seats in the three westernmost provinces.

Emboldened by their large majority and overwhelming support in Eastern Canada, the Trudeau Liberals quickly went back to energy policy as one of their key initiatives. On October 28, 1980, finance minister Allan MacEachen presented the Liberals' first federal budget since their election victory earlier that year. In the budget announcement, MacEachen introduced the idea of the National Energy Program (NEP), a program that would even further fan Western animosity toward Pierre Trudeau and the Liberals and would take the Alberta-Ottawa dispute to new heights. Bumper stickers that read LET THE EASTERN BASTARDS FREEZE IN THE DARK—later the title of a book on Western alienation by journalist Mary Janigan—became a common sight in Alberta during the early 1980s.

The NEP was a program that essentially continued and extended the already established Liberal policy of domestic price controls for oil. It also introduced the controversial Petroleum Gas Revenue Tax (PGRT), whose stated purpose was explicit: to lower the cost of oil to Eastern Canadians by redistributing revenues from the oil industry. It had massive inter-regional redistribution effects, taking tens of billions from the Alberta economy to essentially cross-subsidize oil consumption in Eastern Canada.

In the midst of the political furor and outrage in Alberta over the introduction of the NEP, there was another major story developing in the province, this time in the sports pages. Just six days before Allan MacEachen's infamous budget speech that introduced the NEP, the Calgary Flames and Edmonton Oilers met for the first time ever in an NHL game.[96] While no one knew at the time that this was the first salvo in what would become the decade-long "Battle of Alberta," it was still big news. For many Albertans, it was a signal that hockey in the province was finally coming into its own, being a force on the national level, and no longer being subjected to Eastern interests— the same set of factors that were simultaneously driving Alberta's battles with Ottawa over control of the province's energy resources.

Less than three years later, hockey and Western politics crossed paths again, this time in Saskatchewan, and in an even more direct way. Grant Devine and his Progressive Conservative Party took the province by storm in the spring of 1982, winning a landslide election, and ending the 11-year reign of NDP premier Allan Blakeney. Despite Devine's academic background—he had a Ph.D. in agricultural economics from Ohio State University, and had spent time teaching at the University of Saskatchewan—Devine was a populist. He was a free-market disciple who campaigned on reversing the interventionist policies of the NDP and the staid policy-wonk image that Allan Blakeney presented. Devine also sold himself as a new and more vocal force to protect Saskatchewan's interests in Ottawa, and appealed to many of those who felt the Trudeau government's agriculture and resource policies needed a stronger pushback at the provincial level.

Devine's effusive personality and populist style gave him the public persona of a cheerleader and brash promoter. His government's favourite slogan was that Saskatchewan was now "open for business." It was perfect, then, when Bill Hunter, himself a renowned promoter and one who shared many personality characteristics with

Devine, made a deal to purchase the St. Louis Blues and move them
to Saskatoon into a yet-to-be-built arena. Hunter, the Saskatchewan
native and anti-establishment renegade, had a long track record of
disrupting the status quo—in addition to his integral role in the
founding of the WHA 10 years earlier, his creation of the Western
Canada Hockey League in 1966 had permanently upended Canada's
junior hockey system.

It was a dream come true for Devine. Less than a year after his
upset election win, he was presented with an opportunity to achieve
the unthinkable: to bring the NHL to hockey-mad Saskatchewan. He
and Bill Hunter were simpatico, and pictures of them together were
splashed across provincial newspapers. Devine was more than just
a cheerleader, though; his government became directly involved
by providing loan guarantees for the financial package Hunter had
put together to bring the Blues north. For Devine and Hunter, the
Blues would put Saskatchewan on the map, both politically and in
the hockey world; it would be a sign that Saskatchewan had achieved
"big league" status, and would forever lift the province out of its
hinterland roots.

On May 18, 1983, the dream came crashing down, as the NHL board
of governors resoundingly rejected the sale. For them, Saskatchewan
—despite its deep passion for hockey—was too small and too sparsely
populated. For a league trying to establish itself in the US as a legitimate competitor to the much more popular NFL, NBA and MLB, having
a team located in Saskatchewan was not the image the NHL wanted to
create. Toronto Maple Leafs owner Harold Ballard no doubt contributed to these perception issues, jokingly suggesting that teams going
to Saskatoon would need dogsleds to get around. For the people of
Saskatchewan, the NHL's rejection of the Blues sale simply reinforced
an already held notion that the province would always be subjected
to the forces of the outside establishment, be it in politics or in sports.[97]

The years of battles with the Trudeau government during the 1970s and early 1980s ultimately took their toll in the West. A new phenomenon began to emerge in Canadian politics: Western alienation. Canadian unity now faced two challenges—the long-standing and ongoing constitutional issues involving Quebec, and now the emerging disenchantment of Western Canada.

The 1980 election—with Pierre Trudeau winning a strong national majority despite a complete rejection by the West—revealed to many Westerners their continued political subjugation to the wishes of Central Canada. It also spurred a new political movement in the West—more populist, more radical and more right-wing than in the past—that questioned whether Western Canada still had a place in Confederation.

Several new parties emerged. The Western Canada Concept (wcc) Party was formed in 1980 on the platform of Western separation— that the four Western provinces, along with the Northwest Territories and the Yukon, would leave Canada and form their own independent nation. The party received national attention when one of its candidates—Gordon Kessler—won a provincial by-election in Alberta in 1982, the first-ever Western separatist to be elected to a provincial legislature in Canadian history. In the 1982 Saskatchewan provincial election, the wcc received over 3% of the vote, only one percentage point less than the Liberal Party—a Liberal Party led by future federal finance minister Ralph Goodale.

Also in 1980, former Saskatchewan Progressive Conservative leader Dick Collver formed the Unionest Party, whose primary policy platform was to see the four Western provinces join the United States. The party never fielded candidates in any election, and it soon faded. The Confederation of Regions Party of Canada also entered the Western-alienation fray, forming in 1984 on a platform of greater regional autonomy. In the 1984 federal election, the less-than-six-month-old party surprised many, capturing 2.2% of the popular vote in Alberta—by contrast, the incumbent Liberal Party, now led by Prime Minister John Turner, only captured 12.7% of the Alberta vote. In Manitoba, the Confederation of Regions performance was even more surprising, receiving 6.7% of the vote.

None of these parties lasted long, but collectively they laid the groundwork for the formation of the federal Reform Party, in 1987, a party whose initial slogan was "The West wants in," and whose first leader was Preston Manning, son of long-time Alberta Socred premier Ernest Manning. While, by this point, the Liberals were out of power federally, having lost to Brian Mulroney's Progressive Conservatives in the 1984 election, many in the West felt the Mulroney government had been captured by Eastern interests; in the end, not much was different than the decade and a half of Trudeau rule. The Reform Party became the official opposition in 1997 and eventually morphed into the Conservative Party that governed Canada from 2006 to 2015 under Prime Minister Stephen Harper.

FULL CIRCLE?

The headlines in the *Washington Post* that morning read, "Trudeau's Election Victory Lays Bare Deep Divides in the Canadian Map." The article went on to discuss how Prime Minister Trudeau's Liberals won re-election, largely on the basis of winning two-thirds of the seats in voter-rich Ontario, but that the "oil-producing western provinces of Alberta and Saskatchewan...shut out the Liberals." Surely, a headline from the 1970s or '80s? No, the date was October 22, 2019. This time, "Prime Minister Trudeau" was not Pierre, but his son Justin; to many Westerners, however, this is where the difference stopped. In fact, the *Post* article noted that in "Alberta and

Saskatchewan...the Liberal government's energy policies are inflaming a level of grievance and regional alienation not seen in decades." As baseball's master of malapropisms, Yogi Berra, once said, it was "déjà vu all over again."

Alberta's renewed hostility toward Ottawa was not necessarily something that could have been expected. In the several decades that had passed since the end of the Pierre Trudeau era, Alberta got much of what it wanted.

Pierre Trudeau resigned as prime minister on June 30, 1984. Two months later, his successor, John Turner, led the Liberal Party to a massive and unprecedented defeat in the federal election—at the time, the worst defeat ever for a sitting government. The victorious Progressive Conservatives, under Mulroney, had vigorously campaigned against the NEP. Less than a year after taking power, the PC government introduced the Western Accord on Energy—an agreement between the federal government and the governments of BC, Alberta and Saskatchewan that removed federal regulation of oil prices and allowed for market forces to determine prices.

For much of the next three decades, Alberta's economy boomed, consistently leading all Canadian provinces in GDP per capita, usually by a wide margin. Alberta benefited from Western-friendly governments in Ottawa—Brian Mulroney's Progressive Conservatives ruled from 1984 to 1993, and then Stephen Harper's Conservatives from 2006 to 2015—but even the Liberal governments of Jean Chrétien and Paul Martin largely had a "live and let live" approach to Alberta and its energy. In the four elections won by either Chrétien or Martin, the Liberals won at least two seats in Alberta—granted, a very modest success, but still much superior to eras past.

In recent years, though, a confluence of events transpired to bring to an end, at least temporarily, to the economic heyday of the past three decades. In 2014, world oil prices plummeted, sending

Alberta into a sudden steep and prolonged economic decline. Then, in 2015, Justin Trudeau's Liberals came to power federally, promising a left-of-centre policy agenda not seen since the days of his father's governments. Trudeau's activist approach on environmental and Indigenous issues provided the ideological foundation for the Liberal government's Bill C-69,[98] a bill that met strong opposition in the energy sectors in Alberta and Saskatchewan. The bill increased the level of federal regulation of major infrastructure projects, like interprovincial pipelines and large-scale mining operations, focusing particularly on the environmental, health and social impacts of such projects. Critics of Bill C-69 in the energy sector contended that such increased regulations were onerous, and made it extremely difficult for any future project to be approved.

To make matters worse for Alberta, COVID-19 had a greater impact on its economy than in any other province in the country, adding another devastating blow to an already beleaguered and fragile economy. Then, as if that wasn't enough, the controversial Keystone XL Pipeline, carrying oil from the tar sands of northern Alberta to the US, was abandoned in January 2021 after newly elected US president Joe Biden revoked a critical cross-border permit for the project.

The pipeline project was almost universally opposed by Indigenous and environmental groups, portending more troubles ahead for the province. As Alberta's energy sector operates in what is an increasingly activist world around it, the province's inability or unwillingness to diversify its economy away from that sector leaves it vulnerable to continued future economic decline. One small piece of evidence of this decline is that Calgary, always a city that has appealed to young adults for its opportunities and excitement, is now, for the first time in modern memory, seeing a net outmigration of those in the all-important 20–24 age group—between 2009 and 2019, its population in that age group dropped by 5.5%, at a time when the overall population of the city grew substantially. Its high unemployment rate, heavy concentration of jobs in the energy sector, and overall conservative mindset have all been given as reasons as to why young adults have been turning away from the city in unprecedented numbers.

In the meantime, the political rhetoric of old returned. It was full circle, back to the 1970s and '80s—an outraged Alberta premier attacking the federal Liberals, led by a prime minister named Trudeau, over energy policy. In the aftermath of the October 2019 federal election that saw the Liberals win zero of the 48 combined seats in Alberta and Saskatchewan, Alberta premier (and native of Saskatchewan) Jason Kenney had a blunt assessment in a *New York Times* interview: "For most Albertans, much of this revolves around a basic hostility on the part of the Trudeau government to our energy sector." He went on to say, "You've got at least two provinces [Alberta and Saskatchewan] who have made a hugely oversized contribution to the federation, to prosperity, to fiscal balances, that are feeling increasingly like they're not at home in their own country." Such "not at home in their own country" sentiments have even fuelled renewed talk of Western separation—something thought long-dead. This modern-day "Wexit" movement is still in its relative infancy, but was given a significant boost with the 2019 federal election results.

Whether this confluence of negative (for Alberta) factors that has emerged within the past decade is just a temporary setback for the province, or will have more lasting effects, remains unclear. What *is* clear, though, is that despite the province's future being more clouded now than it's been for decades, the brash and assertive Alberta that emerged from the political turbulence of the 1970s and '80s laid the foundation for what was a spectacular 30-year run of economic prosperity for the province.

It was this same brashness and assertiveness that characterized professional hockey in Alberta during that era. Unlike for the
province as a whole, however, the 1980s for the Flames and Oilers
were *not* a portent of even better things to come; while it was just
the beginning for the province, for the Flames and Oilers it was the
pinnacle to which they would never return. Both franchises would
soon plummet—deeply and rapidly—relegating them to what is
now over three decades on the periphery of the NHL world.

For many of today's fans in Calgary and Edmonton, the 1980s
heyday of the Battle of Alberta occurred before they were even born.
For the others, it is but a distant memory. With either the Flames or
the Oilers appearing in eight consecutive Stanley Cup finals from 1983
to 1990, no one ever expected that such dominance of the NHL could
continue indefinitely. However, neither could anyone have expected
them to fall so far, for so long. In the 30-plus seasons since that era
ended, each team has been to the Stanley Cup finals only once, with
both losing (Calgary in 2004, and Edmonton in 2006). This lack of
appearances and victories in the Cup final only tells part of the story—
in most seasons, neither club was ever a serious contender, either not
making the playoffs, or else being eliminated in the first round.

To that point, the Flames followed their 1988–89 Stanley Cup
victory with 14 consecutive seasons without winning a single playoff series—missing the playoffs in eight of those seasons and being
eliminated in the first round in the other six. For the Oilers, the
serious cracks in their franchise started showing as early as 1992–
93, only three seasons removed from their last Stanley Cup victory.
That year, only four teams in the entire NHL had a worse regular-
season record than the Oilers, and three of those clubs were expansion franchises that had just entered the NHL within the previous
year (San Jose in 1991–92, and Ottawa and Tampa Bay in 1992–93).
The Oilers had abruptly fallen from the heights of five-time Stanley

Cup champions to the depths of a new expansion club, all within a three-year span. The Oilers would go on to miss the playoffs in four consecutive years during the mid-1990s.

As with the other Canadian clubs, the 1990s and early 2000s saw the Flames and Oilers face an increasingly difficult economic environment within the NHL. The digitally driven explosion in TV rights for large-market US-based clubs, combined with the often depressed Canadian dollar, significantly decreased the ability of the Flames and Oilers to compete with clubs like the Red Wings and Rangers in the players' market. When the Rangers won the Stanley Cup in 1994 —their first in 54 years—their roster contained seven players who, four years earlier, were on Edmonton's 1990 Stanley Cup–winning team: Mark Messier, Glenn Anderson, Esa Tikkanen, Adam Graves, Craig MacTavish, Kevin Lowe and Jeff Beukeboom. The Rangers payroll that year was an incredible two and half times higher than the Oilers, approximately $20 million to $8 million. What Edmonton couldn't afford, the Rangers could.

The Oilers payroll during that 1993–94 season came in at only about 60% of the league average, whereas in their last Cup year of 1989–90 it was 121%. By 1995–96 the Oilers bottomed out at only about 58% of the league average, and consistently hovered in the 70% to 75% range for most the 1990s and early 2000s. At these low numbers, putting a contending team on the ice was next to impossible.

The Flames weren't that much different. While their payroll didn't fall as fast through the 1990s as it did for the Oilers, it was nevertheless falling, and by 1999–2000, the Flames payroll was only 71% of the NHL average. Even in the 2003–04 season, their only Stanley Cup appearance since 1988–89, the Flames payroll was less than half of clubs like the Red Wings and Rangers, and only about 80% of the overall league average. They finished with only the 12th-best record in the NHL's regular-season standings that year, but then went on a playoff run that took them all the way to the final.

The Flames' Game 7 loss in the final that year signalled the end of an era: it was the last game ever played in the NHL without a league salary cap. While the Flames improbably overcame large payroll disadvantages that year on their run to the final, there had been a growing sense for over a decade that clubs like the Flames and Oilers needed a financial lifeline if they were to be anything other than perpetual also-rans in the league—or, worse yet, if they were to ensure their mere survivability in these cities. Edmonton had already almost lost the Oilers, in 1998, when owner Peter Pocklington agreed to sell the financially floundering team to Leslie Alexander, owner of the NBA's Houston Rockets, who planned on relocating the club to that city; the deal was staved off when a group of local Edmonton investors moved in at the 11th hour to buy the club.

The Flames and Oilers got that financial lifeline in the summer of 2005, when the NHL and the NHLPA—after an acrimonious year-long dispute that resulted in the cancellation of the entire 2004–05 season—agreed to a new CBA whose primary provision was the introduction of a hard salary cap. As if on cue, the Oilers appeared in the Stanley Cup final in the first-ever capped season of 2005–06. It was their first appearance in the final since they won the Stanley Cup 16 years earlier.

The positive effects of the cap on the Oilers were readily apparent. The cap had levelled the playing field, taking away the payroll advantage that some of the large-revenue US-based clubs had enjoyed for more than a decade. The Oilers' payroll went from being 25% below the league average in 2003–04 (the last uncapped season) to 12% *above* the average in 2005–06 (the first capped season).[99]

Despite the Oilers' early success in that first season of the salary-cap era, the decade and a half since then has seen neither them nor the Flames take advantage of the greater payroll parity in the league. Following that Cup-run season, the Oilers went on to miss the playoffs for the next 10 seasons, and 13 of the next 14. Calgary hasn't been much better—in the 18 seasons of the cap era (through the 2022–23 season), they have missed the playoffs in half (nine) of them, lost in the first-round in seven other seasons, and lost in the second round twice.

Part of the problem is that both clubs were playing in aging facilities, substantially decreasing their revenue-generating potential. The Northlands Coliseum, where the Oilers played, opened in 1974, just in time for the club's third WHA season. The Saddledome in Calgary was somewhat newer—opening in 1983, three years after the Flames' arrival—but by the late 2000s had become dated by the standards of newer NHL arenas.

The Oilers did eventually get their new arena, in 2016, ensuring their long-term existence in Edmonton, something that wasn't necessarily guaranteed up to that point. The Flames were less successful in their pursuit of a new building. Years of back-and-forth negotiations with the city met with no success and got to the point in 2017 where Flames president and CEO Ken King threatened to relocate the club (with Houston, again, as a possible destination) if no agreement could be reached with the city. Finally, in 2019, the two sides did reach an agreement, with the Flames' new building scheduled for opening in 2024. However, that deal fell apart in late 2021—before construction had begun—with the two sides disagreeing on how the significant cost overruns would be covered. The Flames, for now, remain in the Saddledome, with no new arena proposals currently on the table.

Ineffective management on the hockey operations side has also contributed to both clubs' on-ice struggles. With the NHL's reverse-order draft system, a poorer on-ice record in one season leads to a higher draft position, which in turn should lead to better team performance in the future. The Oilers' 10-year run of missing the playoffs gave them high first-round picks in several successive seasons. The Oilers were only the second team[100] in NHL history to have the first-overall pick in three successive seasons—Taylor Hall in 2010, Ryan Nugent-Hopkins in 2011 and Nail Yakupov in 2012.

Hall had a solid career in Edmonton but never developed into a true star and was traded to New Jersey after only six seasons, at just 24 years of age. Ironically for the Oilers, Hall won the Hart Trophy as the NHL's most valuable player in 2017–18 while playing for the Devils.

Nugent-Hopkins has had a long and successful career in Edmonton, but whether he was worthy of the first-overall pick is debatable. There are several players from that year's draft class who have (arguably, in some cases) had more solid careers—including Gabriel Landeskog, Jonathan Huberdeau, Mark Scheifele, Dougie Hamilton, Nikita Kucherov, Johnny Gaudreau and John Gibson.

The drafting of Nail Yakupov in 2012 was the Oilers' low point. In draft parlance, Yakupov was a complete "bust," one of the most underperforming first-overall picks in NHL history. Yakupov scored only 53 goals in parts of four seasons for the Oilers and was then traded to St. Louis for a player that never played a single game for Edmonton (or in the NHL). Yakupov was out of the NHL entirely after just six seasons.

Calgary didn't plummet to the absolute bottom of the NHL standings the way that Edmonton did, so they never had the benefit of drafting from the first-overall position. Nevertheless, many of the Flames' first-round picks in the salary-cap era have proven disastrous, including:

- Matt Pelech, 2005: 13 career NHL games, five with Calgary
- Leland Irving, 2006: 13 career NHL games, all with Calgary
- Greg Nemisz, 2008: 15 career NHL games, all with Calgary

- Tim Erixon, 2009: 93 career NHL games, none with Calgary
- Emile Poirier, 2013: eight career NHL games, all with Calgary
- Morgan Klimchuk, 2013: one career NHL game, with Calgary

Granted, predicting future performance of teenage athletes is far from an exact science, but the Oilers and Flames always seemed to have more than their share of "misses." Building a winning team is about more than just the draft system, though; it is about constructing an entire roster. In the salary-cap era, the Oilers and Flames have generally gotten fewer wins out of their payroll expenditures than have many of their counterparts, leaving open the possibility that deficient player-evaluation systems and/or coaching methods are to blame. While player salaries are capped under the CBA, the salaries of coaches and management are not, meaning that large-revenue clubs are potentially able to hire better talent in these positions than are clubs like the Flames and Oilers.

There may be another factor at work. While the introduction of the salary cap in 2005–06 would seem to have helped small-market clubs like the Flames and Oilers, there was also a potential downside for these clubs. Along with the salary cap, the new CBA that year introduced much more liberalized free-agency rights for players. With the changes, players with six years of NHL service could now voluntarily leave their clubs at the expiration of their contracts, something that was not possible during the peak Battle of Alberta era.

With players today now having more control over where they will play, clubs like the Oilers and Flames (and Jets) that are located on the Canadian Prairies—with their relatively small populations, bitterly cold winters, and general lack of cultural cachet—may find it difficult to attract or retain high-end talent.[101] Of course, players (and their agents) will rarely publicly pronounce that such factors are a reason for them being reluctant to play in these cities, so it becomes difficult to ascertain exactly how widespread and systematic the issue is.

Some high-profile anecdotes come to mind, though. Chris Pronger, one of the most dominant defencemen of his era and a key player on the Oilers' 2006 run to the Stanley Cup final, requested a trade at the end of that season, reportedly because his wife (an American) refused to live in Edmonton. Put in a difficult position, the Oilers accommodated Pronger's request, trading him to Anaheim, where he led the Ducks to the 2006–07 Stanley Cup title. A more recent example is when the Calgary Flames abruptly lost their two star players following the club's (relatively successful) 2021–22 season. Americans Johnny Gaudreau and Matthew Tkachuk, who finished second and eighth, respectively, in NHL scoring that season, both fled to the US. Gaudreau signed a free-agent contract with the Columbus Blue Jackets for less money than he was offered in Calgary, and Tkachuk essentially forced a trade (to the Florida Panthers) when he told the Flames he would not re-sign with the club when he became an unrestricted free agent.

It's almost as if the Flames and Oilers have been in lockstep through their entire NHL existences—with their rapid and explosive rise to the top of the hockey world during the 1980s, and then the equally rapid decline into irrelevance for most of the past three decades. Whereas Alberta was at the centre of the hockey map in the 1980s, it is more of a village outpost today, once again far from the power bases of the large cities in Eastern Canada and the US. While it is true that Alberta has not completely returned to hinterland status in hockey—it still has two franchises in the best league in the world—years of losing by the Flames and Oilers have made the clubs much less points of pride for their cities than in the past.

This raises the question of whether the economic structure of the NHL inherently dooms clubs like the Flames and the Oilers to perpetual second-tier status within the league. If so, would the interests of hockey fans in Calgary and Edmonton be better served

by instead having franchises in some type of made-in-Canada league
—similar to, say, the CFL, or to the domestic soccer leagues found
in every European country—rather than being bit players in a
US–dominated league?

For many fans, the answer would be easy: a perpetually weak
team in the NHL is preferable to a more competitive team in a Canadian domestic league. Part of this is driven by the propensity of many
Canadians—sports fans, in particular—to need American recognition and approval, something not likely to occur with an all-Canadian
league (witness the CFL). Part of this is also that the NHL delivers the
top talent in the world, albeit much of it playing on teams other
than the Flames and Oilers (notwithstanding Connor McDavid and
Leon Draisaitl of Edmonton). At some level, Flames and Oilers fans
over the past 30 years may have come to accept, consciously or not,
that simply being in the NHL is sufficient, and that the occasional
breakout season or unexpected long playoff run is just a bonus.
It would be akin, for example, to soccer fans in Augsburg, Germany,
just being satisfied their team is *in* the Bundesliga, playing with the
big boys like Bayern Munich, even though the fans have no reasonable expectation that their club will ever win the championship.

However, for residents of Calgary and Edmonton, continuing to
keep the NHL in their respective cities has not been without cost.
Under the now-defunct 2019 agreement, the new arena in Calgary
would have cost that city's taxpayers over $290 million in construc-
tion subsidies; in Edmonton, the taxpayer bill was over $300 million.
These are funds that could be used for a variety of other competing
purposes—social programs, public safety, arts and culture, transportation, et cetera—rather than used to subsidize the private, and very
wealthy, owners of the two NHL clubs.

None of this is unique to Alberta. For decades, the closed-league
monopolies in North America have extracted large amounts of

public money from local governments to finance stadiums and arenas. In a closed league, the number and location of franchises are tightly controlled by existing owners, ensuring the demand for franchises always outstrips supply. This allows teams and leagues to hold local governments hostage, essentially forcing these governments to either come up with the subsidies for the new facility or risk having the team relocate to another city. The argument that teams will generate economic benefits for a city well in excess of the subsidy costs has long been debunked by academic economists.[102] It is probably one of the most studied topics in the field of sports economics, and decades of research have consistently shown that the presence of a major sports team has no discernible impact on the host city's local economy.

Nevertheless, the Oilers, at least, did get their new arena, Rogers Place, guaranteeing their continued existence in Edmonton for many years to come. The arena, combined with the NHL's hard salary cap, means the Oilers will survive, if not thrive. Perhaps McDavid and Draisaitl—two of the best players in the world—can bring on-ice glory back to Edmonton. So far (through the 2022–23 season), this has not happened: McDavid and Draisaitl—despite their individual brilliance on the ice—have yet to be able to lift their club out of its now three-decade-long abyss. Or maybe the Flames will still get their new arena and will somehow find the right combination of management, coaches and players to build a club that has sustained success.

What *is* certain, though, is that whatever future successes the Flames and/or Oilers may have, it will never be the same. It can never recapture the magic of the 1980s, when an unlikely combination of economic, political and hockey forces converged in an improbable way to make the Battle of Alberta more than just a hockey story, but a story of the new West challenging the dominance of the Eastern establishment.

CHAPTER 4:
SWEDES, FINNS AND THE SASKATCHEWAN FARM BOY

THE TWO PLAYERS could not have been any more different—in their backgrounds, in their hockey skills, in their on-ice demeanour—and yet both symbolized how the game of hockey during the 1970s was radically transforming. One of the players grew up in rural Saskatchewan, long a rich source of NHL talent; the other migrated from Sweden, one of the first from his country—and from Europe generally—to come to North America to play professional hockey.

The Saskatchewan player was Dave Schultz. Schultz became the symbolic face of a wave of fighting, violence and brawling that would define professional hockey during the 1970s. Nicknamed "the Hammer" for his aggressive playing style, Schultz won two Stanley Cups with the Philadelphia Flyers during the mid-'70s. He was a fighter the likes of which the NHL had not seen before, and was a critical element of the Flyers' on-ice strategy of physical intimidation and violence that earned them the moniker "the Broad Street Bullies." Schultz's 472 penalty minutes in the Flyers' Stanley Cup–winning season of 1974–75—the equivalent of almost eight entire games in the penalty box—is a single-season NHL record that stands to this day, and will almost assuredly never be broken.

The Swede was Anders Hedberg. Hedberg joined the WHA's Winnipeg Jets in 1974, and was everything Schultz was not: a lightning-fast and effortless skater, a deadly accurate shooter and a player with no penchant for physical altercations and violence. In his four years with the WHA's Jets, Hedberg averaged 59 goals a season. He and fellow Swede and Jets teammate Ulf Nilsson were the first Europeans to star in North American professional hockey. However, Hedberg and Nilsson were more than simply good players; they were pioneers of an on-ice style of play—fast-skating, skill-based, dynamic—that came to be associated with the waves of European players that would soon follow them to North America. Hedberg and Nilsson represented the antithesis of Dave Schultz and the Broad Street Bullies.

Professional hockey in the 1970s was the ultimate contradiction. On one hand, fighting and violence, long a part of the game's history, reached an entirely new level; in many ways, fighting and violence became the public face of the game. Simultaneously, however, the decade also saw the early stages of the European hockey migration to North America, with these European players bringing an on-ice style and flair that seemed completely at odds with the North American game at the time.

The fact that players as divergent as Schultz and Hedberg could both make their mark in 1970s hockey is an indication of how the game was struggling to find its identity during that period. Two driving forces—seemingly incompatible and contradictory—were transforming the way in which the game was played. Ironically, and somewhat counterintuitively, it was the exact same underlying force that was ultimately driving both.

THE BROAD STREET BULLIES AND THE BRAWLING '70S

Violence in hockey certainly was not new, but the 1970s saw a radical transformation in the types and prevalence of that violence.

Prior to the '70s, players were expected to be able to "look after themselves"—to fight if necessary and certainly to not back down or allow themselves to be intimidated. Even star players such as Rocket Richard of Montreal and Gordie Howe of Detroit were physically intimidating presences on the ice and didn't need teammates to protect them. In hockey terms, Richard and Howe were as mean and nasty as the rest of the players. The game back then was rough and often brutal, certainly much more so than today. There were several instances of extreme violence, some near-fatal. In one of the most infamous incidents, Eddie Shore of the Boston Bruins—one of the most belligerent and combative players in the history of the NHL, but also a very skilled hockey player—violently attacked the Maple Leafs' Ace Bailey in a game in 1933, with Bailey almost dying from the incident.

By the start of the '70s, however, the violence was beginning to take other forms. In particular, bench-clearing brawls began to proliferate. It was not unusual in these situations for six or eight or even more fights to be occurring simultaneously on the ice. It was also quite common for fans to become involved—in those days, there was usually no protective glass (or just very low glass) between the visiting team's bench and the spectators' seats behind them, sometimes resulting in players going into the stands to confront abusive fans. The brawl would become a spectacle unto itself, almost theatre-like, with the actual hockey seemingly lost in the mayhem; game delays of 30 to 40 minutes were not unusual, as the referees had to first stop all the fighting and restore order, and then go through the long process of sorting out all the penalties and ejections.

The rise of the bench-clearing brawl coincided with teams start-ing to employ what were effectively designated fighters, or enforcers. These players tended to have limited hockey skills, but excelled at intimidation and fisticuffs. Dave Schultz of the Philadelphia Flyers was one such player. It quickly became the norm in the '70s for every team to have one or more fighters on their roster.

Beyond just brawling, other incidents of on-ice violence became commonplace. Some of these even ended up in the judicial system. Roy McMurtry, Ontario's attorney general at the time, took an aggressive approach to violence in hockey, not accepting the long-held notion (promoted, not surprisingly, by the NHL) that such vio-lence should be dealt with as an internal league matter rather than in a court of law. Three separate incidents took place at Maple Leaf Gardens over a two-year period that resulted in assault charges. In 1975, McMurtry charged Detroit's Dan Maloney with assault on a Leafs player; in 1976, he charged four Philadelphia Flyers—Bob Kelly, Don Saleski, Mel Bridgman and Joe Watson—for their actions during a playoff game against the Leafs; and in 1977, he charged hometown player Dave "Tiger" Williams for a stick incident against Pittsburgh's Dennis Owchar.

The WHA wasn't immune from the brawling and violence. With overall talent levels that were lower than the NHL, it probably saw even more of it than the established league. Like the NHL, the WHA experienced judicial intervention in extreme cases of on-ice violence. In Quebec City in 1976, prosecutors charged Calgary Cow-boys player Rick Jodzio with assault for a brutal attack on Quebec Nordiques star (and non-fighter) Marc Tardif. Tardif was the WHA's leading scorer that year, while Jodzio was a journeyman fighter, scoring only 15 goals in his 137-game WHA career, but racking up a staggering 357 penalty minutes. In the incident, Jodzio continued to punch a defenceless Tardif as he lay dazed on the ice. It was an episode that was viewed as particularly reprehensible, even by the standards of the day.[103] Not only was it a particularly savage act, but the difference in talent levels between the two players illustrated how top-tier players were increasingly at risk from players that had negligible hockey skills.

The dramatic growth in violence and brawling that occurred in the 1970s can be attributed to the NHL's decision to rapidly expand—which in turn was triggered by the (ultimately unsuccessful) effort to pre-empt a rival league. It wasn't that the NHL necessarily wanted to expand, at least not to the extent it did; it was that it felt it *had* to expand.

The NHL tripled in size within a span of only eight years—going from six teams in 1966–67 to 18 teams in 1974–75. At an average of 20 players per team, that meant that 240 more players were employed in the NHL in 1974, compared with 1967. Without expansion, these players either would never have played pro hockey or, at best, would have spent their careers in the minor leagues. The result was not only a sudden and dramatic drop in the average talent level in the NHL, but also a corresponding change in the style of play. As a group, the new players generally lacked elite-level talent in one or more of the core hockey skills—skating, stickhandling, shooting; otherwise, they would have likely already been in the six-team NHL. Instead, the new players were forced to rely on a more defensive and physically aggressive style of play to survive in the league.

Exacerbating the effects of this overall decline in average skill in the NHL was the fact that expansion also caused a large decrease in competitive balance in the league. Unlike today, in that era, expansion teams entered the NHL on harsh terms; they had to populate their rosters with players that were essentially rejects of the Original Six clubs. So, most of the approximately 120 new NHL players (six teams of 20 players each) that entered the league with the 1967 expansion played for one of the six expansion teams. In the short run at least, the only way for these expansion franchises to even begin to offset the talent superiority of the established clubs was to play a close-checking and physically intimidating style.[104] Expansion teams, lacking the offensive firepower and talent of the established clubs, could never afford to get into a freewheeling, end-to-end, shootout with these teams.

Fred Shero, who took over as coach of the expansion Philadelphia Flyers in their fifth season (in 1971), took this philosophy to a whole new level. He saw fighting as part of a comprehensive strategy that would not just help a low-talent team survive, but actually help a highly talented team be even better. By the mid-1970s, he and Flyers GM Keith Allen had collected an array of some of the most talented, offensively skilled stars in the NHL—Bobby Clarke, Rick MacLeish, Bill Barber and Reggie Leach. Shero juxtaposed this with a group of players who were on the roster almost solely for their capacity to fight and intimidate—Bob Kelly, Don Saleski, Andre "Moose" Dupont and, most notorious of all, Dave "the Hammer" Schultz. With this approach, the Flyers had tremendous success, appearing in three consecutive Stanley Cup finals during the mid-1970s, winning the first two. As is often the case in sports (and business), success leads to imitation, and other clubs soon began to adopt the Flyers' approach.

The increased violence and brawling in hockey throughout the 1970s earned the league publicity and notoriety, even if it wasn't all good. This was particularly true in the US market, where the league had struggled to gain a national foothold, relative to more "American" sports. An argument could certainly be made that the NHL at the time, while not necessarily promoting violence outright, was not doing much to discourage it either. For some fans, the fighting and violence added an excitement to the game not found in sports like basketball, baseball or football.

Hockey fights got attention in American society and media in a way the game itself could not have. Comedian Rodney Dangerfield's famous quip "I went to a fight the other night, and a hockey game broke out" epitomized the notion that hockey and fighting were deeply intertwined.

Hollywood also took notice. The 1977 comedy *Slap Shot*, starring Academy Award winner Paul Newman, focused on the antics of a minor pro team that used fighting and brawling as its primary on-ice strategy and a means of franchise survival. The movie was a box office hit and, over time, has taken on a cult status.

Whether or not fighting actually increased NHL attendance is questionable. Two opposing forces were at work—while it may have drawn some fans to watch hockey who otherwise would not, other fans may have become disenchanted with the violence and mayhem and turned away from the game.

UNTAPPED TALENT

When the WHA began play in 1972 with 12 teams, another 240 players entered major pro hockey, diluting the overall talent pool even further. The WHA's strategy that first year to build its player rosters was similar to rival leagues in other sports that had preceded it—start with a few star players, and then, to keep costs contained, fill the remaining spots with marginal NHL players and career minor-leaguers. In addition to Bobby Hull, the star players included prominent NHLers such as Derek Sanderson, Bernie Parent, Dave Keon and Gerry Cheevers. But despite these high-profile signings, the WHA's overall talent level in its first season was still relatively low. Part of the problem was that the NHL's rapid expansion in the previous five seasons resulted in an extremely shallow talent pool of available players. By the 1974–75 season, 32 major pro teams—18 in the NHL and 14 in the WHA—were searching for talent, 26 more teams than only seven years earlier, in the final season of the NHL's Original Six era.

Enter the Winnipeg Jets. The club had spent big money to sign Hull in 1972, but for his first two seasons with the Jets they had been forced to surround him mostly with journeyman players. The club could simply not afford to sign more NHL stars and filled out their roster with marginal NHLers and career minor-leaguers. The Jets knew they were not maximizing Hull's potential—they desperately needed more high-end talent, but at a price they could afford.

In a move that would forever change the face of hockey in North America, the Jets turned to Europe. For the 1974–75 season, their third in the WHA, the club brought in seven Europeans, five from Sweden and two from Finland. The approach was truly radical, going completely against tradition. Not surprisingly, it was met with dismay and ridicule within North American hockey circles. Until that point, almost 100% of the players that had played pro hockey in North America were Canadian, and attitudes and approaches were hardened.

In the Jets' view, countries like Sweden and Finland were an unexploited source of talent; both were producing many high-quality players who were not bound by the emigration prohibitions of communism that essentially made Soviet and Czechoslovak players off-limits to North American teams. Prior to the arrival of the WHA, the NHL had completely ignored Europe as a source of talent, even though there was growing evidence that there were many Europeans capable of playing in the NHL. Perhaps part of the trepidation was that Europeans played a more finesse-based and flowing style and were often thought of as being too "soft" to play in the more grinding NHL.

The Jets' gambit proved stunningly successful. The addition of the talented Europeans—particularly Anders Hedberg and Ulf Nilsson—immediately elevated the game of Bobby Hull. Hull went from 53 goals and 95 points in the season prior to the Europeans' arrival, to 77 goals and 142 points the next season. Hedberg and Nilsson also had over 100 points each in their first WHA seasons. The Hull-Hedberg-Nilsson trio made a formidable line combination for four WHA seasons, until Hedberg and Nilsson were lured to the NHL's New York Rangers in 1978, one season prior to the NHL–WHA merger.

By their fourth season, 1975–76, the Jets had an unheard-of nine Europeans on the roster, seven Swedes and two Finns. They won the WHA title that year—one of the three league championships for the team in the WHA's seven-year existence. The following season, they added another elite-level Swedish player, Kent Nilsson (no relation to Ulf). Kent Nilsson registered 107 points in each of his two WHA seasons before going on to become an NHL star with the Calgary Flames, finishing third in NHL scoring in 1980–81 (behind only Wayne Gretzky and Marcel Dionne).

In all, there were 13 Swedes who played in the WHA during the league's final five seasons, with 10 of them playing for Jets.[105] In addition, 10 Finns[106] played in the league over that same period, heavily concentrated on two teams, the Jets (three players) and the Phoenix Roadrunners (four players).

Even witnessing the Jets' success with Europeans, NHL teams were initially still slow to follow suit. While the Toronto Maple Leafs did bring in Swedes Börje Salming and Inge Hammarström in 1973, one year before the Jets brought in their seven-player contingent, four years later there were still only a small handful of Swedes and Finns in the NHL. Eventually, NHL teams did take notice, and by the early 1980s Swedish and Finnish players were becoming fully immersed in the NHL.

While the Jets' approach to finding talent was innovative within a hockey context, it mirrored tactics that rival leagues in other sports had used previously. By their nature, rival leagues increase

the demand for talent, and one way for these leagues to better compete with the (wealthier) established league is to find talent sources
that have been previously untapped or overlooked. By exploiting
these sources, rival leagues can increase their talent levels more
cost-effectively than by relying solely on bidding away existing players in the established league. For example, when the All-American
Football Conference (AAFC) started play in 1946 to challenge the
NFL, an unofficial colour barrier existed in the NFL, as no Blacks had
played in the league since 1933. This provided the new league with
a readily available pool of high-quality talent, and quickly raised
the league's quality of play to a level not otherwise possible. This
same strategy was used by the upstart American Football League
(AFL) in the early 1960s. While by this point the NFL was employing
Black players, their numbers were still relatively low, and the AFL,
like the AAFC before, exploited this to its own advantage.

Rival leagues needed to be innovative to gain a foothold; they
needed some way to counter the natural advantage the established
leagues possessed. For the WHA, tapping into the European talent
market was undoubtedly their greatest innovation.

CHANGING PLAYER DISTRIBUTIONS

Pro hockey was clearly at a crossroads and was witnessing the beginning of a monumental struggle for how the game would be played
moving forward. The struggle would continue for the next several
decades, but it became clear early on as to who would ultimately win.
The WHA's entrepreneurial search for untapped talent that started the
flow of Swedes and Finns to North America showed that Europeans
could indeed play the game very well. North American teams that
initially were reluctant to pursue these players did so at their own
risk and put themselves at a competitive disadvantage.

Even bigger changes were to come. The collapse of the Soviet Union in the early 1990s allowed players from countries such as Russia and Czechoslovakia (now the Czech Republic and Slovakia) to freely leave their countries to play hockey professionally in North America. Canadians had got their first lesson in 1972 about the quality of Soviet hockey. The so-called Summit Series pitted a "dream team" of NHL stars against the Soviet national team. Up to that point, the Soviets had been dominating international competitions like the Olympics and the World Championships. They had won nine consecutive World Championships between 1963 and 1971, along with four out of the previous five Olympic gold medals. However, NHLers had never participated in these tournaments (because of the International Ice Hockey Federation's prohibition on professional players), and the view amongst most Canadians heading into the series was that the NHL stars that comprised Team Canada in 1972 would easily beat the Soviet "amateurs." The expectation was quickly shattered in Game 1 of the eight-game series, with the Soviets handily defeating the NHLers 7–3 at the Montreal Forum. As is legendary in Canada, Team Canada ultimately prevailed, winning the eighth and deciding game in Moscow when Paul Henderson scored with only 34 second left, giving the Canadians a 6–5 victory in the game, and a 4–3 victory in the series (with one game tied).

However, despite the obvious talent of Russian (and Czechoslovak) players, communist rule meant that these players could not voluntarily leave their country to play in the NHL. The only way out was to defect. Almost no Russians ever defected,[107] but many Czechoslovaks did, the most famous of which were the Stastny brothers in 1980, who joined the Quebec Nordiques after a clandestine operation whisked them out of Austria, where they had been playing in a tournament. This started a small wave of Czechoslovak defections during the 1980s, when future NHLers such as Petr Klima, Petr Svoboda and Petr Nedved all left their home country.

The strong identification that Canadians had long had with the game of hockey—including the popular narrative that Canadians, as a group, played the game better than anyone else—meant that the transformative changes in the players' market that began in the 1970s was difficult for many Canadians to accept. Not unrelatedly, the European migrants to the NHL, particularly those who came over in the early years, often faced an unwelcoming environment, both on the ice and off. It was well-documented that players such as Börje Salming, who joined the Maple Leafs in 1973, were the target of much physical and verbal abuse from opposing players. Salming was derisively nicknamed "Chicken Swede" for his unwillingness to engage in the more brutal style of play that existed in the NHL at that time. That 1976 incident at Maple Leaf Gardens that led to the four Philadelphia Flyers being charged was started when the Flyers' Mel Bridgman attacked Salming. This attitude was also broadcast to Canadian hockey fans watching games at home, as influential TV commentator Don Cherry notoriously expressed his negative views toward Europeans because of what he perceived as their lack of toughness.

In addition to this European influx of players, the 1980s and '90s saw the US produce more NHL–calibre players. While there had been a trickle of Americans entering the NHL during the 1960s and '70s, the US's stunning upset of the Soviet Union at the 1980 Winter Olympics in Lake Placid increased interest in the game in America, becoming a catalyst for more youth participation in hockey at the grassroots level, and ultimately leading to a greater representation of Americans in the NHL.

By 2000, the game had become fully internationalized, and was almost unrecognizable from 30 years earlier. Canadians, for so long the only source of NHL talent, were now not even a majority in the league, composing only 49% of players. This was down from 72% in 1990, 84% in 1980, and 97% in 1970. Over the past quarter century, this number has dropped even further, to the point where, by 2023, the number of Canadians in the league is at all-time low of 42%.

To put this in perspective, there are now fewer Canadians, in *absolute* terms, in the NHL in 2023 than there were in 1970, despite the fact that Canada's population has grown by almost 85% during that time (from 21 million in 1970 to 40 million in 2023), and despite the fact that there are now 18 more NHL teams, compared with then. Put differently, in 1970 there were about 15 Canadian NHLers for every one million of Canada's population; today, that rate has been cut almost in half, with only eight NHLers per one million Canadians.

CANADIANS IN THEIR OWN GAME

While the European influence on the NHL has been well-documented, there is another, much more subtle and less visible change in the hockey labour market that has occurred over the last half century: the shift in the geographic source of hockey talent *within* Canada.

Consider this: during the 1950–51 NHL season, players born in Saskatchewan accounted for an astonishing 26% of all players in the league! This, despite the fact the province accounted for less than 6% of the country's population in the 1951 census. In fact, Saskatchewan produced the second-most NHLers that season, trailing only Ontario, who produced 50% more players than Saskatchewan, but whose population was 400% larger. So, on a per capita measure, Saskatchewan was far and away the leading source of NHL talent.

Saskatchewan's dominance was likely attributable to several factors, the most fundamental of which is its climate. In an era before the proliferation of artificial ice, and when natural ice was the norm, Saskatchewan's long, cold winters provided an inherent competitive advantage in producing hockey players.

However, the dominance was due to more than just climate. After all, its neighbouring Prairie province to the west, Alberta, with equally long and cold winters, produced far fewer players. Alberta accounted for only 5% of NHL players that 1950–51 season, compared with Saskatchewan's 26%, despite Alberta having a slightly larger population than Saskatchewan. The third Prairie province, Manitoba, with an almost identical population to Saskatchewan's, produced 12% of all NHLers—more than twice as many as larger Alberta, but only half that of Saskatchewan.

What differentiated Saskatchewan from its two other Prairie counterparts was its significantly higher rural population. About 70% of Saskatchewan residents lived in small towns or on farms. Its two largest cities—Regina and Saskatoon—made up much less of the province's population than did, say, Calgary and Edmonton in Alberta, or Winnipeg in Manitoba. Other than hockey, few outside recreational opportunities existed in winter in these rural Saskatchewan communities, and the sport flourished. For boys and young men growing up in these areas during that era, many did not graduate from high school (or even elementary school), so there were few career choices other than farming and labourer positions, meaning the opportunity cost to pursue hockey was relatively low.

A somewhat similar set of dynamics existed in Northern Ontario, a vast region heavily dependent on industries like mining and forestry, and far removed—culturally, socially and economically— from its more educated and wealthy urban counterparts in the southern part of the province. Like rural Saskatchewan, the cities and towns of Northern Ontario became hotbeds for producing NHLers. During the 1950–51 season, for example, the Northern

Ontario cities of Port Arthur and Fort William (which later combined to form present-day Thunder Bay) composed less than 2%
of Ontario's population, but accounted for more than 15% of that
province's players in the NHL. In fact, the two cities (combined population: 66,000) produced only two fewer NHLers that year than the
entirety of metro Toronto (population: 1.1 million).

The NHL in the mid–20th century was a rough, sometimes brutal
league. Its roster spots were filled by players who were physical and
strong—players who could take care of themselves on the ice and
who would not be easily intimidated. Players from Northern Ontario
and rural Saskatchewan were seen as more likely to possess these
attributes, and more likely to "do what it takes" to reach the NHL. It
wasn't that these players necessarily lacked in hockey talent. In fact,
it was often the opposite. The only two players in NHL history—other
than Wayne Gretzky—to win at least four Hart Trophies (given to
the league's most valuable player) were Eddie Shore and Gordie
Howe, both from rural Saskatchewan, and both feared on the ice.
To this day, Shore is considered one of the most violent players in
NHL history. Howe was far and away the NHL's points leader during
the 1950s, and the statistical achievement of having a goal, an assist
and a fight in one game is named for him—the "Gordie Howe hat
trick." A typical Howe season was 1953–54, when he led the NHL in
scoring, all the while finishing fifth overall in penalty minutes in
the league.

Players from Saskatchewan and Northern Ontario continued to
have outsized impact in the NHL throughout the 1950s and '60s. By
1966–67—the final season of the Original Six era—Saskatchewan
was still producing proportionally more players than any other
province in Canada, and still by a wide margin. That season, it
accounted for 2.34 times as many NHL players as one would expect
from its population. While this ratio was down from the highs of

the early '50s, it still exceeded second-place Manitoba (1.47 times as many NHLers as would be expected) and third-place Ontario (1.34 times as many) by large amounts.

The 1966–67 season wasn't just significant because it marked the end of the Original Six era. It was also the year the Toronto Maple Leafs last won the Stanley Cup. Since then, it has been over 56 years of frustration for the franchise and its fans. The team that year had a roster filled with Northern Ontarians: from Cobalt, Kent Douglas; from Cochrane, Tim Horton; from Copper Cliff, Jim Pappin; from Kirkland Lake, Mike Walton and Larry Hillman; from Port Arthur, Bruce Gamble; from Skead, George Armstrong; from Sudbury, Wayne Carleton and Eddie Shack; and from Timmins, Allan Stanley and Frank Mahovlich. In contrast, the Leafs had only *one* player on their roster from Toronto that season, Brian Conacher.

That 1966–67 season was in many ways the pinnacle for the Northern Ontario hockey player in the NHL. Besides those with the champion Leafs, the other prominent Northern Ontarians in the league that year composed a kind of "who's who" list for that era: Phil Esposito and Chico Maki with Chicago; Dick Duff and Ralph Backstrom with Montreal; Eddie Giacomin, Wayne Hillman and Bob Nevin with the New York Rangers; and Alex Delvecchio, Gary Bergman and Dean Prentice with Detroit.

Kirkland Lake was the epitome of the Northern Ontario hockey town during the '50s, '60s, and early '70s. The iconic *Hockey Night in Canada* broadcaster Foster Hewitt once called Kirkland Lake "the town that made the NHL famous." In the 1970–71 season, for example, 15 NHL players came from Kirkland Lake—an astonishing number, given that the town's population at the time was only 13,000 people. In fact, there were more players in the NHL from Kirkland Lake that year than from the entire province of British Columbia (population: 2.2 million). Kirkland Lake also produced quality, not just quantity.

Of those 15 players in the NHL that 1970–71 season, 10 of them would have careers that exceeded 500 NHL games.

And then it just stopped. In the 40-plus years that have passed since the early 1980s, Kirkland Lake has produced only two players who made it to the NHL, and one of those had an NHL career that lasted only four games.

It wasn't just Kirkland Lake that experienced such a dramatic turnaround. Timmins, a small city 140 kilometres to the northwest of Kirkland Lake, suffered a similar fate. Even though Timmins has produced 39 NHLers during it existence, only four of these 39 entered the NHL in the past 40 years. Like Kirkland Lake, Timmins's heyday as a source of NHL talent has long passed.

Similarly, Saskatchewan's hockey halcyon period has ended. Far removed from its glory days in the mid–20th century, when, at its pinnacle, it produced one quarter of all NHLers that 1950–51 season, the province accounted for less than 3% of NHLers in 2022–23. Part of this decline is due to the influx of Europeans and Americans into the league over the past several decades, something that had an impact on all provinces. But this is far from the full answer. Saskatchewan now accounts for only 6% of *Canadian* NHLers, its lowest total ever, and an indication that it has lost significant ground to other provinces.

POPULATION SHIFTS, URBANIZATION AND AFFLUENCE

So, what happened? The answer to this is complex, but ultimately these traditional geographic sources of NHL talent fell victim to the sea changes that were to occur around them—changes from both outside and inside the game.

Like most liberal democracies in the Western world, Canadian society has undergone a massive transformation since the mid–20th century. For hockey, changing demographics and economic factors in Canada have slowly but steadily shifted the source of talent within the country.

At the most macro level, the population distribution across—and within—provinces has changed considerably. In Northern Ontario, for example, the town of Kirkland Lake is a shell of its former self, going from a population of over 20,000 at the end of the Second World War to less than 8,000 today. With the town being highly dependent on gold mining during its heyday, it suffered greatly when the industry went into decline and most of the town's original mines ultimately closed. This was to be the plight of many Northern Ontario towns, as the Canadian economy began a decades-long journey away from a heavy dependence on resource-based, primary industries and toward the modern, technology- and knowledge-driven economy that it is today.

Long-term population shifts also negatively affected Saskatchewan. In the 1941 Canadian census, Saskatchewan was the third-most populous province in the country, trailing only Ontario and Quebec. Saskatchewan's population had boomed in the early part of the 20th century, with the federal government providing free land to immigrants under the Homestead Act. Saskatchewan's climate and rich, fertile farmland were very conducive to growing wheat and other grain crops, and the province established itself as one of the leading producers in the world.

By the 1951 census, Saskatchewan had lost its third-place standing for population in the country and had been surpassed, albeit ever so slightly, by its two neighbours to the west, Alberta and BC. Over the 80-year period from 1941 to 2021, Canada's population grew at an average annual rate of about 1.4%, from 14 million to 37 million. BC led the way with an average annual growth rate of 2.3%, followed by Alberta at 2.1%, and Ontario at 1.7%. Of the 10 provinces,

Saskatchewan was dead last—by far—at a miniscule 0.6% per year. In fact, over the entire 80-year span, Saskatchewan added only 237,000 residents in total; during that same period, BC grew by 4.2 million residents, and Alberta by 3.5 million.

The numbers are clear: Saskatchewan got left behind. But why?

Several factors exist. Technological advances in the farming industry shifted the labour-capital mix, with modern machinery greatly reducing the number of farm workers needed to produce a given amount of product. At the same time, Saskatchewan seemed unable or unwilling to sufficiently diversify outside its agriculture-based origins, and the more emerging, cutting-edge industries often seemed to bypass the province.

As well, Regina and Saskatoon had "prairie town" atmospheres and lacked the cultural cachet that many other Canadian cites had. Combined with their bitterly cold winters, this put them at a distinct disadvantage in attracting in-migration, whether from other parts of Canada, or of new Canadians. Related, there was also constant outmigration; many young adults who had been raised in Saskatchewan moved west to Alberta, where jobs were more plentiful and paid better (particularly in the oil industry), and where life was seen to be more exciting.

Politics may have also been a factor in this shift. In 1944, the voters of Saskatchewan elected the first socialist government in Canadian history, as Tommy Douglas's Co-operative Commonwealth Federation (CCF) won an overwhelming majority in the provincial legislature. The CCF would go on to introduce a universal health insurance program in the province, the first of its kind in Canada, and Douglas would forever afterward be known as the "Father of Medicare."

The CCF—and its descendant, the New Democratic Party (NDP)—would go on to lead Saskatchewan for 20 straight years, until 1964, and then, after a seven-year break during the mid- and late 1960s when Ross Thatcher's Liberal Party governed, another 27 out of the next 36 years after that. The CCF/NDP was more focused on wealth redistribution than wealth creation, and the party was often unabashedly interventionist. In the late 1940s, soon after Douglas was first elected premier, the CCF created government (Crown corporation) monopolies in electricity, automobile insurance and telephones.

The 1970s version of the NDP under Premier Allan Blakeney nationalized the potash industry in Saskatchewan, expropriating the assets of private producers and creating a monopoly Crown corporation in their stead: the Potash Corporation of Saskatchewan. The move made national and international headlines, since Saskatchewan was (and still is) the largest supplier of potash in the world. Blakeney's government also created Crown corporations in mining (Saskatchewan Mining Development Corporation) and fossil fuel energy (Saskatchewan Oil and Gas Corporation), all the while implementing high taxes and royalties on many segments of the natural-resource sector.

The extent to which this interventionist political climate in Saskatchewan affected population growth in the postwar period is difficult to measure in any precise way. What is certain, though, is the province developed a reputation amongst many private corporate leaders, justified or not, as being unfriendly to business, particularly compared with much more free-market Alberta just to its west.

Saskatchewan's precipitous population decline—relative to the rest of Canada—over the past 80 years is no doubt a major factor in its much-reduced ability to produce NHLers. But it may not be the only factor. Changes within the game of hockey itself have also worked against the province.

Saskatchewan's rural and farming heritage has long produced tough, physical players—Shore, Howe, Schultz and Dave Williams.

These types of characteristics were highly sought-after in the '50s, '60s and '70s, given the NHL's rough style of play. However, the European influx into the NHL changed all of that. The Saskatchewan player's traditional competitive advantage was beginning to become less valued in the "new" NHL. Players from Europe were seen to be more skilled and dynamic. They could skate better, they could stickhandle better, and they could score more often.

This doesn't mean that there weren't any prolific offensive talents coming out of Saskatchewan over the years—Howe and Bryan Trottier are the most prominent. Howe is still fourth on the all-time NHL scoring list, despite not having played in the league for over 40 years and having played in an era when there was less scoring than today. Trottier was the scoring leader of the dynastic New York Islanders teams of the late '70s and early '80s, winning the NHL points title in 1978–79 and finishing runner-up to Guy Lafleur a year earlier. When he retired in 1994, he was sixth on the NHL's all-time points list.

But it was really the physical side of the game where Saskatchewan players excelled. Take the 1974–75 season, the height of the fighting and brawling era of the NHL. The Philadelphia Flyers would win their second consecutive Stanley Cup, combining skill and intimidation in a way that had not been done in the past. While the NHL had always been a rough and physical league with plenty of fighting, it had now reached an entirely new level. That season, of the NHL's leading point producers, Saskatchewan had only one player in the top 40—Gregg Sheppard of the Boston Bruins, at a fairly distant 23rd. In contrast, eight of the top 40 penalty-minute leaders were from Saskatchewan.

This was not a one-season anomaly. Taking the decade of the '70s as a whole, no Saskatchewan players were in the top 30 in scoring, but five were in the top 30 in penalty minutes, including the first three spots on the list. The wild-west, brawling nature of hockey during that decade seemed to particularly suit the Saskatchewan player. It certainly gave notorious fighters like Dave "the Hammer" Schultz and Dave "Tiger" Williams a level of fame that went well beyond what their hockey skills would have normally generated, and both became household names in Canada. Between the two of them, they led the league in penalty minutes in six out of seven years.

It wasn't just Schultz and Williams, though. Saskatchewan produced some of the toughest players of the era: Clark Gillies of the Islanders, Dennis Polonich of the Red Wings, Keith Magnuson and Terry Ruskowski of the Black Hawks, and Don Saleski and Ed Van Impe of the Flyers, to name only a few. NHL teams of the '70s wanted players who were, above all, *tough guys*, and there was no better place in the country than Saskatchewan to find them.

Much has changed since that time, both for the game of hockey and for Saskatchewan. Today's NHL is almost unrecognizable from its 1970s predecessor. It's now a game that seeks players with speed, puck skills and "hockey sense," the latter being the ability to innately "read" the fast-paced action in real time and then react accordingly. Whereas the NHL of the '70s had no room for the undersized but highly skilled player, today's NHL features smaller stars like 5'9", 157-pound Johnny Gaudreau, 5'7", 165-pound Alex DeBrincat, and 5'7", 174-pound Cole Caufield.

The European invasion of the NHL that had begun as a trickle in the '70s grew into a torrent in the '80s and '90s, forever changing the league's style of play and ultimately relegating to the league's scrap heap the plodding, one-dimensional player that relied solely on physicality and fighting. This natural evolution of the game toward speed and skill was given a further boost in 2005 when the NHL made several critical rule changes designed to increase offensive output in the league.

The league was coming out of a devastating labour lockout that resulted in the cancellation of the entire 2004–05 season. The NHL wanted to win fans back, and fast. League officials believed this could be achieved by making the game more exciting, by bringing back speed and scoring. In the years leading up to the lockout, games had often gotten bogged down in defensive struggles as many clubs patterned their play after the New Jersey Devils' neutral zone trap—a tight-checking, defensive system that essentially shut down the opponent's offensive attack in the neutral zone. While this method was successful for the Devils (they won the Stanley Cup in 1995 and 2000, and were runners-up in 2001), it tended to produce a slow, boring game to watch for the casual fan.

The league responded by implementing a variety of rule changes. This included decreasing the size of the neutral zone, eliminating the red line for two-line offside calls, and introducing an instigator penalty for fights that occur in the last five minutes of regulation time. Perhaps most importantly, referees were ordered to have zero tolerance for obstruction penalties, such as hooking, holding and interference.

None of these changes were advantageous to the type of hockey player Saskatchewan typically produced. The province's traditional comparative advantage in producing toughness and aggression—at least as stand-alone attributes—was becoming less relevant in the new NHL.

However, even more importantly, factors are at work that make it difficult for Saskatchewan to change course—to explicitly shift its focus toward producing more highly skilled players with attributes closer to what today's NHL is seeking. As the NHL game has become increasingly about speed and skill, the nature of player development at the minor hockey level has changed with it. To have a chance to play in today's NHL, youth players generally now need exposure to advanced, sophisticated training methods, access to modern facilities, high-quality coaching, and the opportunity to face top-level competition on the ice. Geographically, all of these elements are more likely to be found in affluent, high-population urban areas, rather than in, say, smaller, more isolated communities dependent on primary industries like agriculture or mining. The latter often no longer have the necessary resources and infrastructures to consistently produce NHL–calibre players.

Instead, the advantage has decidedly shifted to large metropolitan areas, the most prominent of which is the megalopolis of the Greater Toronto Area (GTA). The GTA has produced some of the best players in the game over the past decade. As a case in point, six of the top 15 (40%) Canadian-born point leaders in the NHL during the 2021–22 season came from the GTA—a group that includes first-overall draft picks John Tavares, Steven Stamkos and Connor McDavid, along with fourth-overall pick Mitch Marner. The GTA had another first-overall pick in 2021, with Owen Power being selected by the Buffalo Sabres.

In contrast, Saskatchewan had only one player that season in the top 90 in NHL scoring (Chandler Stephenson—hardly a household name for most hockey fans—at 58th). Nor does there seem to be much young talent on the horizon. The province has only two players under the age of 27 who played at least 60 NHL games in 2021–22. Ironically, Saskatchewan seems to have even lost its comparative advantage in producing toughness, with only one player in the top 70 in penalty minutes during 2021–22—something that would be unthinkable in the era of Schultz and Williams.

The evolving hockey world has left behind both the Saskatchewan farm boy and the Northern Ontario miner's son—the foundations of the NHL a half century ago. Back then, these types of players put many small towns on the map that would have otherwise been unheard of without hockey. Their prominence in the NHL is now greatly diminished—by Europeans, by Americans and by their Canadian counterparts in places like the GTA.

But this is far more than just a hockey story. These changes are simply manifestations of the massive transformations that have occurred in society over the past half century. At its core, it is really a story about the perceived efficiencies of globalization and urbanization, and, relatedly, about technology's impact on labour productivity. The verdict is in: the metropolis has won, the hinterland has lost.

CHAPTER 5:
EASY MONEY

IN A DECEMBER 2001 story that was widely reported in the Canadian media, the Ottawa Senators' director of player personnel, Jarmo Kekäläinen, was said to have told a Finnish newspaper that the junior hockey system in Canada amounted to an "exploitation of child labour."[108] It was a searing indictment of one the oldest institutions in Canadian sport, and of a system that has historically been the primary feeder of amateur players to the NHL.

While Kekäläinen—who is now GM of the Columbus Blue Jackets—seemed to be simply stating what many outside observers had been arguing for years, his comments were particularly noteworthy because such criticism of junior hockey had rarely come from someone inside the game. Not surprisingly, there was rage and fury in the junior hockey establishment, with Western Hockey League commissioner Ron Robison telling the *National Post* that Kekäläinen was "so out of touch, it's ridiculous," and the controversy was soon buried.

Almost 30 years before Kekäläinen's comments, renowned University of Toronto professor Bruce Kidd and his co-author John Macfarlane essentially made the same argument in their 1972 book

The Death of Hockey, in which they devoted an entire chapter to what they termed "child buying." They noted that, even then, the issue of child buying in hockey was certainly no secret, and that many institutions—including the federal government, the Alberta government, the Synod of the Anglican Church and the United Church *Observer*— had already acknowledged and/or condemned the practice.

For the first half century of the NHL's existence, the Canadian junior hockey system was effectively the *only* feeder system of amateur players to the NHL; almost every single player that entered the NHL through the early 1970s came from that system. In more recent decades, it has lost its exclusive status, with increasing numbers of players entering the NHL from US colleges, from the US junior system, or directly from European leagues, but the Canadian junior system still remains the single largest provider of talent to the NHL —in the 2021 NHL draft, for example, 40% of the players selected were from the Canadian junior system, compared with 25% from US college hockey.

While junior hockey has undergone many structural changes during its long history, it seems to have always had fierce critics. The nature of the criticisms has been remarkably consistent, no matter the era, and revolve around the same basic theme: junior hockey players, many of whom have not yet reached the age of majority, are unilaterally subjected to practices and treatment that create economic gains for others, but simultaneously receive very little of these gains themselves.

Juxtapose these notions of "child labour" and "child buying" with a comment made in the early 2000s by a general manager in the Ontario Hockey League, who told the *National Post Business* magazine that "making money in junior hockey is like falling out of a boat— anybody should be able to do it." There is a critical interconnection here—it's always much easier for a business to make money when it doesn't have to pay a salary to its most important labour inputs. As former Mississauga IceDogs owner Mario Forgione once told TSN, junior clubs make millions on the "backs of kids," then "wash their hands of them."

Despite the consistency of these criticisms through time, junior hockey has shown a remarkable ability to withstand external pressures. Kidd and Macfarlane wrote at a time when junior hockey was undergoing a fundamental and transformative change in the late 1960s and early 1970s, a change driven entirely by the NHL's elimination of the sponsorship system. Hence, many of their specific criticisms pertained to the treatment of players during the sponsorship era—an era when NHL teams had an almost complete control over the amateur hockey system in Canada.

That era ended in the 1960s, but was immediately replaced by a very different, yet equally exploitive system. With sponsorship ending, junior teams and leagues had the freedom to act independently—as such, they quickly transformed themselves into business-oriented, profit-seeking entities. In the process, junior hockey leagues adopted what economists would call cartel-like behaviours, similar to their NHL counterparts. These behaviours include highly restrictive labour practices, including a draft system (of bantam-age, 14- and 15-year-old players, designed to prevent junior teams from competing against each other for these players), and "reserving" players so that they were unable to voluntarily move between clubs in the league. Such a reservation system is similar to long-past eras in most professional sports leagues, when players (even veterans) lacked any free-agency rights, and were hence subjected to "take-it-or-leave-it" type offers from their employers. Thus, the end of the sponsorship system did not end the monopsonistic control of junior hockey players and their families, it simply changed the source of this control.

Junior hockey's history in Canada is as long and complicated
as it is controversial. Understanding this history in some detail is
critical to understanding the controversies of today. Three different
eras of junior hockey can be identified: the pre-1967 sponsorship
years, the transition years from 1967 to 1980, and the post-1980
modern era.

THE SPONSORSHIP YEARS

Until the late 1960s, NHL teams exerted direct control over all of
Canadian amateur hockey—including junior hockey—by sponsoring, originally, individual junior players and then, later, entire
junior clubs. As early as the 1920s, NHL teams began sponsoring individual amateur players in Canada, whereby NHL teams compensated
players in return for a promise from the player that, if he turned pro,
he would sign only with the sponsoring NHL team. NHL teams used
these arrangements to ensure a steady supply of incoming players.
The inducements took many forms: paying retainers to the player,
finding the player a job or paying to keep a player in school. For
example, Conn Smythe, upon buying the Toronto St. Pats (forerunner
to the Maple Leafs) in 1926, brought many young players from across
the country to Toronto, covering their tuition at St. Michael's College,
in exchange for the player playing hockey at St. Mike's or for the
Toronto Marlboros.

During the Depression, several amateur hockey clubs in Canada
began to experience financial hardship. By the end of the Second
World War, many clubs and leagues in the country faced severe
financial difficulties, with some on the verge of collapse without significant funding injections. In light of this, the NHL and Canadian
Amateur Hockey Association (CAHA) entered into an agreement in
1947 that would change the face of junior hockey for the next 20 years.

The CAHA's stated purpose was to develop amateur hockey in Canada. That goal was served through various means: by encouraging the development of local governing bodies across the country, by standardizing a set of playing rules, by developing tests of amateur status and by developing inter-regional competitions. The agreement committed the NHL to providing funding to the CAHA and to junior teams, in exchange for the NHL effectively being given control of the entire amateur hockey system in Canada. Prior to 1947, the CAHA was an independent body, with no affiliation with the NHL—in fact, some of the senior (i.e., adult) leagues within the CAHA system sometimes competed with the NHL for players.

The agreement between the NHL and CAHA allowed each NHL team to sponsor two amateur clubs of midget category or higher. However, the term *club* was very broadly defined, so as to include all categories of teams within a given city—senior, intermediate, Junior A, Junior B, midget and bantam, as well as all "house league" players affiliated with those teams. Thus, when a team sponsored a Junior A club (at that time, there was no major junior category, so Junior A was the highest junior level) in a community, it effectively controlled every registered amateur player in that community. As Kidd and Macfarlane noted in their book, this led, for example, to every boy growing up in, say, Winnipeg to be automatically the property of the Boston Bruins, and to be perpetually bound to that team.

One of the problems, according to Kidd and Macfarlane, was that the practices tended to be accepted by the boys themselves, and by their parents. They relate a story from the sponsorship era where the sports editor of the *Edmonton Journal* asked members of the Edmonton Oil Kings if they had any objections to being bound to the NHL's Detroit Red Wings. Apparently, the players had no objections, and one player reportedly said, "If this is slavery, let's have more of it."

In those Canadian communities where no NHL team was involved in sponsorship, control was exerted in other ways. Promising players in these communities could be placed on an NHL team's "negotiation list," whereby the player would immediately and perpetually become property of the "listing" team. This listing process was unilateral, in that the NHL team did not need the boy's—or his parents'—permission to list the player. In fact, players were often listed by NHL teams without the player's knowledge. Only if and when the player was eventually promoted to a more advanced level would the player become aware of which team owned his rights. Even for the few players of that era who opted to go to university, the clutches of the listing system could not be avoided. Players opting for this route would be placed on an NHL team's "inactive list," denying the player any ability to become a free agent and ensuring that the player was bound to the team should he ever wish to pursue an NHL career.

As Kidd and Macfarlane document, under the sponsorship system, NHL teams could unilaterally move young players from team to team within their system. For example, at age 13, Bobby Hull was sent by the Chicago Black Hawks from Point Anne, Ontario, over 500 kilometres to Dresden, in far southwestern Ontario. Many moves were cross-country. For instance, the Detroit Red Wings moved Gordie Howe from his hometown of Saskatoon to Galt, Ontario, a distance of 2,700 kilometres, when Howe was only 15 years old. While the CAHA did have regulations governing interprovincial transfers, these regulations were relatively impotent. Furthermore, any change to these regulations required NHL approval. To get a sense of just how important interprovincial transfers were, there were 104 interprovincial transfers in 1965–66 alone, with 38 of these involving boys under the age of 18. Most often, these transfers involved boys leaving their homes in Western Canada to play Junior A hockey in the Ontario Hockey Association (OHA). Given this, it is not surprising that OHA teams dominated the Memorial Cup during the sponsorship years, winning the championship in all but six seasons.

While each NHL team directly controlled only two junior teams, it also *indirectly* controlled numerous other junior teams. Each NHL club maintained affiliations with teams in what could be termed the minor pro leagues in the US—leagues such as the Central Hockey League (CHL), the Western Hockey League (WHL—not the current junior league of the same name), and the American Hockey League (AHL). Generally, each NHL team would have an affiliate team in each of these minor pro leagues and would send players to these teams for development. However, because each of these minor pro teams also maintained affiliations with junior teams, the NHL team indirectly controlled the junior franchises of the minor pro team.

Take as an example the Montreal Canadiens. The club directly sponsored two junior teams—one in Peterborough, Ontario, and the other in Montreal. In addition, the Canadiens maintained affiliations with three minor pro teams: Quebec City of the AHL, Houston of the CPHL, and Seattle of the WHL. Each of these minor pro teams, in turn, had affiliations with junior teams. Quebec City had affiliations with junior teams in Regina and Quebec City, Houston had affiliations with junior teams in Chatham, Ontario, and Lachine, Quebec, and Seattle had affiliations with junior teams in Fort William, Ontario, and Hull, Quebec. In effect, Montreal had monopsonistic control over eight junior teams.

At the height of the sponsorship system in 1967, junior hockey was highly dispersed and unconsolidated, with 231 clubs in existence across the country, of which 96 were operating at the highest level at the time—Junior A. Those 96 elite-level clubs in 1967 compare with only 60 elite clubs today (now called major junior clubs), despite Canada's population almost doubling in size

over that more than 50-year period. This consolidation and ratio-
nalization at the elite level of junior hockey is not coincidental.

There was also a geographic pattern in the sponsorship of
junior teams. Not surprisingly, the majority of sponsored junior
teams were in Ontario and Quebec—not only the largest provinces
in terms of population and, correspondingly, in the volume of amateur talent being developed, but also relatively close geographically
to the six NHL teams in existence at the time, a fact that allowed NHL
teams to follow their amateur prospects more closely.

Overall, the NHL's imposition of the team-sponsorship system
on the CAHA in 1947 was never popular in amateur hockey circles.
It made stark the perception of many that junior hockey's primary
purpose was simply to act as a training ground for NHL teams. In
his 1996 book, Bruce Kidd quotes CAHA secretary-manager Gordon
Juckes as saying in the 1960s, "The money barons of the NHL have
relegated Canada to the role of gigantic hockey slave farm."

The 1947 agreement resulted in junior hockey becoming less
about offering recreational and participatory opportunities for
young men, and more about athletic elitism, with junior teams
quickly dispensing of any players not deemed to have NHL prospects.
As Kidd argues, the sponsorship system significantly decreased the
opportunity for boys older than 15 to continue to play hockey, except
for those who were most talented. While an NHL team might sponsor
multiple peewee-, bantam- and midget-age teams in a given city,
rarely did an NHL team sponsor more than one junior team in
that city. The commonly held view was that, by about the time
a boy turned 15, most NHL scouts could determine whether or not
the boy had any potential to ultimately play professionally. For
those who were deemed to not have this potential, the NHL really
had very little further interest in them, and thus had no reason to
continue to sponsor their development. For these boys, it became

very difficult, if not impossible, to be able to continue to play organized hockey.

THE TRANSITION YEARS: 1967 TO 1980

With the end of the sponsorship system, junior hockey clubs became independent entities—no longer were they affiliated with an NHL club. However, this shift did not materially diminish the degree to which the NHL could control amateur hockey in Canada, since the CAHA continued to play a subordinate role to the NHL. What did change was the *manner* in which the NHL controlled Canadian amateur hockey. Under the sponsorship system, the NHL's control was direct, visible and high-profile. With the move to the draft system, and with NHL teams divesting themselves of their junior affiliates, the NHL's control became less direct and less transparent, but no less effective.

In 1967, the two parties signed a new agreement—often referred to as the Pro-Am Agreement—that saw the NHL commit to paying various grants and fees to the CAHA, in recognition of the developmental service provided by the Canadian amateur hockey system. As part of this agreement, the age limit for junior players was lowered from 21 to 20. This accommodated the NHL's desire to have earlier access to the best junior players, but was detrimental, of course, to owners of junior teams, who now had their players leaving one year earlier. Furthermore, if the NHL was not satisfied with the quantity or quality of talent being produced by junior hockey, the agreement required the CAHA to remedy the situation by establishing a program of "accelerated player development," or risk, in the words of then NHL president Clarence Campbell, the NHL reverting back to a sponsorship system.

The 1967 agreement also included a system of financial transfers from the NHL to the CAHA. Provisions of the agreement required the NHL to make various payments, including annual assessments, player development grants and draft claim payments. With the latter, the agreement specified a formula by which the NHL would make payments to the CAHA for each drafted player, with the amount of the compensation varying by the round in which the player was drafted. In turn, the CAHA would distribute these payments to the junior team from which the player had been drafted. Between 1969 and 1973, a total of $7.3 million dollars—or about $1.2 million per year—was paid by the NHL to the CAHA.[109]

The NHL–CAHA agreement of 1967 met with harsh criticism from many observers of the amateur hockey system in Canada, with various reports condemning the CAHA's relationship with the NHL. A 1967 report from the government of Alberta was critical of the CAHA's financial dependence on the NHL and suggested that the NHL–CAHA agreement was a restrictive conspiracy between the CAHA and the NHL, designed to serve the self-interests of the two organizations, as opposed to the interests of amateur hockey players and communities. While suggesting that a federal response, particularly through amendments to the Combines Investigation Act,[110] would be welcomed, it argued that provincial action was even more essential.

Another 1967 report—this one from Canada's National Advisory Council on Fitness and Amateur Sport—called for an end to the NHL's influence in Canadian amateur hockey and recommended greater autonomy for the CAHA in its player development programs. The report argued for the enactment of federal legislation to guarantee "amateur hockey freedom from any kind of interference from the National Hockey League." The report also recommended the draft age be kept at 21, but allowed for the possibility that exceptional 18-to-20-year-olds should be allowed to turn pro.

Two years later, in 1969, yet another study was released on the matter: the *Report of the Task Force on Sports for Canadians,* prepared for the federal government's Department of National Health and Welfare. This report expressed particular concern about the decline in participation in amateur hockey for those over the age of 15, and attributed it to the NHL's influence, whose interest was solely directed at developing elite players, and not at the broader promotion of the game as a recreational activity. The report noted "the irony that the ruling body of a national sport, the CAHA, should have to have an agreement with an international industry, most of which operates in the United States, as to when its players reach the end of a certain stage in their hockey careers." A key recommendation of the report, later accepted and implemented, was that the federal government provide financial support to the CAHA to assist with administrative expenses, thus reducing the CAHA's dependence on the NHL for funding.

The reports continued in 1973, with a widely publicized study by Alberta's Department of Culture, Youth and Recreation—commonly referred to as the *Downey Report*, after its lead researcher, L.W. Downey —that focused on the Alberta Junior A Hockey League, but could have equally applied to the more elite Western Canada Hockey League. The report was extremely critical of how clubs in that league treated their players, and its analysis centred on the individual rights, or lack thereof, of players. It found particularly "offensive" the practice of clubs entering into contracts with "infants" (as legally defined). It also criticized the unreasonable restraint of "one-sided contracts, which served to deny individuals the right to bargain or transfer, but which, instead, assigned to the league or team the right to seek or trade individuals." In essence, these contractual specifications truly did give teams complete ownership over player services. In Downey's view, the standard player contract imposed unreasonable limitations on the freedom of young hockey players—limitations that would simply not be found anywhere else in society.

Downey also objected to the use of "protected lists" in junior
hockey. Here, the issue was not so much what happened to players
once they signed with a team, but rather how a player got to a team
in the first place. Junior hockey clubs at that time used a system
similar to what the NHL used prior to 1963, whereby prospective
players would be unilaterally placed on a team's protected list, often
without their knowledge. In other words, the player and his family
had no choice as to where he would play. These lists, with apparently as many as 70 names on them per team, were referred to by
Downey as, alternately, "conscription lists" or "slave lists," leaving no
doubt as to how he felt these lists had an impact on personal freedom
of choice.

One year before the *Downey Report* was released, the market
power of junior players increased somewhat, as the WHA began
operations as a direct competitor to the NHL. Downey noted that,
on the positive side, the competition for junior players offered by
the emergence of the WHA could potentially serve to break the NHL's
control of amateur hockey in Canada. But, at the same time, he was
sceptical of the WHA's actual impact, arguing that it was in the WHA's
best interest to not disrupt the status quo and to ensure positive
relations with the CAHA and the junior hockey establishment.

In fact, some of both happened. At one level, the WHA attempted to
follow the practices established by the NHL–CAHA agreement, in the
sense that the WHA agreed to pay draft and development fees to the
CAHA and/or directly to individual junior clubs. However, the emergence of the WHA did alter the landscape of junior hockey in one very
important and long-lasting way, in that many underage players signed
with the new league. The term *underage* referred to those junior players under the age of 20 and, according to the terms of the NHL–CAHA
agreement, were thus not eligible to be drafted or signed by NHL teams.
Officially, the WHA, as a league, observed this age limit, but a problem

arose when some of the league's teams refused to abide by the rule and unilaterally signed underage players to professional contracts.

When the WHA attempted to enforce league rules to prevent this from happening, a US federal court decision ruled against it. In *Linseman v. World Hockey Association,* the court determined that such league rules were an illegal restraint of players' freedom, contrary to US antitrust law. The player in question was Ken Linseman, a junior star with the Kingston Canadians of what was then the Ontario Major Junior Hockey League (now the OHL), who had signed with the WHA's Birmingham Bulls in 1977. Following the decision, the Bulls went ahead and signed many other underage players—including such future NHL players as Mark Napier, Gaston Gingras, Rob Ramage and Rick Vaive. Many other underage players were signed by the WHA, including future NHL superstars Wayne Gretzky and Mark Messier. For these star-quality junior players, the emergence of the WHA was a financial boon. Not only did the presence of the WHA increase NHL salaries dramatically, but some junior players were now able to earn a return on their skills at a younger age.

Not surprisingly, junior hockey operators strongly opposed this signing of underage juniors, or "raiding," as they often called it, since it resulted in the early exodus from junior hockey of many star players who had significant revenue-generating ability for their junior teams. Junior hockey operators often grounded their opposition in an apparent concern for the boys, and would argue that the signing of underage players would interfere with those players' development. However, in his 1996 book *Sports and the Law in Canada,* John Barnes debunks this argument as insincere, saying the underage player's development, particularly educational and personal, is already compromised by the gruelling schedules of junior hockey, and by living away from home to play in "quasi-professional" leagues that ultimately serve the NHL.

A 1978 report for the Minister of State (Fitness and Amateur Sport) expressed the view that junior hockey was "professional," and, as such, players should be able to bargain for remuneration and choice of team. It also raised questions about whether the entrepreneurial gains of owners justified the level of exploitation that was occurring in junior hockey. The report called for a federal study on the issue. The resultant *Canadian Hockey Review*, initiated in 1979, recommended a complete public inquiry into the practices of major junior hockey. However, with the changes brought by the federal election in February 1979, the review was terminated by the new Progressive Conservative government, and the inquiry into junior hockey never occurred.

The 1979 merger of the WHA and NHL ended the labour market competition that had existed for seven years—once again, the NHL had a monopsony. With the merger, and fearing legal ramifications, the NHL relaxed its rules regarding the draft age. For the first time, it allowed, albeit with restrictions, 18-year-olds to be drafted. By 1992, all restrictions on drafting underage juniors were removed—any player 18 years and older was eligible to be drafted. However, in an effort not to gut junior hockey of all its best players, the policy required that drafted players with junior eligibility remaining had to either play in the NHL or be returned to their major junior team—they could not be sent to the minor pro affiliate of the NHL team.

One year after the NHL–WHA merger, an equally major restructuring occurred in junior hockey. In 1980, the three top-tier junior leagues—the Western Hockey League (WHL), the Ontario Hockey League (OHL) and the Quebec Major Junior Hockey League (QMJHL)—made the momentous decision to split from the CAHA and instead form their own governing body, the Canadian Hockey League (CHL). For club owners in the three CHL leagues, the primary benefit of the split was that they now had freedom to pursue their commercial interests, to be profit-seeking and to operate their leagues in ways typically found in the monopoly pro leagues. The shackles of having to maintain the façade of amateurism were now removed.

THE MODERN ERA: THE EMERGENCE OF THREE MAJOR JUNIOR LEAGUES

During the sponsorship era, amateur hockey in Canada was highly fragmented and decentralized. With the sponsorship system ending and NHL clubs divesting their amateur clubs to private owners, there was bound to be a consolidation. From a business perspective, junior hockey simply had too many teams, in too many different leagues, in too many small centres for it to be operated profitably. What quickly emerged was a consolidation of the elite-tier of junior hockey into three "super-leagues," the forerunners of today's OHL, WHL and QMJHL.

Of the three current leagues, the roots of the OHL go back the farthest—as far as the late 1800s. The OHL's predecessor was the Ontario Hockey Association (OHA), which was formed in 1896 as the governing body for all amateur hockey in the province. Originally, the OHA simply categorized teams as either junior or senior, with players 20 years of age or younger being eligible to play junior hockey. In 1933, the OHA, in an effort to better recognize that the junior division housed teams and leagues of widely differing qualities, subdivided that division into Junior A and Junior B levels. With this realignment, only teams in the Junior A category were allowed to compete for the OHA championship and the right to contend for the Memorial Cup.

During the 1930s, '40s and '50s, several prominent Junior A teams were established, including the Toronto Marlboros, St. Michael's Majors, Oshawa Generals, Barrie Flyers, Guelph Biltmore Mad Hatters, Kitchener Greenshirts (forerunner to the Peterborough Petes) and St. Catharines Teepees. Throughout this era, there was a steady turnover of franchises, with many new teams entering the league, some relocating to other cities, and some simply disbanding.

In 1963, Junior A teams faced competition in the form of the Metro Junior A League. This upstart league was founded by Toronto Marlboros owner Stafford Smythe, who pulled the Marlboros from the OHA to make them the flagship team of the new league. The other members of Metro Junior A were generally teams that had previously played at the Junior B level. As a result, the quality of hockey was inferior to that of the OHA, and the new league folded after only two seasons, as the Marlboros returned to the OHA. The Oshawa Generals, who had entered the Metro Junior A League in its second season, also moved to the OHA.

With the CAHA's overhaul of the junior hockey system in 1971, the OHA further subdivided the Junior A level into two additional levels, Tier I and Tier II. The Tier I portion became known as Major Junior A, with teams in this division continuing to compete for the Memorial Cup. The Tier II portion became known as Minor Junior A, with teams in this division dropping out of the Memorial Cup chase and instead competing for a new national trophy known as the Centennial Cup. Two cities that had teams in the Northern Ontario Junior Hockey League—Sudbury and Sault Ste. Marie—were also granted franchises in the OHA's Major Junior A tier. In Sudbury's case, the team was the former Niagara Falls Flyers franchise, which relocated to Sudbury for the 1972 season.

Within two years, teams in this tier adopted a radically different organizational structure, establishing a quasi-independent league. This new Ontario Major Junior Hockey League operated with considerable autonomy from the OHA, adopting an organizational structure complete with its own commissioner and league office staff. Perhaps most importantly, the creation of the new league allowed teams to gain increased control over their financial matters.

This disengagement from the OHA became complete in 1980, when the league changed its name to the Ontario Hockey League (OHL), and officially severed all remaining ties with the OHA. This separation allowed the OHL to completely control all of its financial matters—an issue that was becoming increasingly important in a business environment where the revenue-generating ability of major junior teams was beginning to show significant increases. The terms of the agreement also allowed the OHL to continue to be the only Ontario junior league to compete for the Memorial Cup. In return for these benefits, the OHL agreed to pay a yearly $30,000 "affiliation" fee to the OHA.

Since 1980, the league has grown from 12 franchises to 20. It expanded into the US market in 1990, when the Detroit Compuware Ambassadors joined the league, a franchise that operates today as the Flint Firebirds. There are now two other US–based franchises in the league, located in Erie, Pennsylvania, and Saginaw, Michigan, respectively.

The WHL's history is shorter, going back to only 1966 with the formation of what was then known as the Western Canada Junior Hockey League (WCJHL). The league subsequently dropped the word *junior* from its name in 1968 (becoming the WCHL), and took on its current name in 1978 when the word *Canada* was also dropped, in recognition of the entry of the first US–based franchise (in Portland, Oregon) into the league two years earlier.

The roots of junior hockey in the West, however, go back well before 1966. Prior to that year, each of the four Western provinces had their own junior systems. In Alberta, for example, the Alberta Junior Hockey League (AJHL) began operations in 1963 with five teams—the Lethbridge Sugar Kings, Calgary Buffaloes, Calgary Cowboys, Edmonton Safeway Canadians and Edmonton Maple Leafs.

Ironically, and somewhat confusingly, however, the most dominant and successful junior team in Alberta in the pre–WHL era—the

Edmonton Oil Kings—did not actually play in the AJHL. The Oil
Kings existence predated the formation of the AJHL, and the Oil Kings'
pre-eminence within the province of Alberta generally allowed
them to capture all of the best junior-age players in that province.
The Oil Kings won the Memorial Cup in both 1963 and 1966 as
members of a senior men's league known as the Central Alberta
Hockey League. In both those years, the Oil Kings were required
to defeat the AJHL champions in a playoff for the right to represent
Alberta. The Oil Kings also made it to five other Memorial Cup finals
during the early 1960s, losing each time to teams from Ontario.

In some sense, the AJHL was formed directly in response to the
lack of Junior A playing opportunities for Alberta players. The Oil
Kings were the only elite-level team in Alberta, so many talented
Alberta players had no regional opportunities to hone their skills.

The Edmonton Oil Kings franchise would go on to play a central
role in the formation of the modern WHL. The Oil Kings' general manager at the time, Bill Hunter—co-founder of the WHA and original
owner of the WHA's Edmonton Oilers—felt junior hockey in Western
Canada needed to be consolidated. In his view, the fact that each
province operated its own independent junior hockey system put
teams from Western Canada at a distinct competitive disadvantage
when competing nationally with junior teams in the larger Quebec
and Ontario leagues. Hunter envisioned what amounted to a type of
Western Canada super-league that would consolidate talent and also
—no doubt, given Hunter's widely acclaimed entrepreneurial skills
—make junior hockey in Western Canada a more marketable product.

This super-league took the form of the WCJHL, which began play
in the fall of 1966 as a seven-team league. Hunter's Oil Kings were
the centrepiece of the new league. The league's other founding members included five teams that had defected from the Saskatchewan
Junior Hockey League—the Regina Pats, Saskatoon Blades, Moose

Jaw Canucks, Weyburn Red Wings and Estevan Bruins—as well as the Calgary Buffaloes.

In its early years, the new league was embroiled in controversy, largely because its founders were viewed as renegades who acted outside the long-established power structure of the Canadian amateur hockey system. The CAHA did not officially recognize the new league, and considered it an "outlaw" league. As such, the champions of the new league were not allowed to compete for the Memorial Cup.

Nevertheless, the new league was not deterred and continued on a path of rapid growth. In 1967, it added three Manitoba teams: the Winnipeg Jets, Flin Flon Bombers and Brandon Wheat Kings. One year later, the Swift Current Broncos entered the league, and in 1970, the Medicine Hat Tigers were granted a franchise. In 1971, the league entered the British Columbia market, with expansion franchises granted to the Victoria Cougars and Vancouver Nats, and with the later relocation of the Estevan Bruins to New Westminster.

The league encountered a minor setback in 1968, when the Pats, Bruins and Red Wings all elected to return to the Saskatchewan Junior Hockey League. The Pats subsequently reversed this decision in 1970, once again leaving the Saskatchewan league to join the new league.

By the early 1970s, it was becoming apparent that the various Western Canadian provincial junior leagues were losing the competitive battle to the WCHL. The CAHA's decision in 1971 to create a major junior tier signified a truce between itself and the WCHL. It also meant that, while the provincial junior leagues such as the Alberta Junior Hockey League and the Saskatchewan Junior Hockey League would continue to function, they would now be designated as Tier II junior leagues.

With these administrative battles behind it, the WCHL was now free to move forward and focus on building an even stronger league.

A particular milestone for the league occurred in 1976, when the Edmonton Oil Kings—unable to compete with the WHA's Edmonton Oilers—relocated from Edmonton to Portland. This relocation was significant not only because it signified the end of the league's original flagship franchise, but also because it marked the first foray of any Canadian junior league into the US market. The Portland market proved to be particularly lucrative for the league and was the beginning of further expansion into US cities. Over the past three decades, the league has experienced numerous expansions and franchise relocations, to the point where, as of the 2022–23 season, it now operates with 22 franchises: two in Manitoba, five each in Saskatchewan, Alberta and BC, four in Washington state and one in Oregon.

The Quebec Major Junior Hockey League (QMJHL) was founded in 1969, spurred by a similar motivation to Bill Hunter's when he formed the WCJHL three years earlier: to improve the quality of play at the junior level by consolidating a fragmented system into a single league aimed at elite players. Prior to 1969, the Quebec Junior Hockey League (QJHL) had been the primary junior league in Quebec, but this league was generally not considered a "major junior" type of league. In fact, the flagship franchise of the QJHL—the Montreal Junior Canadiens—had actually left the QJHL in 1962 to join the higher-calibre OHA.

In its initial season in 1969, the QMJHL consisted of 11 teams, most of which had transferred from either the QJHL or the Metropolitan Montreal Junior Hockey League. The league also included one Ontario team—the Cornwall Royals—who had previously been a member of the Central Junior A Hockey League. However, with the Montreal Junior Canadiens playing in the OHA, the QMJHL was without a team in its largest market, an issue that was a large aggravation for the new league. In 1972, under the threat of a lawsuit from the

QMJHL, the Junior Canadiens franchise decided to leave the OHA to join the QMJHL, where the franchise became known as the Montreal Bleu Blanc Rouge.

Like both the WHL and OHL, the QMJHL has experienced considerable franchise growth since its formation, some of which has included placing franchises in locations outside its original geographic boundaries. In fact, as of the 2022–23 season, only two-thirds of the league's 18 franchises are actually located in the province of Quebec. The remaining six franchises are located in Atlantic Canada—three in New Brunswick, two in Nova Scotia and one in Prince Edward Island. The league has also had forays into the US market, the first being in 1984 in Plattsburg, New York; that franchise was very short-lived, though, folding only 17 games into its first season. It would be almost 20 years, in 2003, before the league again re-entered the US market, with the transfer of the Sherbrooke franchise to Lewiston, Maine. The Lewiston Maineiacs lasted eight seasons before disbanding after the 2010–11 season.

For the QMJHL, it has been the Atlantic Canada market, rather than the US market, where the league has focused its expansion interests. Prior to the mid-1990s, the Atlantic Canada hockey market had long been dominated by the American Hockey League (AHL)—a professional league that is the top farm league for the NHL. Gradually, however, AHL teams began relocating out of Atlantic Canada, leaving a void in the market for high-calibre hockey. The QMJHL's first move into Atlantic Canada occurred in 1994, when the Halifax Mooseheads were awarded an expansion franchise. Since then, the league has placed teams in all major Atlantic Canada cities, including Saint John's, Moncton, Saint John and Charlottetown.

THE ECONOMICS OF THE CHL: ADOPTING NHL-STYLE PRACTICES

During the sponsorship era, junior teams were generally an organic outgrowth of the minor hockey associations in the cities in which they were located. Each club would then voluntarily join together with other clubs in the area to form local leagues. In other words, cities did not have a junior club because some outside third party deemed that the city was a "good market"; rather, it was the other way around, with teams naturally forming at the local level and then finding other teams to play against.

However, the three new super-leagues that emerged out of the sponsorship era did not follow this model. In fact, these leagues adopted a "closed" system favoured by the Big Four pro leagues in North America. This system was not the bottom-up, organic system of days past in junior hockey, but instead was a system where profit potential became key, and where all aspects of team and league behaviour were centrally planned and controlled. The three major junior leagues became mini-NHLS in almost every aspect of the operations.

Like their brethren in the pro leagues, the junior leagues adopted policies that use a league's market power to both increase revenues and decrease costs, often by employing what would be considered anti-competitive techniques if they were used in almost any other industry. The revenues and, ultimately, the franchise values of CHL teams are enhanced by the fact that the CHL has considerable monopoly power in the output market. This monopoly power is rooted in the closed-league nature of the three CHL leagues. The entry of new teams is tightly controlled, and new franchises are only admitted to a league with the approval of the existing league members. In addition, territorial rights are granted to league members, whereby no new franchise can locate within a specific geographic radius of an existing franchise, without that existing franchise first granting its approval. These rules allow the leagues to tightly ration the supply of new teams that enter the league.[111] In 2002, for example, WHL[112] governors voted against expansion, even though the league had formal applications from groups in six different cities. Even more revealing, in the two decades since that time, the league has added only three additional franchises—increasing the league size from 19 to 22—despite the continued high demand from prospective owner groups seeking expansion clubs. For the WHL, however, by artificially inducing a scarcity of franchises, the market values of existing franchises are enhanced.

Emerging from the sponsorship era, junior hockey operators clearly understood the concept of artificial scarcity. The number of top-tier teams in Canada fell from 96 in 1967, the last year of the sponsorship, to only 30 in 1970.[113] Not only did this consolidate the country's elite players into many fewer teams, thus allowing the leagues to market themselves as having only the "best-of-the-best" players, but it created an excess demand for franchises—in other words, there were now more cities that wanted major junior franchises than there were franchises available. While all three CHL leagues have expanded over the past half century, this expansion has failed to keep up with population growth. As a result, today there are even fewer Canadian-based CHL franchises per capita than there were in 1970.

This shortage of franchises creates the opportunity for existing franchises to relocate in response to profit opportunities, just as in pro leagues like the NHL. Junior clubs of today are no longer an outgrowth of their city's amateur hockey system and hence inherently bound to that location, but instead are independent commercial enterprises searching for a location that will provide the club's owner with the best financial arrangement. Teams struggling at the gate may move in hopes of increasing attendance in a different city, or they may move to secure a more favourable arena lease with their municipal landlord. When many markets are intentionally left unserved by a league, it encourages franchise "free agency," with club owners continually scanning the market for more profitable locations.

In the over half a century since the sponsorship era ended, the three existing CHL leagues have seen an astounding 57 different franchises shifts—21 in the WHL and 18 in each of the OHL and QMJHL (see charts below). To put this in context, with 60 CHL clubs operating as of 2021–22, this means that, on average, about one CHL club relocates each and every year.

Franchise Relocations: Western Hockey League, 1971 to 2022

Year	From	To
2019	Cranbrook (Kootenay Ice)	Winnipeg
2011	Chilliwack (Bruins)	Victoria (Royals)
1998	Edmonton (Ice)	Cranbrook (Kootenay Ice)
1995	Tacoma (Rockets)	Kelowna (Rockets)
1994	Victoria (Cougars)	Prince George (Cougars)
1988	New Westminster (Bruins) (2nd version)	Kennewick, WA (Tri-City Americans)
1987	Calgary (Wranglers)	Lethbridge (Hurricanes)
1986	Lethbridge (Broncos)	Swift Current (Broncos)
1985	Kelowna (Wings)	Spokane (Chiefs)
1984	Winnipeg (Warriors)	Moose Jaw (Warriors)
1983	Nanaimo (Islanders)	New Westminster (Bruins) (2nd version)
1982	Billings, MT (Bighorns)	Nanaimo (Islanders)
1981	New Westminster (Bruins) (1st version)	Kamloops (Jr. Oilers, later Blazers)
1979	Edmonton (Oil Kings) (2nd version)	Great Falls, MT (Americans)
1978	Flin Flon (Bombers)	Edmonton (Oil Kings) (2nd version)
1977	Calgary (Centennials)	Billings, MT (Bighorns)
1977	Winnipeg (Monarchs)	Calgary (Wranglers)

1976	Edmonton (Oil Kings) (1st version)	Portland (Winter Hawks)
1974	Swift Current (Broncos)	Lethbridge (Broncos)
1973	Vancouver (Nats)	Kamloops (Chiefs)
1971	Estevan (Bruins)	New Westminster (Bruins) (1st version)

Franchise Relocations: Ontario Hockey League, 1971 to 2022

Year	From	To
2015	Plymouth, MI (Whalers)	Flint, MI (Firebirds)
2015	Belleville (Bulls)	Hamilton (Bulldogs)
2013	Brampton (Battalion)	North Bay (Battalion)
2007	Mississauga (IceDogs)	Niagara Falls (IceDogs)
2007	Toronto (St. Michael's Majors)	Mississauga (St. Michael's Majors and then Steelheads)
2002	North Bay (Centennials)	Saginaw, MI (Spirit)
1996	Niagara Falls (Thunder)	Erie, PA (Otters)
1994	Newmarket (Royals)	Sarnia (Sting)
1992	Cornwall (Royals)	Newmarket (Royals)
1991	Hamilton (Dukes)	Guelph (Storm)
1989	Toronto (Marlboros)	Hamilton (Dukes)
1989	Guelph (Platers)	Owen Sound (Platers)
1989	Hamilton (Steelhawks)	Niagara Falls (Thunder)
1984	Brantford (Alexanders)	Hamilton (Steelhawks)
1982	Niagara Falls (Flyers) (2nd version)	North Bay (Centennials)
1978	Hamilton (Fincups)	Brantford (Alexanders)
1976	St. Catharines (Black Hawks)	Niagara Falls (Flyers) (2nd version)
1972	Niagara Falls (Flyers) 1st version	Sudbury (Wolves)

Franchise Relocations: Quebec Major Junior Hockey League, 1971 to 2022

Year	From	To
2011	Montreal (Juniors)	Blainville-Boisbriand (Armada)
2008	St. John's (Fog Devils)	Montreal (Juniors)
2003	Sherbrooke (Castors) (2nd version)	Lewiston , ME (Maineiacs)
2003	Montreal (Rocket)	Charlottetown (PEI Rocket)
1998	Laval (Titan)	Acadie-Bathurst (Titan)
1997	Granby (Prédateurs)	Sydney (Cape Breton Screaming Eagles)
1997	Beauport (Harfangs)	Quebec (Remparts) (2nd version)
1996	Saint-Hyacinthe (Laser)	Rouyn-Noranda (Huskies)
1995	Saint-Jean (Lynx)	Rimouski (Océanic)
1993	Longueuil (Collège Français)	Verdun (Collège Français)
1992	Trois-Rivieres (Draveurs)	Sherbrooke (Faucons)
1989	Verdun (Jr. Canadiens)	Saint-Hyacinthe (Laser)
1987	Longueuil (Chevaliers)	Victoriaville (Tigres)
1982	Sherbrooke (Castors) (1st version)	Saint-Jean (Lynx)
1981	Sorel (Black Hawks)	Granby (Bisons)
1979	Verdun (Black Hawks)	Sorel (Black Hawks)
1977	Sorel (Black Hawks)	Verdun (Black Hawks)
1971	Rosemont (National)	Laval (National)

With the lure of increased profits driving relocations, any commitments that CHL clubs may profess to have for their existing communities are often insincere and self-serving, or, at best, transitory and fleeting. Major junior hockey is a business, and sentimental community considerations impede the commercial interests of club owners. Fans pay the price, seeing their local team—one they have financially supported and become emotionally invested in—up and leave for more profitable locales.

Take, for example, the WHL's Kootenay Ice, who played in Cranbrook, BC, from 1998 to 2019. The Ice were big news in Cranbrook, a city of just 20,000 people. They had immediate success on the ice and built a strong local fan base. In their first four seasons in Cranbrook, the club won two WHL championships (in 2000 and 2002) and one Memorial Cup (in 2002). The club won another WHL championship in 2011 and again advanced to the Memorial Cup. In their later years in Cranbrook, though, the club struggled on the ice, and attendance waned, dropping from peaks of 3,500 per game in their early years in the city down to around 2,000 per game. Even with that drop, 2,000 fans per game was still impressive—it meant that about 10% of Cranbrook's 20,000 residents were regularly attending Ice games.

Had the club been a non-profit, community-owned entity, as were most junior clubs in the sponsorship era, it probably would have stayed in Cranbrook, even with the limited financial potential in that market. After all, there were three other clubs in the league, all in Saskatchewan cities—Swift Current, Moose Jaw and Prince Albert—that had long operated in small markets as community-based clubs. However, the private ownership that dominates CHL clubs changes the financial dynamics. Investors in these clubs must do better than just break even; they must be able to earn a return sufficiently large to justify their capital investment.

For the WHL, the Ice franchise was more valuable to the league and its owners by *not* being in Cranbrook. In 2017, the Chynoweth family—owners of the Ice—cashed out their investment, selling the club to a Winnipeg group. The new owners were reportedly exploring the possibility of moving the franchise to Nanaimo, BC, but that idea fell through when local taxpayers defeated a proposal that would have seen the City of Nanaimo issue debt for the construction of a new arena. Cranbrook's reprieve was short-lived, however, and the club left for Winnipeg in 2019, despite having a lease on the arena in Cranbrook that ran for four more years. The City of Cranbrook sued, and the matter remains tied up in the courts.

Fans in many cities have had to get accustomed to a revolving door of franchises. For example, take Edmonton—a city on the opposite end of the WHL population spectrum compared with Cranbrook. Edmonton's big-city status has not insulated it from franchise instability. The city's original junior club, the iconic Edmonton Oil Kings, were founded in 1950 and had tremendous national success, reaching the Memorial Cup final in seven consecutive seasons during the 1960s, winning twice. Despite this history of success, local interest in the club began to wane in the mid-1970s, with the WHA's Oilers now presenting competition for the consumer dollar. This, combined with the fact that Portland offered the club a much more favourable arena deal than it was getting in Edmonton, prompted Oil Kings owner Brian Shaw to move the club south of the border.

The Oil Kings left Edmonton in 1976, but were quickly replaced two years later when the Flin Flon Bombers moved to Edmonton. The Bombers franchise—despite being located in a small northern Manitoba mining town—was noted for producing a plethora of NHL players during the 1960s and early 1970s, including such future NHL stars as Bobby Clarke and Reggie Leach. Upon the move to Edmonton, the Bombers were renamed the Oil Kings, despite having no connection to the franchise that had just left for Portland. The new Oil Kings had a short life in Edmonton, lasting only one year before moving to Great Falls, Montana. It would be almost 20 years before the WHL returned to Edmonton, this time in the form of an expansion franchise, the Edmonton Ice. The Ice lasted only two years in Edmonton before relocating to Cranbrook in 1998. Then, a decade later, yet another Edmonton franchise appeared in the WHL, again as an expansion club. This latest and current Edmonton-based WHL club chose to revive the "Oil Kings" nickname, hoping to evoke a nostalgic connection with the great Oil Kings teams of past eras.

Like Edmonton, Niagara Falls, Ontario, was home to an iconic junior hockey team during the 1960s, but has since seen a steady stream of franchises come and go. The Niagara Falls Flyers put the city on the junior hockey map, losing the 1963 Memorial Cup final to the Edmonton Oil Kings, but then defeating the Oil Kings two years later in the 1965 final. The Flyers were part of the Boston Bruins sponsorship system, and that Memorial Cup–winning roster included a who's who of Bruins prospects who would go on to become long-time NHLers: Bernie Parent, Derek Sanderson, Jean Pronovost, Don Marcotte, Gilles Marotte, Jim Lorentz, Doug Favell and Rick Ley. The links between the Bruins and the Flyers were particularly close; the Flyers' long-time owner and general manager, Leighton "Hap" Emms, also served as Bruins GM for two seasons during the mid-1960s, doing both jobs simultaneously during the 1965–66 and 1966–67 seasons.

The Flyers' success continued. In 1968, and for the second time in four years, the club would again bring the Memorial Cup back to Niagara Falls, this time defeating the Estevan Bruins in the best-of-seven final. Like the Flyers, and as their name would suggest, the Estevan club was also sponsored by the Boston Bruins, making the 1968 Memorial Cup a clash of two Boston farm clubs.

Despite these accomplishments, it all ended abruptly for Flyers fans. Just four years after their 1968 championship, the iconic Niagara Falls Flyers were no more. Owner Hap Emms sold the team in 1972, with the new owner immediately relocating the franchise to Sudbury, where the club was rebranded as the Sudbury Wolves. It was a clear reminder to those in Niagara Falls that junior hockey was a business and any notion that a club had some type of deeper connection with the community in which it played was simply naive.

The Flyers' departure was only the beginning of what has been a tumultuous half century of major junior hockey in Niagara Falls. The city regained a franchise in 1976 when the St. Catharines Black Hawks—owned, ironically, by Hap Emms—relocated to Niagara Falls. Emms, undoubtedly in an attempt to recapture the positive feelings of the glory years, revived the "Flyers" nickname for the franchise, even though this version of the Flyers had no connection to the 1960s version. Emms sold this second version of the Flyers just two years later, but the club stayed in Niagara Falls until 1982, when it was relocated to North Bay to become the Centennials (who are now the Saginaw Spirit of Michigan). After seven years with no junior club, Niagara Falls was back in the OHL in 1989, when the Hamilton Steelhawks (formerly the Brantford Alexanders, and, before that, the Hamilton Fincups) moved to the city. The Niagara Falls Thunder, as they were known, lasted eight seasons in the city, but they too eventually left, becoming the Erie Otters of Pennsylvania in 1996. The Thunder were the last OHL team to be located in Niagara Falls, although the name "Niagara" still lives on in the league with the Niagara IceDogs—the IceDogs, however, play in nearby St. Catharines, albeit while marketing themselves as the team of the broader Niagara region.

The IceDogs franchise in St. Catharines was itself a transplant, moving from Mississauga in 2007. The Mississauga IceDogs had entered the OHL as an expansion franchise in 1998, owned by the long-time *Hockey Night in Canada* commentator Don Cherry. In its early years, the franchise became known for recording some of the singularly worst seasons in the history of junior hockey, winning only 16 regular-season games (out of 206) in its first three seasons combined. Ottawa Senators owner Eugene Melnyk bought the club from Cherry in 2006, but flipped the club after only one season, with new owner Bill Burke then moving the club from Mississauga to St. Catharines.

Before the Burke purchase, Melnyk had entertained offers from Toronto businessman Tom Bitove to buy the club and move it to Niagara Falls (which would have been the fourth junior club in that city), but Niagara Falls city council rejected a plan to construct a new arena for the club, killing the deal and paving the way for the sale to Burke. Four years later, in 2011, St. Catharines city council approved a brand new $50 million arena, which, upon completion in 2014, became the home of the IceDogs. So, in the end, the franchise did get its new arena, just not in Niagara Falls.

The IceDogs story illustrates two important characteristics of modern-day junior hockey. First, like their NHL counterparts, junior hockey clubs play the "arena game," using the artificial undersupply of franchises in a league to create leverage with local governments. Cities are at a distinct disadvantage when dealing with these clubs. If a team relocates, the city may not ever see another junior team, at least not until taxpayers fund a new or renovated arena.

In the OHL, a flurry of arena construction occurred in the decade spanning 1998 to 2008, with no less than nine franchises (of the 17 Ontario-based franchises) getting new publicly funded arenas. In Oshawa, threats by the OHL's Oshawa Generals to move that franchise were followed by the City of Oshawa agreeing to build a new state-of-the-art $45 million facility. The arena opened in 2006 and includes 5,400 regular seats, 200 club seats, and 23 private boxes.

In North Bay, owners of the OHL's Centennials actually followed through on their threats—the franchise was sold in 2002 to a group that relocated the team to Saginaw, Michigan. Despite a strong grassroots campaign to the keep the team in North Bay, owners sold the team when the City of North Bay refused to renegotiate the team's lease on the city-owned arena.

Also in 2002, Windsor city councillors, in a controversial and narrow 6–5 vote, approved a $400,000 bailout package for the OHL's

Windsor Spitfires—the vote was in response to a claim by the team's owner that he had a $4.5 million offer for the team that would have resulted in the team leaving Windsor. Just four years later, the public largesse flowing to the club got even greater when city council approved a new $71 million arena for the club.

If junior leagues were instead required to be operated as open leagues, similar to what is seen in the European club system, even if a team left a city there would still be the opportunity for a new team to emerge in the city, perhaps through grassroots initiatives. However, the CHL leagues would never voluntarily agree to such an open system, since it would largely eliminate the monopoly power over cities that the leagues and their teams now possess.

A second broad storyline that emerges from the IceDogs saga is that junior hockey has been increasingly attracting high-profile owners—not only successful business leaders like Melnyk, but also celebrities like Cherry. In addition to Melnyk, NHL owners who have owned junior hockey clubs include Peter Karmanos Jr., former owner of the NHL's Carolina Hurricanes and the OHL's Plymouth Whalers; Murray Edwards, co-owner of the NHL's Calgary Flames and the WHL's Calgary Hitmen; and Daryl Katz, owner of both the NHL's Edmonton Oilers and the WHL's Edmonton Oil Kings. Beyond just NHL owners, junior hockey has also attracted the likes of industrialist Robert K. Irving of the venerable Irving family dynasty of New Brunswick. He has owned the QMJHL's Moncton Wildcats since 1996.

On the celebrity side, undoubtedly the biggest name is renowned crooner Michael Bublé, who has had a minority stake in the WHL's Vancouver Giants since 2008. Junior hockey has also drawn many former NHL players to its ownership ranks—"hockey celebrities," in a sense. Prominent ex-players who have had, at one time or another, ownership stakes in current or past CHL teams include: Dino Ciccarelli with the Sarnia Sting; Guy Carbonneau with the Chicoutimi

Saguenéens; Bobby Smith with the Halifax Mooseheads; Patrick Roy with the Quebec Remparts; Rob and Scott Niedermayer with the Kootenay Ice; Brent Sutter with the Red Deer Rebels; and Basil McRae, Mark Hunter and Dale Hunter with the London Knights.

Whatever the reasons individuals seek to invest in junior hockey—the potential profit opportunities, the public visibility ownership provides, the pure entertainment value of owning part of a hockey team, et cetera—it is clear that having a stake in a junior hockey club has become fashionable within a certain segment of affluent society. Gone are the days when junior hockey was a cottage industry, guided by franchise owners who were rarely known outside their local communities. So, while junior hockey is now attracting owners with wealth, status, power and influence, an inevitable question arises: How do the players fare in all of this?

THE PLAYERS

Being a CHL player is a gruelling, all-consuming venture.

First, there is the length of the season. With revenue maximization always at the forefront of league decision-making, CHL teams play nearly NHL–length schedules. In the WHL, for example, teams play a 68-game regular season (scaled back from 72 in 2017), only 14 games shorter than the NHL's regular season. By contrast, most US college hockey teams play about a 35-to-40-game regular season.

In addition, 16 of the 22 WHL teams make the playoffs, with all playoff series being best-of-seven competitions. Thus, the two teams that advance to the league final will play a total of four playoff series, and with each series going a possible seven games, these teams could play a maximum of 28 playoff games. When combined with the 68 regular-season games that each team plays, it is conceivable for a team to play almost 100 games in a season. This does not count pre-season games, nor does it count games in the Memorial Cup tournament, should a team make it that far.

However, what makes the WHL's season even more demanding is that, unlike the NHL, travel is almost always by bus. Distances between WHL cities can be very large. Geographically, the league spans an area from Winnipeg, Manitoba, to Portland, Oregon, a distance of 2,365 kilometres. Without taking into account stops, that amounts to an almost 50-hour round-trip bus ride.

Then there is the controversial player allocation system. CHL leagues have also mimicked the NHL, using a draft system to assign players to member teams, with players themselves having no say in where they will play. The WHL, for example, conducts a draft of all bantam-age players (14 and 15 years old) each year, in which all players in the four Western provinces (and 20 US states) who turn 15 before the end of that year are eligible to be drafted. As in the NHL, the draft is conducted in reverse order of the standings of the previous season.

However, unlike pro-sports leagues, where undrafted players become free agents and can sign with any team, players not selected in the bantam draft can then be unilaterally "listed" by any league team. If a team lists a player, that team then has the exclusive major junior rights to that player. Teams are allowed 50 players on their list at any one time. The team that drafts a player has exclusive rights to that player within the league—either the player plays for the team that drafted him, or he does not play in the league.[114]

The team holds the rights to that player for as long as the player is of junior age. The player himself cannot voluntarily move between teams, although the team can initiate a transaction by trading or releasing a player. Trades do, in fact, frequently occur. Many of these trades occur just before the mid-January trading deadline in CHL leagues, with some seasons seeing as many of 10% of a league's players changing teams during this period. Mid-season trades can be particularly damaging to players still in high school (of whom there are many in the CHL leagues), as it necessitates a transfer to a new high school, in a different city, partway through the school year.

Players not wishing to play for the team that owns their rights have few options. In essence, the only options for the player are either to refuse to report to the team that drafted him and attempt to force a trade to a preferred team, or to elect not to play major junior hockey.[115] With the former option, few players, other than perhaps stars, have sufficient bargaining power to force a trade. While a player like Eric Lindros—who ultimately became a Hall of Fame NHL player—was successful using this strategy in the OHL in 1989, it is not a realistic option for most players.[116]

With the latter option, players who do not play major junior still have, in theory, US college hockey as a possible alternative. In practice, however, the great majority of elite Canadian players do not take this route. There are several possible reasons for this. The first is simply tradition: junior hockey has been an important part of the social fabric of Canadian communities for over a century, and for many Canadian boys and their families, it is unquestioningly seen as the only route to the NHL. Second, for those players who do not have the interest and/or the aptitude for post-secondary education in a US college environment, junior hockey is the only real alternative. A third factor is that major junior hockey offers the attraction of allowing the elite player to experience a high level of play at a younger age. High-quality players often begin their major junior careers at 16 years of age. Playing US college hockey requires the player to wait until they are at least 18 (i.e., until they graduate from high school), without providing any assurance that they will actually receive a scholarship offer when they do reach that age. Furthermore, players cannot play major junior hockey in the interim. Under National Collegiate Athletics Association (NCAA) regulations, any player who has played major junior hockey is ineligible to play NCAA hockey.[117] In general, then, junior hockey allows a more immediate entry into high-level hockey and thus maintains a strong appeal for many players.

The overwhelming evidence supports the notion that most elite, high-potential Canadian players do not see US college hockey as an option. For example, in the 2020 NHL draft, of the 22 Canadian-born players selected in the first two rounds, 21 of them played CHL hockey; in the 2019 draft, 18 of the 19 Canadians selected in the first two rounds were from CHL clubs.

With most young Canadian hockey players and their families apparently seeing the CHL as the only route to the NHL, enormous power is automatically conferred on the CHL leagues to do largely as they please with respect to their internal player allocation systems. The draft system these leagues employ ensures that member teams do not compete with each other to attract players—in economic terms, it grants the team that drafted the player a monopsony.

Removing from players the ability to choose where they will play is profit-enhancing for teams and leagues. One effect is that it ensures that leagues can locate franchises in cities that generally do not produce junior hockey players, but are nevertheless cities that offer strong revenue potential—cities (all in the WHL) such as Portland, Spokane and Seattle. These cities are very important to the league in a revenue sense. Without the league controlling player allocations, teams in these three places would have difficulty attracting young, high school–age players from Canada.

The monopsonistic player allocation system also has other benefits for leagues. For example, it has the potential to increase competitive balance within a league, which, in turn, enhances the overall revenue-generating capacity of the league. Perhaps most importantly, it reduces recruiting costs and avoids multiple teams in the same league competing against each other for the services of any given player. An orderly allocation of players to teams, with players having no choice but to play for the team that drafts them, effectively eliminates any bargaining power a player and his family may have with the team, and sets up a straight take-it-or-leave-it scenario.

The control over player movement in the CHL is even more absolute than in pro leagues. While all major pro leagues in North America also employ a draft system for incoming players, this is done only with the consent (through collective bargaining agreements—CBAS) of players' unions. Without this player consent, the drafts would be subject to prosecution under US antitrust law. The players agree to the draft as a bargaining concession to owners, in return for players gaining mobility rights (i.e., free agency) later in their careers. This mobility not only increases players' bargaining power, thus allowing them to capture a much greater share of the revenue they generate, but it also allows players to better serve their non-pecuniary interests by allowing them, for example, to have some choice as to the city in which they and their families will live. In junior hockey, however, there are no players' unions and no CBAS, allowing CHL leagues to unilaterally impose their player allocation and mobility rules.

Even the NCAA in the US—the college athletics governing body that itself has come under intense criticism over the years for monopsonistic practices toward its players—doesn't go nearly as far the CHL leagues. In the NCAA, there is no draft, so athletes still have the right to select the school of their choice. That choice may be influenced by many factors—the quality of the team's coaching staff, the opportunity to play regularly, the distance from the player's hometown and so on. If he so chooses, a sought-after high school football player from, say, Columbus, Ohio, is free to attend his hometown school of Ohio State University, and doesn't have to be concerned about being drafted by a school in California or Texas or Florida, et cetera.

The CHL leagues offer athletes and their families no such choice. The draft systems that these leagues employ results in incoming 16-year-old players being involuntarily relocated to clubs not of their choice, often far from their childhood homes, and all the while still being minors in a legal sense. This is particularly a problem in the WHL, where the league's geographic sprawl across the four western provinces and the US Pacific Northwest can mean that players are living hundreds, if not thousands, of kilometres from their families.

In most cases, there are reasonable alternatives to forcing players to endure these long-distance relocations; it's just that leagues like the WHL refuse to entertain these alternatives. The WHL's geographic footprint is now so extensive that no incoming player should ever have to move that far from home in order to play in the league—BC, Alberta and Saskatchewan all have five franchises each, while Manitoba has two. And yet, this doesn't happen. Long-distance relocations are the norm, not the exception.

As an example, take the WHL's 2021 crop of bantam-age players. The top prospect in the group was considered to be Berkly Catton, a 15-year-old from Saskatoon. However, rather than being able to choose to play for his hometown Blades or, for that matter, any one of the other four WHL franchises in Saskatchewan, Catton was instead subjected to the WHL draft system, where he was chosen first overall in 2021 by the Spokane Chiefs, thereby forcing a move of more than 1,200 kilometres—to another country, no less—for the high-schooler.

In fact, of the 16 players selected in the 2021 draft whose hometown was Saskatoon, only one was selected by the local Blades, and only three others were selected by another Saskatchewan-based club. Clubs in far away BC and Washington state accounted for seven of the city's 16 players drafted. But the movement went the other way as well. Of the 10 players the Blades drafted in 2021, almost half (four) were from BC, requiring of these players a long-distance move in the opposite direction.

The 2021 draft was in no way an anomaly. One year earlier, Connor Bedard of North Vancouver was the top bantam prospect, but instead of being able to remain in the Lower Mainland with the Vancouver Giants—or even being able to remain in BC with one of the league's four other franchises—he was forced to move 1,700 kilometres east to endure the frigid Prairie winters, when the Regina Pats made the 14-year-old the first overall selection in the draft.

Over 30 years of evidence suggests that elite bantam-age players almost never see the NCAA as an alternative to the WHL. Since the inception of the WHL bantam draft in 1990,[118] there has been only one instance of the first-overall pick in the draft spurning the WHL for NCAA hockey. That occurred in 2003, when the Tri-City Americans drafted a player out of Winnipeg. Instead of making the 1,800-kilometre move to Kennewick, Washington, the player waited two years and finished high school, then played college hockey at the University of North Dakota, just 235 kilometres from his home in Winnipeg. The player in question was Jonathan Toews, who went on to become one of the greatest NHLers of his era, captaining the Chicago Blackhawks to three Stanley Cups and helping lead Team Canada to a gold medal in the 2010 Winter Olympics.

Toews took somewhat of a risk by waiting two years and hoping for a US college scholarship, rather than playing junior hockey more immediately. However, for someone of his immense talent, this was undoubtedly a fairly low risk. For most other players, though, this is not a risk they are willing to take, and as evidenced by the data, they strongly gravitate to the more immediate and certain opportunity.

The mandatory, large-scale relocations of high school–age boys that is so prevalent in the WHL inherently impose costs on players and their families. Such a system reduces parental and other family influences at a time when these boys are particularly vulnerable and impressionable. With many players living far from home, family life is disrupted, parental monitoring—of not only the child, but also the team and its coaches—is reduced and parental enjoyment is lessened in the sense they are less able to regularly watch their children play.

Furthermore, the long regular season in the wHL, the large distances between cities and the use of buses as the primary mode of travel mean that players are often "on the road" and away from even their adopted "homes" for considerable amounts of time. For those players still in high school, academic performance will inevitably decline for many. In their book *Hockey Night in Canada: Sport, Identities, and Cultural Politics*, academics Richard Gruneau and David Whitson argue that only the most extraordinarily disciplined junior players can make progress in school. They quote a Portland Winterhawks (of the wHL) player as saying that team management always emphasizes a hockey-first approach, and with players living away from home and beyond the direct influence of their parents, education often suffers as a result.

Other academics have been critical of the social and cultural milieu of junior hockey and its effects on impressionable boys and young men. Sociologist Kristi Allain argues that the representation of Canadian dominant hockey masculinity within the cHL has the effect of marginalizing European players. She contends that this masculinity, which emphasizes aggression, hard hitting and a highly physical type of play, is portrayed in the cHL as the only legitimate form of masculinity, and is contrasted with the undesirable masculinity of the "soft" Europeans.

Journalist Laura Robinson goes even further and argues in her book *Crossing the Line* that junior hockey is plagued by a wide range of abuses and social dysfunctions—the existence of a "rape culture" within the sport; instances of the sexual assault of young women by players, with teams then rallying to protect these players from prosecution, often by discrediting the accuser; degrading and often sexually violent hazing rituals, et cetera—all of which are given a greater chance to flourish and develop when the adolescent males are physically removed from their home environment.

One of the impetuses for her book was the 1997 conviction of Graham James on charges that he sexually abused one of his (underage) players when James was coach of the WHL's Swift Current Broncos. The abuse charges shocked the country; James had been a hockey celebrity in Canada, having led the Broncos to a Memorial Cup championship in 1989, less than three years after the club had suffered a devastating bus crash on an icy Saskatchewan highway while travelling to a game in Regina. Four Bronco players died in the crash, and James was hailed for his leadership in helping the club and city recover from the tragedy. He was even named "Man of the Year" in 1989 by the influential publication the *Hockey News*.

The player who levelled the charges was Sheldon Kennedy, saying that James abused him hundreds of times, beginning when Kennedy was in his mid-teens. Kennedy, who would go on to play over 300 games in the NHL, was a Broncos hero at the time of the abuse—he was a survivor of the 1986 bus crash[119] and three years later was the leading goal scorer on the 1989 Memorial Cup–winning team. His story garnered international attention, with Kennedy appearing on Oprah Winfrey's TV program, and also testifying before the International Olympic Committee and a US Senate committee.

The allegations against James continued even after he went to prison in 1997. A 1999 civil suit by an unnamed Swift Current teammate of Kennedy's was ultimately settled out of court three years later. The suit named not only James, but also the WHL, the CHL and the Broncos hockey club, amongst many others. Then, in

2010, former NHL star Theoren Fleury revealed that he too had been repeatedly sexually assaulted by James, when both were with the WHL's Moose Jaw Warriors in the mid-1980s. James was convicted on these new charges and ended up returning to prison for two more years.

While child sexual abuse can happen anywhere and in any setting, major junior hockey, with so many underage boys playing for teams far from home, would seem to provide a climate that is ripe for abuse to occur. As Sheldon Kennedy told the *Ottawa Citizen* at the time of James's conviction, "The coach is so respected. Your parents send you away and say, 'Do what he says.' At that age, you listen. That's your first step if you want to play pro."

ECONOMIC EXPLOITATION

In addition to the high social costs that CHL players and their families potentially face, they are also subject to large-scale economic exploitation. While the on-ice talents of CHL players can generate yearly multi-million-dollar revenues for CHL teams, very little of this revenue flows to players or their families, resulting in a substantial wealth transfer away from players and to team owners.

To determine the magnitude of the economic exploitation that major junior hockey players suffer, it is first necessary to know the level of revenues generated by CHL teams. This step is not as easy as it may first appear, since most CHL teams are operated as privately owned businesses and are therefore not required to publicly report their financial information. Furthermore, junior hockey owners, like their counterparts in professional sports, are notoriously guarded and secretive about their financial affairs. Thus, any insight into the financial aspects of these firms must be ascertained through estimation.

Gate receipts compose the majority of revenues for CHL teams, and such receipts can be estimated using publicly available data. For example, take the WHL's 2017–18 season, the last season the league played a 72-game schedule (it's now 68), and just before the onset of COVID. Attendance that year averaged 4,415 fans per game across the league. With each team playing 36 home games during the regular season, and conservatively assuming an average ticket price of $25, the average WHL team would have earned about $3.9 million in regular-season gate revenues. In addition, each team played an average of four home playoff games that season, adding a further $400,000 in revenue, and making the average club's combined regular season and playoffs gate receipts about $4.3 million. This figure does not include sponsorship revenues, media-rights revenues or concessions/parking revenues, all of which are difficult to estimate without direct access to team financial information, but are undoubtedly worth several hundred thousand dollars. As well, for teams whose attendance was well above the league average (of 4,415) that season—like Edmonton at 8,154 and Calgary at 7,570— team revenues could easily exceed $7 million.

Since the talents and skills of a club's players are a major factor in generating these revenues, basic economics tells us that the players should commensurately receive a portion of these revenues. In the NHL, for example, the collective bargaining agreement between the owners and players calls for players, as a group, to receive 50% of the league's revenues. In essence, what this means is that NHL clubs allocate 50% of total revenues to players and still generally make a profit. The 50% that does not go to players must be used to pay all other expenses first, with any residual then going to owners in the form of profits. Presumably, the league would not negotiate such a percentage going to players if most or all teams in the league were unable to make reasonable profits.

Using this 50% split, and applying it to the estimated $4.3 million revenue figure, players should collectively capture about $2.15 million per year in remuneration, or, given a 20-player roster, about $108,000 per player. However, not all players are equal, and some players will capture a disproportionate share of this amount, since player productivity (and hence salaries) are not uniformly distributed across all players. For example, the NHL CBA allows individual star players to capture up to 20% of their team's total payroll (and many have, over the years). Applied to the WHL, this would mean that some star players could have values of about $430,000 (i.e., 20% of $2.15 million) per year to their team.

Compare these figures with the actual compensation that players receive. WHL players receive no salary, and although they do receive a weekly "allowance," this amount is very small (usually less than $100). Furthermore, WHL teams are forbidden by league policy to even provide disability insurance to their players.

The only significant compensation that a player may receive is through the educational scholarships that each CHL league maintains.[120] For example, the WHL's scholarship program will pay for a year of post-secondary education (tuition and books) for each year the player plays in the league. For those players who take advantage of this program (not all do), its monetary value is probably less than $10,000 per year—an amount that is still dramatically lower than many players' economic value to their teams. Furthermore, the scholarship is only available to those players who do not sign a professional contract, further reducing the universality of the program.

Taking the $108,000 estimate of what the average player should be compensated, and optimistically assuming the player receives about $10,000 in compensation (through the education program and through the weekly allowances), there is still a net wealth transfer of almost $100,000 (per year, per player) away from the player and his family, and to the team owner. Over a typical three-year junior hockey career, the total transfer would thus be around $300,000. For top-tier players, whose gross value could exceed $400,000 per year, the educational scholarship is almost completely insignificant, relative to the value these players are generating for their team.

These large wealth transfers from players to team owners are driven by the cartel-like policies of the owners, primarily the unspoken agreement amongst owners to, essentially, not pay their players. As with any cartel, economic theory predicts that there will be an incentive amongst cartel members to "cheat" on the agreement, particularly when a superstar player could have a yearly value to a team that exceeds $400,000. Thus, owners might be willing to make covert payments to certain players as inducements to play for that team (as opposed to, say, playing NCAA hockey). A good example is Patrick Kane, who was the first-overall pick in the 2007 NHL draft. Kane played one year in the OHL, for the London Knights, won the league scoring title and was as close to a superstar as one could envision in junior hockey. Some media reports suggested that the Knights made covert payments to Kane of approximately $100,000 (about $150,000 in 2023 dollars). If this were true, and if the estimates in this chapter of a superstar's value are reasonably accurate, the Knights would still be getting a good deal, paying Kane an amount that was still less than half his value to the team. However, even if a few superstars may be able to extract these clandestine (i.e., outside of league rules) payments from junior teams, most players simply do not have such bargaining power, and are essentially left with a take-it-or-leave-it stance from team owners.

INERTIA

Half a century ago, professors Kidd and Macfarlane's book *The Death of Hockey* excoriated the state of junior hockey at that time. The core element of their argument—that junior hockey players are exploited economically and socially—remains as true today as it was then. Junior hockey players are still not paid, and player allocation systems still force many high school–age boys to relocate far from home.

The CHL and its owners have used various justifications over the years for resisting meaningful change. One argument, espoused by WHL commissioner Ron Robison, is that players are not paid because junior hockey is an "apprenticeship" for the NHL. However, the idea that most players will ever recoup their earnings losses in junior hockey by later earning NHL salaries is deeply fallacious and misleading. The reality is that most CHL players, even the elite players, do not play in the NHL, and the economic exploitation they incur in the CHL is not recoverable.

CHL leagues also justify their player allocation systems and their economic exploitation on the grounds that such monopsonistic practices are needed to protect small-market teams in the league. This argument, which has been made by professional leagues for decades, lacks economic validity. Quite simply, if small-market franchises are financially unable to compensate their players at the appropriate level, then these franchises should either fold or relocate, or they should be subsidized (through, perhaps, a revenue-sharing scheme) by their larger-market (and more profitable) partners in the league—it is not the role of players and their families to provide such a subsidy.

There has been no serious efforts by players and/or their families to act collectively—for example, to form a players' association—even though it is the players and their families who directly bear the cost of the monopsonistic practices. Because the potential monetary payoff from achieving an NHL career is so large, many players and their families are no doubt lured by such a prospect, even though so few CHL players ever actually achieve an NHL career. Players and their families may be unwilling to challenge the CHL, for fear that such challenges could result in some type of retribution. Such retribution (like, for example, the blacklisting of "troublemakers") could not only jeopardize the player's CHL career, but conceivably jeopardize any possible NHL aspirations the player may have. Furthermore, collective action—such as some type of unionization—is difficult to organize because CHL careers are very short (usually three years, at most), with large-scale player turnover occurring each year.

Taken as a whole, and looking through the years, junior hockey has seemingly always been in the spotlight, most often for the wrong reasons. That continues to this day. In 2014, a group of former CHL players filed a $180 million lawsuit against the CHL, arguing that players should be treated as employees and therefore be paid at least a minimum wage. As would be expected, the CHL clubs pleaded poverty (as their professional counterparts have often done over the years), and even opened their financial statements (as required by a court ruling) to show that many clubs were financially incapable of paying. The fallacy of using these statements as evidence of financial well-being is that there are many (perfectly legal) ways for clubs to hide profits. Paul Beeston, former Toronto Blue Jays president and CEO, said it best over 30 years ago: "Anyone who quotes profits of a baseball club is missing the point. Under generally accepted accounting principles, I can turn a $4 million profit into a $2 million loss, and I can get every national accounting firm to agree with me."

For those economists who study the spectator-sport business, the Beeston quote is legendary. It also directly relates to the minimum-wage suit. Forensic accountant Rob Smith, who was retained by the plaintiffs in the case, pointed out in his report, for example, that the

Red Deer Rebels' 2016 financial statements included as an expense $1.49 million in unexplained "management fees." Smith surmised that a significant amount of the fees was likely a distribution of profits to owners. When contacted for clarification by the *Hockey News*, Rebels owner Brent Sutter did not respond.

Smith's report also pointed out another incongruence. The Prince George Cougars sold for $6.4 million in 2014, despite their financial statements showing a combined loss of $2.1 million in the three previous years. Another WHL franchise, the Regina Pats, sold about the same time, for $6.8 million, all the while reporting combined losses of $605,000 during the previous three seasons. On the surface, these sales defy basic financial logic—why would someone pay over $6 million for an asset (the club), when that asset consistently loses money? The answer? The financial statements are obviously not reflecting the true profitability of the club. In the Paul Beeston sense, profits are being (legally) turned into "losses." CHL team owners, like their NHL brethren, have a strong interest in making their businesses appear less profitable than they actually are. In the sports business, high profits attract unwanted attention—players want to be paid more (or at all), local governments are more reluctant to provide public funds for new arenas, and so on.

In the end, the players in the class-action suit won the battle but lost the war. In 2020, the two sides agreed to a $30 million settlement, vindicating the players' basic claims that they were employees. But there was a downside to the win. During the five-year period that the case was in progress, every Canadian province passed legislation that exempted major junior players from employment standards laws, effectively prohibiting any such lawsuits from arising in the future. It was a big legislative win for the CHL and its member clubs, and illustrated the enormous lobbying power of junior hockey owners in their local communities.

Ironically, just as the minimum wage class-action suit was resolved in early 2020, the CHL faced yet another challenge. In December of that year, a group of former OHL players filed suit, claiming they were victims of horrific physical and sexual abuse during hazing rituals with their teams.

These are just the latest chapters in the controversial history of junior hockey—the lawsuits, the scandals and the fervent criticisms of its policies are the threads that bind together the eras. What is remarkable, though, is that through the years, junior hockey and its NHL collaborators have shown an uncanny ability to withstand such controversies, and continue unabated, and largely unfazed, by outside pressures.

EPILOGUE:
THE DISNEYFICATION OF AN UNTIDY HISTORY

IT WAS A 15-YEAR SPAN—from the late 1960s to the early 1980s—that changed the game of hockey in Canada forever. It was a period of great tumult, unlike anything the game has seen before or since. This was by no means a natural evolution of the game. Evolutionary changes tend to be organic, incremental, barely perceptible at the time. In contrast, this change was the outcome of specific and deliberate business decisions of the NHL, decisions that would upend the very foundations of the game.

The NHL's 1967 expansion and corresponding abolishment of the sponsorship system were the primary catalysts. Many of the transformative changes that have occurred in hockey over the past half century have, in some form or another, had their roots here.

Expansion was a logical response to the economic environment at the time; with only four US–based franchises, the NHL was falling behind other major pro leagues in the efforts to capture the growing discretionary budget of the postwar consumer. Adding new franchises not only brought immediate windfall expansion fees to the existing owners, but also increased the league's overall revenue

base into the future. In the NHL's mind, expansion was also needed
to pre-empt the entry of a rival league, something about which the
NHL had become increasingly concerned, given the recent emergence
of the AFL and ABA to challenge the NFL and NBA, respectively.

However, the history-altering significance of expansion had less
to do with the fact that more teams were added to the league, and
more to do with the NHL using expansion as a justification for abolishing the sponsorship system in favour of the draft system. It was
this that truly changed the game forever.

The NHL's argument was that continuing the sponsorship system
would have put the six new expansion clubs of 1967 at a large disadvantage, since, unlike the Original Six clubs, the expansion teams
did not have a network of clubs in the Canadian amateur system.
The argument, though, doesn't withstand scrutiny, since the NHL
could have required existing clubs to divest themselves of some of
their amateur teams, allowing expansion clubs to build their own
networks. The real problem with the sponsorship system for the
NHL was it involved its member clubs potentially competing against
each other to sign young amateur players, as was so starkly illustrated by the recruiting of 14-year-old Bobby Orr in 1962.

Ending the sponsorship system signalled the NHL's definitive move
to a US-style league-management system. Both the NFL and the NBA had
long had drafts. In contrast, the NHL's sponsorship system had more
closely resembled a European model of player acquisition, where
amateur players were free to sign their first contract with any club. By
introducing the draft system, individual NHL clubs were given monopsony power over the players they drafted, giving clubs the exclusive
right to bargain with those players, and eliminating the ability of
players and their families to trade one offer off against another.

The most direct and obvious impact was on the Canadian amateur hockey system itself. With the NHL divesting itself of direct

control, junior hockey quickly consolidated itself nationally into only three elite leagues, and within a decade these leagues had left the amateur system of the CAHA altogether to form the Canadian Hockey League (CHL). But instead of this change benefiting junior players, it actually further increased their exploitation. Prospective junior players became subject to league drafts when they were 15 years old, giving them no choice in where they would play. To add insult to injury, they were compensated at levels far below their economic value to teams, similar to what pro players suffered in the pre–free agency era.

At the NHL level, the Montreal Canadiens franchise almost singularly bore the brunt of the change. No longer able to freely sign young incoming francophone players, the draft system spelled the beginning of the end for the club's on-ice dominance. By the early 1980s, the venerable club was no longer "special"—the last of the sponsorship-era francophone players were gone, and more recently formed clubs like the New York Islanders and Edmonton Oilers had become the dominant forces in the league, between the two of them winning nine Stanley Cups in 11 seasons.

But the end of the sponsorship system also cost the Canadiens their unique identity within the North American sport scene. Throughout the mid–20th century, when Quebec society, still very insular, was increasingly talking about sovereignty and francophone self-determination, the Canadiens not only represented a point of great pride for French Canadians, but also exemplified a resistance to the outside, anglocentric world. Their roster, then dominated by francophone players, represented an unparalleled (at least in North America) synergy between a sport club and the social, cultural and linguistic makeup of the community in which it operated.

The draft system eroded this synergy—albeit gradually. But it also induced a domino effect for francophone *players*. With the Canadiens losing the ability to control these players, and with rapid NHL expansion in the US, it wasn't long before most francophones in the league were playing in an anglo environment, either in the US or in English Canada. They often faced language and cultural barriers, ultimately making them vulnerable to discriminatory treatment. This all came at a time of rising French-English tensions in Canada—the FLQ crisis in 1970, the 1976 election of the Parti Québécois's René Lévesque as premier, and the first of two sovereignty referendums in 1980. The NHL at that time was a league (outside of the Canadiens and, briefly, the Nordiques) that was dominated almost entirely by English Canadians—as GMS, as coaches and as players—making the transition of francophones to clubs outside Quebec particularly difficult for many of these players.

There was also an undercurrent of Canadian regional politics a decade later, when the Battle of Alberta took centre stage. In the midst of Alberta premier Peter Lougheed's bold moves to take on Ottawa and the Pierre Trudeau Liberal government, and driven by a growing sense of Western alienation, the Battle of Alberta represented hockey's version of a new, much more assertive Alberta, a province no longer willing to play a "poor cousin" role to the Central Canadian power brokers.

The parallels between politics and hockey in Western Canada were not merely coincidental. The roots of the Battle of Alberta can ultimately be traced back to the NHL's 1967 expansion, when all six of the new teams were based in US cities, and when the growing and hockey-mad Canadian Prairie cities of Edmonton, Calgary and Winnipeg were never given any serious consideration for expansion franchises. Nor were they given any serious consideration in the smaller subsequent NHL expansions of 1970 and 1972.

Hockey's version of an anti-Eastern, anti-establishment mindset developed, eventually leading to the formation of the WHA, with

Winnipeg, Edmonton and Calgary being flagship charter franchises in the renegade league. While the original Calgary franchise (the Broncos) never did play a game in the new league (largely due to ownership issues), the Jets' and Oilers' success in the WHA paved the way not only for their absorption into the NHL in 1979, but also for Calgary being viewed as a viable NHL market.

In turn, the formation of the WHA was a primary catalyst for massive changes in the players' market. The WHA's pursuit of Europeans forever changed the style of play in North American hockey, moving the game away from its physical, often brutal history, and toward a flowing, offensive-minded style, emphasizing skill. Over the ensuing half century, Canadian players saw their dominance of the game decline dramatically, going from composing almost 100% of the players in the league in 1967, down to under 45% today. The modern-day emphasis on speed and skill also changed the geographic source of NHLers within Canada. More advanced skills require higher-level training methods and technologies, better coaching and a more intense competitive environment—all of which are more likely found in highly populated urban areas, in contrast to the hinterlands of rural Saskatchewan and Northern Ontario, the primary sources of Canadian hockey talent in eras past.

The disruptive and transformative changes that occurred in the years following the Toronto Maple Leafs' magical 1967 Stanley Cup win have long filtered through the system, and a "new normal" in hockey has now been in place for decades. The NHL of today is simply part of the broad American commercial entertainment system—an Americentric league that just happens to have a handful of franchises in Canada. The league's Canadian social, political and cultural roots seem to have long been forgotten. The news of today is rarely placed in any type of historical context. The Montreal Canadiens advanced all the way to the Stanley Cup final in 2021 (albeit under a COVID-induced modified playoff system whose integrity could be questioned). It was the club's first appearance in the final since 1993. The fact that the iconic franchise had a unique place in North American sports seemed to be a near-forgotten storyline. A similar situation happened the following (2021–22) season, when the club finished, for the first time since 1940, with the worst-overall record in the NHL—the 32nd-best team in a 32-team league. There was a time when the hockey world would have been shocked—an event equivalent to, say, Manchester United finishing last in the English Premier League, or Real Madrid finishing last in La Liga. Iconic franchises are not supposed to tumble this far.

The 2021–22 season was significant also because the Flames and Oilers met in the playoffs for the first time since 1991, a 31-year gap. But this Battle of Alberta bore little resemblance to the 1980s version. This wasn't about two upstart clubs (one from a renegade league), from an upstart province, challenging both the hockey and political establishments. Now, the Flames versus the Oilers is just a typical regional rivalry between two teams in geographic proximity to each other, like dozens of other rivalries across the sports world. In the 1980s, it was more than just the Flames versus the Oilers, it was the Flames *and* Oilers together, versus the establishment.

Canada is to hockey what England is to soccer—the birthplace of the modern game, and its spiritual home. But the professional game developed much differently in Canada than in England. In the latter, despite the massive commercialization of the game over the last several decades, the community, grassroots foundations of most pro teams remain strong. With an open-league system, clubs are natural, organic outgrowths of their communities, with many players traditionally having ties to the surrounding region. The significance of soccer to English culture was reinforced by pro leagues being domestic, not transnational.

In contrast, pro hockey in Canada quickly became transnational; when the Boston Bruins joined what was then the four-team, all-Canadian NHL in 1924, it was the beginning of the gradual Americanization of the game. In five years, the NHL added five more US–based teams, leaving the league with six out of its 10 franchises in the US, and forever changing the face of the game.

Hockey was, and still is, a niche sport in the US, but owners soon realized that small market shares in large (US) markets were more lucrative than large market shares in small (Canadian) markets. In short, Canada supplied the players, and the US provided the spectator dollars. The NHL's 1947 agreement with the CAHA codified the NHL's access to, and control of, the large Canadian amateur talent pool, something that was particularly important to US–based clubs, who had no homegrown talent of their own to draw from.

With head offices in New York, a New York City–born commissioner for the past 30 years, and 25 of its 32 franchises in the US, today's NHL is very much an American institution. With its slick marketing and branding, and carefully scripted messaging, it presents a highly sanitized and palatable product for its consumers, free of any uncomfortable and untidy Canadian historical narratives on hockey—in essence, a Disneyfied version of the game of hockey.[121]

For Canadians, though, it's not just about the game on the ice. It's about how hockey has been inextricably intertwined with everything else Canadian—its social and cultural dynamics, its politics, its economy and its distinct regions. The stories in this book have attempted to highlight some of these, but there are certainly many more. In Canada, hockey goes far beyond mere entertainment. It is the essence of the country itself.

ACKNOWLEDGEMENTS

As always, a project of this nature is only possible with the assistance and support of many individuals.

Most importantly, I wish to thank my wife, Susan Griffin. She has always been unfailingly supportive of my career, and has made many sacrifices for me throughout the years. Without her, this book would not have been possible. To Susan, I owe a tremendous amount.

On the professional side, I have been positively influenced over the years by many colleagues and co-authors in sports economics, in both North America and Europe. They have always been important sources of intellectual engagement and support.

More specifically, some of my early work pertaining to this book was presented at a 2018 colloquium of the Canadian Studies program at the University of California, Berkeley. I'd like to thank the attendees at that invited lecture for their helpful comments and feedback.

I am also particularly grateful to the folks at Douglas & McIntyre, who showed confidence in the book, and whose support has been invaluable. Gratitude is also owed to my editor, Derek Fairbridge. Derek's deep knowledge of hockey history fit perfectly with the book's content. His detailed comments and suggestions were always spot-on and have made this a better book.

NOTES

1   The Chicago NHL team was originally known as the Black Hawks (two words), but the name was changed in 1986 to Blackhawks.

2   While the term *original* was a misnomer—of the six teams, only the Canadiens and Leafs (known then as the Toronto Arenas) were charter NHL members in the league's founding year of 1917—it has come to represent a period when the modern NHL game formed its true roots, centred on six stable franchises that survived the league's more uncertain early years.

3   The six expansion franchises were the Philadelphia Flyers, Pittsburgh Penguins, Minnesota North Stars, St. Louis Blues, Los Angeles Kings and California Seals.

4   To avoid potential antitrust implications in the US, the absorption of the four WHA teams into the NHL (the Hartford Whalers were the sole US team of the four) was officially referred to as an NHL "expansion," rather than a merger of the two leagues.

5   Technically, the NHL's first draft was in 1963, but the only players eligible for that draft were those not already owned by an NHL team (through the sponsorship system). It wasn't until the 1969 draft that the effects of the sponsorship system had fully dissipated—i.e., that all draft-age players were available. For that reason, the 1969 draft is considered the NHL's first "true" draft.

6   Of course, the French and English were settling on land already inhabited by Indigenous peoples.

7   Organization of the Petroleum Exporting Countries.

8   Prior to the stagflation years, most macroeconomists believed there was a trade-off between unemployment and inflation—so, if unemployment was low, inflation would be high, and vice versa. The presence of the twin evils of high unemployment and high inflation caught economists off guard, seemingly unaware as to how to deal with the problem.

9   The Stanley Cup was first awarded in 1893 as a "challenge" trophy for Canadian amateur hockey teams and leagues. The NHL essentially commandeered the trophy as its own in 1926.

10 While there were francophone minority populations in New Brunswick and other provinces, these populations tended to be small compared with that found in Quebec.

11 The Canadiens maintained a delicate balance of players during that era: while most of the stars were French Canadian, the club still had a significant group of anglophone players, such as Doug Harvey and Dickie Moore, and coach Toe Blake.

12 The Bretton Woods Agreement was signed by all 44 allies, including Canada, in anticipation of both the end of the Second World War and the subsequent efforts to begin to rebuild the world economy.

13   While the AFL and NFL agreed to a merger in 1966, it did not become official until
     1969. In the meantime, the AFL expanded to Miami (Dolphins) and Cincinnati
     (Bengals), so it was actually 10 AFL teams that joined the NFL.
14   Major League Baseball also faced a potential competitive threat in the form of
     the Continental Baseball League, which was scheduled to begin play in 1960, but
     folded before its first season. More discussion of the league is provided in Chapter 3.
15   More detail on the sponsorship system is provided in Chapter 5.
16   The NFL introduced its draft in 1936 and the NBA in 1946. Major League Baseball
     was the last of the Big Four to implement a draft, doing so in 1965.
17   There have been a few instances where existing clubs have voluntarily agreed
     to allow a competitor franchise (either an expansion club or a relocated team)
     to enter their territory in return for monetary compensation. In 1972, for exam-
     ple, the NHL, concerned that the new WHA would put a franchise on Long Island,
     granted an expansion franchise to the New York Islanders, after the Islanders'
     owners agreed to pay the Rangers a reported $4 million. In 1982, the new Bren-
     dan Byrne Arena in East Rutherford, New Jersey, was seeking an NHL franchise as
     a tenant. The New York Rangers were reported as interested in making the move
     across the Hudson River, but ultimately chose not to, and the flailing Colorado
     Rockies franchise was allowed to relocate to New Jersey to become the Devils. The
     Devils move encroached on the territory of three teams—the Rangers, Islanders
     and Philadelphia Flyers—who were paid, collectively, a reported $30 million as
     compensation by the Devils.
18   Moving to an international league would also decrease a player's exposure in
     North America, reducing endorsement opportunities.
19   This was no more evident than when the energy drink manufacturer Red Bull
     bought a small club in Leipzig, Germany, in 2009 and converted the club into a
     marketing behemoth for its brand. Most fans in Germany were outraged at the
     flagrant corporatization of the club and the seeming disregard for the organic
     and grassroots foundations of professional soccer in that country.
20   Because European clubs have evolved from "bottom-up," organic beginnings,
     rather than from the "top-down" franchise model of modern North American
     leagues, fan support for individual European clubs can be highly fragmented
     along a wide array of factors not typically found in North America (except for
     the sponsorship-era Montreal Canadiens). For example, while Athletic Bilbao's
     strategy of employing only local players is an extreme case, grassroots connec-
     tions between sports clubs and the local communities in which they are located
     are generally commonplace in European soccer. These club-community synergies
     are built on a variety of factors, like ethnicity, politics, religion and social class.
21   The Big Four have always argued that draft systems were necessary to prevent
     large-revenue teams from signing all the best young talent. However, decades
     of research by sports economists have generally failed to find any evidence that
     draft systems improve competitive balance.

22　There were two francophones at the top of the 1971 draft class—Lafleur and Marcel Dionne. So, even if the Seals finished second-last, not last, Pollock was still assured of getting a premium francophone player. Like Lafleur, Dionne went on to have a Hall of Fame career.

23　Organizationally, the Canadiens imploded almost immediately after their 1979 Cup win. Pollock retired at only 52 years old, without explanation. His head coach, Scotty Bowman, desperately wanted the job, but Pollock instead chose Irving Grundman, his assistant GM. Grundman went on to be, in the minds of most Canadiens fans, a complete disaster.

24　As measured by games played.

25　The 1993 club did, however, have two notable francophones on the roster—goalie Patrick Roy won the Conn Smythe Trophy, and dependable, if not flashy, Guy Carbonneau was team captain.

26　Cloutier never played a game for the Black Hawks, and he would stay with the Nordiques throughout the remainder of the WHA's existence.

27　Pollock had actually stepped down as general manager at the end of the 1977–78 season, but stayed with club for one more season as a member of their board of directors.

28　The 1983–84 season was salvaged somewhat by the club going on a playoff run, surprisingly reaching the conference finals.

29　Ironically, Lafleur played his last two seasons (1989–90 and 1990–91) with the Nordiques. Nearing 40, his skills had greatly dimished, and he scored only 24 goals combined in those final seasons.

30　Terry Vaios Gitersos, in his 2011 Ph dissertation at the University of Western Ontario, analyzed French and English newspaper articles from the early 1980s and found the Nordiques were celebrated by sovereigntists as an institution that better reflected and advanced their cause, with the Canadiens seen as failing to keep current with the province's social and political changes.

31　As measured by games played, and as calculated by the author.

32　For those seven years, Bob Gainey was GM, from June 2003 to February 2010. His appointment as GM was no doubt an acknowledgement by the club of his critical role in the Canadiens' numerous Stanley Cup wins during the 1970s.

33　Two anglophones have been "interim" coaches of the Canadiens during that period: Bob Gainey (on two different occasions) and Randy Cunneyworth.

34　Ethnicity and language issues are clearly still important to the club. When the Canadiens appointed Randy Cunneyworth as interim coach in December 2011 to replace the fired Jacques Martin, fans and the media in Montreal railed against the selection because Cunneyworth, an English Canadian, could not speak French.

35　The Toronto Maple Leafs' financials were not reported at the congressional hearings. The Leafs were a subsidiary of the Maple Leaf Gardens Limited and the hockey club's financials were not separable from the parent company.

36   This was at a time when little was publicly known about the finances of NHL clubs; NHL teams, like those in the other major professional leagues, were privately held entities that closely guarded their finances. Other than during the congressional hearings of the 1950s, the finances of pro-sports teams remained largely a mystery until the early 1990s.

37   After *Financial World* went out of business in the late 1990s, *Forbes* magazine took over the pro-sports data stream. It still releases annual estimates of the finances of individual clubs.

38   In economic terms, team values represent what a buyer would pay for the club if it were sold today. These values are a function of the estimated future cash flows (discounted to current dollars) that the club is expected to generate.

39   Prior to Bettman's appointment, the NHL's top position was titled *president,* not *commissioner.*

40   The Carolina Hurricanes were initially based in Greensboro, North Carolina, for their first two years of existence, while they awaited the completion of a new arena in Raleigh.

41   Gillett also experienced the perils of being an outsider during his brief tenure (2008 to 2010) as co-owner of Liverpool FC of the English Premier League. Fans of the historic club were outraged by the American ownership of a British sports icon; Gillett was the target of frequent fan protests, and even reportedly received death threats.

42   The 1989–90 season is the first season for which the NHL Players' Association released official salary data for all players. Prior to that, any salary and payroll estimates reported in the media were unofficial and were often educated guesses.

43   The Canadian dollar increased from $0.62 USD in 2003 to $0.94 by 2007.

44   The points-percent reported here is for regulation time only so as to make it comparable through different eras as the rules regarding overtime and shootouts changed.

45   Two other professional leagues—both based in Western Canada—existed in the early part of the 20th century as competitors to the NHA/NHL. The Pacific Coast Hockey Association (PCHA) was founded by Ontarians Lester and Frank Patrick in 1911, while the Prairie-based Western Canada Hockey League (WCHL) began play in 1921. The PCHA started as a three-team league, with franchises in Vancouver, New Westminster and Victoria, but it, too, quickly Americanized, expanding to Portland in 1914 and Seattle in 1915. The league struggled for years, and was eventually absorbed by the WCHL in 1924, only to see that league fold two years later.

46   The 1947 agreement between the NHL and CAHA is discussed in much more detail in Chapter 5.

47   In Canada, there *were* Blacks playing the game, with Willie O'Ree from Nova Scotia being the first to ever play in the NHL (for the Boston Bruins in 1958). However, their numbers were small, and there was no critical mass of Black talent vying to play

in the NHL, unlike the situation at the time in the NFL, NBA and MLB with respect to American Blacks. The first Black American to play in the NHL was Val James in 1981–82 with Buffalo. His NHL career was short, only eleven games, with no goals and no assists. Over the next 15 years, there would only be two other Black Americans to play in the NHL.

48 Defencemen Pierre Pilote of the Black Hawks and Marcel Pronovost of the Red Wings were two other francophone NHL players from this era who had long and noteworthy careers, for teams other than the Canadiens. Both were inducted into the Hockey Hall of Fame—Pilote in 1975 and Pronovost in 1978.

49 Noel Picard's NHL career is probably best-remembered for his presence in the iconic photo of Bobby Orr flying through the air after scoring the Stanley Cup–winning goal in overtime in May 1970. The goal gave the Bruins a four-game sweep of the Blues, as Boston won their first Stanley Cup in 29 years. Picard was the player who tripped Orr in front of the Blues net, propelling Orr through the air as he scored. Picard can be seen in the photo as the Blues player dejectedly skating away, as a still-airborne Orr is already beginning his celebration.

50 As measured by games played, and as calculated by the author.

51 In 1979, the issues surrounding French Canadians playing "at home" in Quebec took a different turn when the Quebec Nordiques became one of four WHA teams to be absorbed into the NHL.

52 Marple's seminal research, which focused on the 1972–73 NHL season, was often overlooked and underappreciated. It was published in a French-language journal, perhaps part of the reason it tended to receive little attention amongst researchers in English Canada.

53 Lavoie et al also examined the NHL's entry draft and found that, for a given draft position, the future NHL performance of francophones exceeded that of anglophones, again a signal of possible discrimination against the former.

54 The Selke Trophy is an annual award given to the best defensive forward in the NHL, determined by a vote amongst members of the Professional Hockey Writers Association.

55 The measures were "adjusted plus/minus" and "short-handed participation."

56 In an updated follow-up study by Lavoie in 2003, he continued to find evidence of the underrepresentation of French Canadians, 16 years after he and his colleagues published their original study.

57 Again, the 1989–90 season was the first in which official salary data was available. Prior to that, any research relating to salaries was forced to use estimates obtained from media reports.

58 There was, however, one notable outlier to these generally consistent findings across studies. William Walsh of Victoria and his colleagues found no evidence of salary discrimination against French Canadians in their study of the 1989–90 season.

59   When the NHL faced competition from the rival WHA in the early 1970s, the plight
     of francophone players improved immensely, at least for a short few years—an
     outcome that could have been predicted from economic theory. During the WHA's
     seven-year existence, the proportion of hockey players in the NHL and WHA that were
     francophone increased from about 10% to about 15%, meaning the influx of new
     players into pro hockey was disproportionately French Canadian (as opposed to
     English Canadian, the only other player group at the time). It implies that French
     Canadians were underrepresented in the pre–WHA NHL—in essence, of the pool
     of players not in the pre–WHA NHL, French Canadians were of better average
     quality than were English Canadians. Then, when the WHA arrived and provided
     labour-market competition, French Canadians were a better "buy" than were
     English Canadians—they provided more talent for a given wage. Curiously, and
     perhaps surprisingly, even clubs based in English Canada became more likely to
     employ French Canadians during the early WHA years.

60   My research examining the decade of the 1990s showed that it wasn't just the
     ethnicity of the club's local fans that differed between English Canadian and
     US-based clubs; the ethnicity patterns of the coaches and GMS also differed. In
     particular, US clubs were somewhat less likely to employ English Canadians in
     these positions (and instead employed more Americans and French Canadians).
     By extension, then, it is theoretically possible that the underrepresentation of
     francophones on English Canadian teams is attributable to biases of those teams'
     coaches and GMS, rather than their fans. However, further analysis dispelled this
     possibility—English Canadian GMS and coaches of US-based teams were no less
     likely to employ francophone players than were their francophone and American
     counterparts on those US clubs. This is not surprising, since even if some English
     Canadian coaches and GMS did hold biases against French Canadian players, the
     intense competitive pressure of the NHL would prevent them from indulging
     these preferences for fear of lowering team quality and ultimately losing their jobs.

61   During that period, francophone Marc-André Fleury—a goaltender—also went
     first overall, going to the Pittsburgh Penguins.

62   St. Louis was elected to the Hockey Hall of Fame in 2018.

63   However, Martin St. Louis was not the only hidden gem on the University of Ver-
     mont teams of the mid-1990s. Goalie Tim Thomas, St. Louis's college teammate,
     gained little NHL interest coming out of Vermont, and started his professional career
     in Europe. He eventually found his way to the NHL and went on to have a stellar
     career, leading the Boston Bruins to the 2011 Stanley Cup, and winning the Conn
     Smythe Trophy in the process.

64   The one area where francophone players have made a mark in recent decades
     is at the goaltender position. During the 1990s and into the 2000s, players like
     Martin Brodeur, Jean-Sebastién Giguère, Marc-André Fleury and José Théodore
     were some of the best goalies in the game.

65 The percentage of Canadians identifying as being of European origin fell from 96% in 1970 to just 73% by 2016.

66 Calculated from the author's own analyses.

67 Historically, all four of the major North American leagues had some form of the reserve clause—a provision in players' contracts that allowed clubs perpetual control over that player and preventing them from voluntarily moving between clubs. Baseball players were the first to gain free-agency rights, in 1975, with the other three leagues eventually falling suit. Hockey players were the last to gain full free-agency rights, in 2005, an outcome of a labour dispute that saw the cancellation of the entire 2004–05 season.

68 Gilbert's popularity in New York was so great that he was the subject of a 1977 artwork by Andy Warhol.

69 Since NHL statistics do not recognize "own goals," the goal was officially credited to Calgary's Perry Berezan.

70 In 1941, Saskatchewan had the largest population of any of the four western provinces. Today, it has the smallest.

71 This growth trajectory for the two westernmost provinces continued. Today, BC and Alberta, combined, compose 25% of Canada's population.

72 Canada's high tariffs on many manufactured goods—invoked to protect Central Canadian manufacturing jobs from foreign competition—had long been one of the sore points for many Western Canadians. Tariffs raised the price of goods for Western Canadians (as they did for all Canadians), but most of the job-preserving benefits of the tariffs accrued to those in Central Canada. Western Canadians paid the price, but got few benefits, at least as they saw it. Conversely, the agriculture- and resource-based economics of the West were export-dependent and relied on open access to foreign markets. For these industries, a world of freer trade, not protectionism, was crucial.

73 This was the original version of the Oil Kings. The franchise relocated to Portland, Oregon, in 1976, where they became the Winterhawks. A second version of the Oil Kings, the relocated Flin Flon Bombers, played one season in Edmonton, 1978–79. The current Edmonton WHL team is the third version of the Oil Kings, entering the league as an expansion franchise in 2007.

74 While the Canadian Football League did occasionally bid away players from the NFL in the 1950s, it had no presence in any American market during that time, and therefore was not a true rival league.

75 The NBA's decrease was at least partially attributable to the fact the league was brand new in 1950, with the league experiencing serious difficulties early in the decade, and ultimately seeing a few franchises fold.

76 Established leagues would (and still do) grant "territorial rights" to its franchise owners. These territorial rights—covering roughly a 100-kilometre radius around a team's stadium, depending on the league—prevented other owners

within the league from relocating into the territory. So, for example, owners of small-market clubs, like, say the 1950s Kansas City A's in baseball, could not unilaterally choose to move the franchise to New York. While this often gave large-market owners windfall profits, because they were protected from any internal competition, it also provided an incentive for rival leagues to enter these markets and siphon off some of these excess profits.

77 Again, the merger did not take effect until 1969.

78 The players' associations of both the NBA and ABA opposed the merger, feeling it would reduce competition in the players' market, and would ultimately lead to lower salaries. This was still the era when the "reserve clause" was present (i.e., there was no free agency) and their only means of gaining bargaining leverage was to change leagues.

79 The Toronto Northmen were a charter WFL franchise in 1974, but never played a game in the city after the Trudeau government barred the WFL from operating in Canada, feeling it would destroy the CFL. The franchise moved to Tennessee and became the Memphis Southmen before the league's first season.

80 There were a couple of exceptions to this. The stillborn Continental League in baseball was scheduled to have a franchise in Toronto; as well, the aforementioned Toronto Northmen were to be part of the WFL.

81 Howard Baldwin, the co-owner of the charter New England Whalers franchise, says that in an early version of the WHA bylaws (developed by Davidson himself) the ice surface is referred to as the "court."

82 While Scotty Munro had been the public face of the Calgary franchise, the "money man" (i.e., majority owner) behind the scenes was actually Brownridge. The same was true of the Alberta Oilers franchise, where Bill Hunter was the face, but Charles Allard was actually the majority owner.

83 Gary Davidson claimed that when Brownridge died, Munro "walked away" from the franchise and never again contacted the WHA, even though Davidson later stated that he could have helped Munro find another owner in Calgary to replace Brownridge's money.

84 By comparison, Hull's annual salary in the NHL was estimated to be only about $150,000.

85 Most of the other owners ended up not paying their share of Hull's signing bonus, leaving the Jets and a few other clubs to make up the difference.

86 Instead, his Pats teammate, Greg Joly, was the first pick overall in the draft. The Pats were loaded with talent that year, with winger Clark Gillies going fourth overall to the New York Islanders. Gillies was elected to the Hockey Hall of Fame in 2002.

87 Again, the entry of the WHA clubs was referred to as an NHL "expansion," rather than a merger, so as to avoid antitrust issues.

88 Pocklington had bought partial ownership of the Oilers one year earlier, in 1976, and then gained full control in 1977, when he bought out the shares of Nelson Skalbania, who then went immediately on to buy the WHA's Indianapolis Racers.

89 Ballard and John W. H. Bassett (John F. Bassett's father) had a long history of animosity toward each other, going back to the early 1960s, when they were both co-owners of the Toronto Maple Leafs.

90 The franchise was originally slated for Miami, Florida, as the Screaming Eagles, but relocated to Philadelphia before the WHA's first season.

91 At the time, the NHL required its arenas to have a minimum capacity 14,500. The Stampede Corral held roughly half that.

92 The Flames would play three years in the old Stampede Corral, awaiting the construction of the Saddledome.

93 After the NHL vote rejecting the sale of the Blues to Bill Hunter, Ralston Purina walked away from the franchise. The Blues quickly became rudderless, to the point where they even failed to participate in the 1983 draft.

94 The WHA was founded as business entity on September 13, 1971, but began play a year later, in October 1972.

95 Davey also briefly served as commissioner of the CFL, resigning in 1966 after only two months on the job.

96 The Oilers won the game, 5–3.

97 In retrospect, the Devine era in Saskatchewan became primarily known for its scandals, rather than the failed attempt to secure the Blues. Less than one year into Devine's first term, the ex-wife of Colin Thatcher, Devine's first minister of energy and mines, was found bludgeoned and shot to death in the garage of her upscale Regina home. Thatcher was arrested and eventually convicted of first-degree murder in connection with her death and served 25 years in prison. In a separate scandal several years later, 12 of Devine's former MLAs were charged with fraud pertaining to their use of public funds, with several serving jail time.

98 Bill C-69 was given royal assent in June 2019, and came into law at that point.

99 Even with the Oilers' large increase in relative payroll that season, they were never expected to reach the final, finishing as the eighth (and lowest) seed to make the playoffs in the Western Conference that year.

100 The Quebec Nordiques were the only other team in NHL history to have the first pick overall in three successive seasons—1989, 1990 and 1991.

101 The issue relates to what economists term "compensating differentials." In this context, it means that NHL clubs in cities that are deemed less "desirable" by many players will have to pay a salary premium—over and above what clubs in more desirable locations would have to pay—in order to attract players to the club. This notion, taken to its logical conclusion, means that, in a league governed by a hard salary cap, clubs in less desirable locations will attract less talent per dollar of payroll expenditure, all else equal.

102 The findings of academic economists on the issue are generally counter to the "economic impact studies" done by consultants. These private consulting studies almost always show large net benefits for these stadium projects, but suffer from a conflict-of-interest criticism, since they are generally commissioned by the project's political supporters and/or by the team itself.

103 The Jodzio-Tardif incident in the WHA happened the same week in April 1976 as the NHL incident in Toronto involving the four Philadelphia Flyers who were charged with assault.

104 Some of the obvious effects of this imbalance were reduced because the six expansion clubs were all placed in the same division, thus predominantly playing each other, and ensuring that four of the six expansion clubs were guaranteed to make the playoffs that first year.

105 In 1974, the same year the Jets signed Hedberg and Nilsson, the New England Whalers brought in twin brothers Thommy and Christer Abrahamsson, both of whom played three years in the WHA.

106 This does not include Juha Widing, who was Finnish-born but who moved to Canada with his family when he was a teenager.

107 In the *perestroika* era of the late 1980s, when greater openness was taking place in the Mikhail Gorbachev–led Soviet Union, a few select veteran Soviet players, such as Viacheslav Fetisov, Sergei Makarov, Alexei Kasatonov and Vladimir Krutov, were allowed to come to the NHL to finish out their careers. The waning days of the Soviet Union also saw the first two defections of Soviet players to the NHL—Alexander Mogilny in 1989 and Sergei Federov a year later. Both were young, emerging stars, and both would ultimately go on to have long and successful NHL careers.

108 After the story broke, Kekäläinen, while admitting that he was critical of junior hockey in the interview, claimed that some of his statements were incorrectly translated. George Johnson of the *Calgary Herald*, for one, didn't buy Kekäläinen's "backtracking" (in Johnson's words), saying it was the usual "I was misquoted… or, I was misinterpreted" defensive tack.

109 In 1974, the NHL began paying junior clubs directly, bypassing the CAHA, as concerns arose that the practice of paying the CAHA was a possible violation of US antitrust laws.

110 The Combines Investigation Act, forerunner to today's Competition Act, prohibited a variety of anti-competitive practices in the marketplace.

111 Monopoly power is further enhanced by the fact that many CHL teams face little competition from other spectator sports in the same city. Most CHL teams are located in small- to medium-sized Canadian cities, where major junior hockey is the premier sports entertainment outlet. Lower-tier junior leagues, such as Junior A and Junior B hockey, tend to locate franchises in smaller communities. Furthermore, college hockey offers little competition in the output market for CHL

teams, since college hockey programs in Canada are largely comprised of players without professional prospects, and hence generate little widespread fan interest. On the opposite side, while CHL teams are located in all Canadian NHL cities except Montreal, the two leagues should be viewed as complements to each other rather than competitors, not only because of the close association between the leagues (with the NHL having a strong vested interest in ensuring the success of the local CHL franchise), but also because the CHL tends to serve more the lower end of the consumer demand spectrum—i.e., a fan base that cannot either afford or gain access to NHL tickets.

112 Throughout this discussion, the WHL is used as an illustrative focal point, although all the core issues apply to both the OHL and QMJHL.

113 The top tier was Junior A in 1967 and Major Junior in 1970.

114 Additionally, there is a separate CHL-wide draft of European players each year, which also has a reverse-order selection process.

115 The legality of the OHL's draft was upheld in a 1984 case, *Greenlaw v. Ontario Major Junior Hockey League*. The court ruled that the draft was necessary to allow teams in smaller, remote areas to compete with teams in large centres.

116 The Sault Ste. Marie Greyhounds made Lindros the first-overall pick in the 1989 OHL draft, but Lindros, from Toronto, refused to report to the Northern Ontario city, subsequently forcing the Greyhounds to trade him to the Oshawa Generals. Lindros then led the Generals to the 1990 Memorial Cup championship.

117 The NCAA considers major junior players to be "professionals."

118 Before 1990, the unilateral "listing" system was used by WHL teams, equally unfavourable from the players' perspective.

119 Colorado Avalanche icon and Hall of Famer Joe Sakic was a teammate of Kennedy's in Swift Current and was also on the bus the night of the crash.

120 While CHL teams do incur costs to billet players with local families, such payments cannot be viewed as a "benefit" to players, since such costs would not have been incurred had the player not been forced to move away from his family.

121 The "Disneyfication" of the NHL isn't simply a metaphor. It was no better exemplified in real life than in the 1993 awarding of an expansion franchise to Anaheim, California, home of Disneyland. The franchise owner, the Walt Disney Company, named the team the Mighty Ducks, which was taken from a 1992 Disney movie about a children's hockey team, blurring the lines between the reality of the NHL and the fictional world of Disney.

REFERENCES

Baldwin, Howard. *Slim and None: My Wild Ride from the* WHA *to the* NHL *and All the Way to Hollywood* (Anansi International, 2014).

Barnes, J. *Sports and the Law in Canada,* 3rd edition (Butterworths, 1996).

Blake, Jason and Andrew Holman. *The Same but Different: Hockey in Quebec* (McGill-Queens University Press, 2017).

Cole, Stephen. *Hockey Night Fever* (Doubleday Canada, 2015).

Cole, Stephen. *The Last Hurrah: A Celebration of Hockey's Greatest Season* (Penguin, 1996).

Committee on the Judiciary, House of Representatives, *Organized Professional Team Sports* (85th Cong. 1st sess. Part 3, 1957).

Cox, Damien, and Gord Stellick. *'67: The Maple Leafs, Their Sensational Victory, and the End of an Empire* (Wiley, 2004).

Davidson, Gary, and Bill Libby. *Breaking the Game Wide Open.* (Atheneum, 1974).

Dryden, Ken. *The Game* (Macmillan of Canada, 1983).

Gruneau, Richard, and David Whitson. *Hockey Night in Canada: Sports, Identities and Cultural Politics* (Garamond Press, 1993).

Joyce, Gare. *Future Greats and Heartbreaks: A Year Undercover in the Secret World of* NHL *Scouts* (Doubleday Canada, 2007).

Longley, Neil. *An Absence of Competition: The Sustained Competitive Advantage of the Monopoly Sports Leagues* (Springer, 2013).

Longley, Neil. "The Economics of Discrimination: Evidence from Hockey." In *The Oxford Handbook of Sports Economics: Volume 2, Economics Through Sports,* edited by Leo Kahane and Stephen Schmanske (Oxford University Press, 2012).

Kidd, Bruce. *The Struggle for Canadian Sport* (University of Toronto Press, 1996).

Kidd, Bruce, and John Macfarlane. *The Death of Hockey* (New Press, 1972).

Quirk, James, and Rodney Fort. *Pay Dirt: The Business of Professional Team Sports* (Princeton University Press, 1992).

Ransom, Amy. *Hockey* PQ: *Canada's Game in Quebec's Popular Culture* (University of Toronto Press, 2014).

Robinson, Laura. *Crossing the Line* (McClelland & Stewart, 1998).

Whitson, David, and Richard Gruneau. *Artificial Ice: Hockey, Culture, and Commerce* (University of Toronto Press, 2006).

INDEX

Aberhart, William, 84
Alberta, 117–19
    Keystone XL Pipeline, 118
    Leduc oil reserve, 82–84
    politics, 84–85
        See also Clark, Joe; Lougheed, Peter
Alberta, Battle of
    See Calgary Flames; Edmonton Oilers
American Basketball Association (ABA), 11–12, 88, 93–94, 222n78
American Basketball League (ABL), 11, 93
American Football League (AFL), 11, 88–91, 216n13, 222n77
Americanization, 44
    See also National Hockey League (NHL)
Avery, Sean, 56

Ballard, Harold, 104, 114, 223n89
Bassett, John F., 104–5
Bassett, John W. H., 223n89
Bedard, Connor, 193
Bergeron, Patrice, 74–75
Berry, Bob, 32
Bettman, Gary, 36
Big Four (leagues), 11, 13–14
Birmingham Bulls, 101–2
Bloc Québécois, 53–54, 72
Boudrias, André, 61–62

Calgary Broncos, 97
Calgary Cowboys, 105
Calgary Flames, 79–80, 80–82, 107, 113, 120–23, 125–26, 223n92
    first-round picks, 124–25
California Golden Seals, 17
Canadian Amateur Hockey Association (CAHA), 43, 218n46
Canadian Hockey League (CHL), 168–69, 176–78, 200–203, 206–7, 224–25n111
    revenues, 196–97
    player value, 198–99
Cannon, Billy, 90

Gainey, Bob, 217nn32–33
Gaudreau, Johnny, 126
geographics, xiii, 51
    source of hockey talent, 141–45
Gilbert, Rod, 78, 221n68
Gillett, George, 37, 218n41
Gillies, Clark, 222n86
Goulet, Michel, 28
Gretzky, Wayne, 102
Grundman, Irving, 32, 217n23

Hall, Taylor, 124
Hatskin, Ben, 86–87, 95–96
Hedberg, Anders, 130, 136–37
Houle, Réjean, 24–25
Howe, Gordie, 143, 149, 160
Howe, Mark, 101
Hull, Bobby, 98–99, 136–37, 160, 222nn84–85
Hunt, Lamar, 89–90
Hunter, Bill, 86–87, 95–97, 113–14

IceDogs franchise, 184–85
immigration, xv, 75–76
industries (Western Canada), 7–8, 83–84, 215n12

James, Graham, 195–96
James, Val, 219n47
Jodzio, Rick, 132
Joly, Greg, 222n86
junior hockey, xi–xii, 155–58
    draft system, 163–69, 224n109
    Junior A teams, 169–70
    sponsorship system, 158–63
    underage juniors, 100–102, 166–68
    See also long-distance relocations

Kane, Patrick, 199
Kekäläinen, Jarmo, 155, 224n108
Kennedy, Sheldon, 195–96
Keystone xl Pipeline
    See Alberta